PRAISE FOR
MAKE PARTNER AND
STILL HAVE A LIFE

"After the recent economic turmoil, during which we have seen downsizing partner numbers across all professional service firms, this is a timely and indispensable no-nonsense guide to what it takes to make partner in today's environment. This is about partnerships as they really are, not as we might like them to be: and giving yourself the best possible chance to get to the top. This book doesn't pretend that the route to partnership isn't tough nor does it pull any punches on the demands placed on those who do make it to partner. What is does do is to present an honest account of the upsides and downsides of partnership life and a practical framework to assess how much you really want it." **Jeremy Horner, Former Global Chief Executive, Davis Langdon**

"Crystal clear. Razor sharp. And intensely practical. This book is an absolute must for anyone who wants to become a partner, wants to make themselves a better partner, or wants to grow future partners as part of their succession plan."
Steve Pipe, Professional Service Firm Strategist and Author of
The UK's Best Accountancy Practices

"Highly recommended read for aspiring partners and HR professionals. Inspirational advice for creating a new generation of successful partnerships."
Yvonne Hardiman, Partner and HR Director, Pictons Solicitors LLP

"This book sets out what you need to do to objectively decide you want to be a partner and then guides you through the process to get you there."
Darryn Hedges, Global Finance Director of Marks & Clerk LLP

"*How to Make Partner and Still Have a Life* provides practical guidance on the things you need to think about and do as you develop your career. It is a valuable contribution to the very limited guidance on what you need to do if it's your ambition to make partner."
Wendy Walton, Partner BDO LLP

"Another must-have read from Heather Townsend. A book that looks at the reality of what it is to be a Partner and provides essential practical advice for anyone considering promotion." **Claire Martin, Solicitor**

"As an award winning and people development focused firm, I have to say that this book will become required reading for our aspiring people. The insight and avoidance of "guru-speak" make the case studies very real. An essential read for anyone at or seeking a senior position in a professional practice." **Peter Gillman, Managing Director, Price Bailey LLP**

"Original, clear, concise and brilliantly written, this handbook is packed with invaluable insights. An absolute must-read (and potential life saver) for anyone pursuing a professional career. From long experience, Larbie and Townsend explain exactly how to reach both success AND that elusive work-life balance many top professionals so desperately need." **Sunny Stout-Rostron DProf, Executive Coach; Director: Sunny Stout-Rostron Associates, and Research Mentor with the Institute of Coaching at Harvard/McLean Medical School**

"There is so much of value to partners and future partners in this book that I don't know where to start! It is a book, like Heather's first, that I will recommend to all my professional services clients. Heather and Jo's experience of working on the inside of a professional firm shines through and every chapter contains something of practical value. The real-life case studies will convince you that you can make partner and still have a life. I'm even putting some of their tips into practice in my own life." **David Tovey, Author of *Principled Selling***

"Life is about choices. If you know of this book and choose to ignore it, you do so at your peril! This book is the bible for every ambitious person in professional services. Too many would be partners 'live to work'. *How To Make Partner and Still Have A Life* makes an outstanding contribution towards getting control of your time and thinking in order to 'work to live'. It is a must buy." **Ian Cooper, Author of *The Financial Times Guide To Business Development* and *How To Be A Time Master***

"Packed with practical tips, exercises and advice from partners who have already made it, this is an essential career guide for any professional, whether aiming for partnership or unsure about their future direction. Highly recommended reading!"
Phil Gott, Director Peopleism Ltd

"All partners and potential partners should read this book. The few who follow the advice and take action will succeed."
Jamie Pennington, Managing Director, Pennington Hennessy Ltd

"I wish this book had been around when I was a junior lawyer – it's a brilliant and practical guide to the issues surrounding partnership – how to work out if you really want it as well as helping you to create a road map to get it. It will also help a lot of partners gain some focus in these challenging times and treat partnership as the beginning, not the end of a journey. I particularly like the action points at the end of each chapter. I'm going to put it in our firm's library with a big 'Read Me' sticker on it!"
Nicky Richmond, Joint Managing Partner of Brecher Solicitors

"If you have aspirations to make Partner and you only purchase one book this year – make this that one. It could quite literally change your life."
Drew Moss, Senior Learning and Development Manager, BDO Australia

"Too many people get part-way through their career with no clear ambition or idea of where it is going. This book is an essential tool for anyone within the professions – and in other areas too – to help them understand and work out what they want to achieve, and how best to achieve it." **James Mendelssohn, Chairman of MSI Global Alliance and founder of Firm Management**

How to Make Partner and Still Have a Life

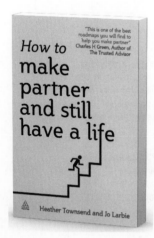

How to Make Partner and Still Have a Life

Heather Townsend
and Jo Larbie

KoganPage

LONDON PHILADELPHIA NEW DELHI

First published in Great Britain and the United States in 2013 by Kogan Page Limited

120 Pentonville Road	1518 Walnut Street, Suite 1100	4737/23 Ansari Road
London N1 9JN	Philadelphia PA 19102	Daryaganj
United Kingdom	USA	New Delhi 110002
www.koganpage.com		India

© Heather Townsend and Jo Larbie, 2013

The right of Heather Townsend and Jo Larbie to be identified as the authors of this work has been asserted by them in accordance with the Copyright, Designs and Patents Act 1988.

ISBN   978 0 7494 6655 8
E-ISBN   978 0 7494 6656 5

British Library Cataloguing-in-Publication Data

A CIP record for this book is available from the British Library.

Library of Congress Cataloging-in-Publication Data

Larbie, Jo.
   How to make partner and still have a life / Jo Larbie and Heather Townsend.
      p. cm.
   ISBN 978-0-7494-6655-8 – ISBN 978-0-7494-6656-5 (ebook)   1. Strategic alliances (Business)
2. Partnership.   3. Business enterprises.   I. Townsend, Heather.   II. Title.
   HD69.S8L37 2012
   650.14–dc23

                                                                                    2012028983

Typeset by Graphicraft Limited, Hong Kong
Print production managed by Jellyfish
Printed and bound by CPI Group (UK) Ltd, Croydon, CR0 4YY

CONTENTS

Foreword   xiii
Acknowledgements   xv

Overview and introduction   1

PART 1 Is partnership right for you?

01   **What does being a partner in the 21st century actually mean?**   10

What makes a partnership environment different from a limited company?   11
The changing world of professional services firms   13
What does it take to be a partner in a firm today?   14
Summary   16
Action points   17
Further resources   17

02   **What do you want from your career and life?**   18

Taking responsibility for your career   19
Who are you, and why does this matter?   21
The importance of your firm's values to you and your career   27
Summary   37
Action points   37
Further resources   38

03   **The four different routes to partnership**   39

Differences between small firms and large firms   39
The four different routes to partnership   41
The three different types of partner   46
Summary   47
Action points   48
Further resources   48

04   Is partnership for you? Making the right choices 49

Becoming a career manager 49
Moving out of professional services into industry: taking
an in-house role 51
Career change 53
Is partnership for you? 55
Summary 56
Action points 56
Further resources 56

PART 2 Building a firm foundation for partnership

05   How to become partnership potential 58

What is partnership potential? 59
How to be perceived as having partnership potential 60
Summary 72
Action points 73
Further resources 73

**06   How to develop yourself on the route to
partnership** 75

How we learn and develop new skills and behaviours 76
The importance of playing to your strengths 80
How to identify gaps in your skill base 81
How to keep your knowledge up-to-date 84
Summary 85
Action points 85
Further resources 86

07   Creating and writing your own career action plan 87

Why set goals? 88
How to get started 88
Writing your own career action plan 95
The importance of gaining feedback from others 98
Summary 98
Action points 99
Further resources 99

08   Building your support team   100

Why do you need a support team?   101
The crucial role of a mentor   102
Mentoring and diversity   103
What do mentors do?   103
What to look for in a mentor   104
What should you expect from a mentoring relationship?   105
How to get the most from your mentor   108
Summary   109
Action points   110
Further resources   110

09   How your firm makes money   111

Building your understanding of your firm's financial
performance   112
How does the firm make money and profit?   115
Summary   122
Action points   122
Further resources   123

10   How to be seen as 'one of the club'   124

The firm's culture – warts and all   125
How to navigate and survive the firm's politics   126
Join 'the club'   132
Summary   133
Action points   133
Further resources   134

11   How to find the time to fit it all in   135

The challenge of having to do it all   136
Adopt the right mindset to be productive   136
Why you need to be assertive   137
How to make sure you make time for the 'right' stuff   139
Conquering distractions   145
Stopping meetings wasting your time   148
Delegation   149
Summary   151

Action points 151
Further resources 152

12 How to look, sound and be the part 153

What do we mean by effective communication? 154
Positively influencing others 158
How to handle a difficult conversation 162
How to give and receive feedback 163
How to dress the part 166
Delivering a presentation with impact 167
Summary 168
Action points 169
Further resources 170

PART 3 Surviving the early years

13 How to build your network for life 171

What is networking? 172
Common concerns and myths around networking 173
How to design and build your network 174
How to network effectively 179
Summary 188
Action points 189
Further resources 190

14 How your role will change as you move upwards 191

Pre-qualification 192
Qualified 193
Manager or associate 194
Director or senior associate 195
Partner 195
Summary 196
Action points 196
Further resources 197

15 Keeping your eyes on the prize 198

How to stay focused when you are too busy to think 198
How to keep yourself constructively busy and motivated when work
is light 201
Summary 205
Action points 206
Further resources 206

PART 4 How to build your own client
portfolio and team

**16 How to keep your body working at peak
performance** 207

The Health Audit 208
Pressure vs performance 209
Feed your soul 210
Alternative asset management 212
Summary 215
Action points 215
Further resources 216

**17 How to become the 'go to' expert for your firm and
profession** 217

What do we mean by profile? 218
How to build your personal profile and become the 'go to' expert in
your field 223
Relationship management 226
Summary 231
Action points 232
Further resources 233

18 Building your own client portfolio 234

The business development process 235
How to build your own personal marketing plan to build your client
portfolio 237
The sales process 240

The importance of keeping in touch   242
Summary   243
Action points   243
Further resources   243

19   Managing and leading your way to success   245

What are 'management' and 'leadership'?   246
How to build and develop a team   247
What motivates people   250
How to develop your people   251
How to run a performance review and set goals   254
How to coach   258
Quality controls   260
Summary   260
Action points   261
Further resources   262

PART 5 How to make it through your firm's partnership selection process

20   Overcoming the final hurdles to making partner   263

Undertaking your own due diligence   263
The partner admission process   267
Your moment of truth – is partnership right for you at this firm?   276
Summary   278
Action points   279
Further resources   279

21   First steps as a partner   280

Your first few steps as a new partner   280
Creating your legacy   286
Summary   287
Action points   287
Further resources   288

Index   289

FOREWORD

So, you think you want to be a partner. How can you decide for sure? And if the answer turns out to be yes, how do you go about getting there? (And, if you don't want to be a partner, what do you want to be?).

Those are probably your motivations in picking up this book. In which case, you've made a good choice. If you're reading it for other reasons (you're a new partner and want to review expectations, you're a senior partner and want to think about leadership development), these perspectives will be valuable to you as well. Because in order to get there, you have to understand what success looks like – including such things as how your firm makes money, and how you contribute to strategy.

Having spent 20 years in professional services and another 15 as an advisor to them, I wish I'd had access to a book like this before I became a partner. It would probably have accelerated my promotion, most likely improved my performance, and certainly reduced my level of angst. I have every confidence it can do the same for you.

In fact, I'll go out on a limb: if you are looking to make partner, have the basic qualifications, and take half the suggested actions in this book – you are very likely to earn your partner status. But, if you have the basic qualifications and *don't* take half the suggested actions in this book, it's probably a good indication that you really don't *want to be* a partner – and you'll recognize that as a fact; and that too is a very positive outcome – there are partners out there who shouldn't have applied, and shouldn't have been admitted, and they are a sorry lot indeed. There is a fate worse than not making partner, and that is making partner and hating it.

This is very much *a how-to book*, in the best sense of the word. What are the four paths to partnership? What are the three main alternative career paths to partnership? What are the five characteristics at which a firm looks to determine partner potential? These are the kinds of structured questions that the authors – Jo and Heather – ask; they proceed to not only give answers, but a structured pattern of stories, tips, questions and exercises to help you provide your own personal, customized choices to the options raised. The authors are well-read, and have taken significant perspective and ideas from some of the best authors and practitioners in the field of professional services leadership and management.

Most of the book, appropriately, is devoted to the 'how do I become a partner?' question. This is one of the best road maps you will find to help you make partner. In the brief space I have here, I want to underscore a critical part of the book – the big picture, the stage-setting, the 'soft stuff.' This is covered in Chapters 1–4, particularly Chapter 2, 'What Do You Want From Your Career and Life?'

I emphasize this because if your motivation is 'I want to become a partner,' this is precisely the material you're likely to skip over. I know I would have. If you're a smart, hard-working, highly industrious lawyer, consultant, actuary, accountant or other professional, your eyes probably glaze over at 'understanding who you are and what makes you tick,' or thinking about what you want in life. You want to get to the 'hard stuff.'

Well, listen up. You've been warned. This *is* the hard stuff.

Your life is about to move at lightning pace, and the decisions you make now will have literally life-changing effects on you, and on those close to you. *Don't live your life by default.* Don't be like the lawyers in this book who, when asked by Jo what they wanted from life, answered that it was 'too early to tell.' It's your life to live, or to default. It's not a dress rehearsal. In this matter, no decision is a decision. Make the decision, and make it intentionally. As John Lennon memorably said, 'Life is what happens to you when you are busy making plans.'

Yes, this book is a how-to manual. It's also a chance to viscerally try on for size a possible life, to envision an alternative reality without having to live it in full. Grab the opportunity. Read this book as a way to decide whether you want to be a partner, and what kind of life you'll want with it or without it.

If you read it that way, making partner will be only one of the benefits you gain.

Charles H Green,
co-author of *The Trusted Advisor* and author of *Trust-based Selling*

ACKNOWLEDGEMENTS

This book has been a labour of love for both of us and the process of writing it pushed us personally to question our own lives and careers. If we can help just one professional 'feed their soul' rather than having to 'sell their soul' to achieve their true potential and career ambition within professional services, then it will all have been worth it.

We would like to thank the following individuals who participated in our interviews and shared their experiences and insights of working in and with professional services firms. They include among others: Jan Allenby, Jonathan Beck, Robert Chambers, Sarah Craggs, Simon Dawkins, Suzanne Dibble, Peter Gillman, Stuart Gould, Charles H Green, Darryn Hedges, Jeremy Horner, Toni Hunter, Janet Legrand, Suzanne Lines, Mike Mister, Amber Moore, Myfanwy Neville, Jeremy Newman, Antoinette Oglethorpe, Alan Pannett, Heena Pattni, Jamie Pennington, Patrick Raggett, Rakesh Shaunak, Dona and Andrew Skaife, Alan Smith, John Stylianou, Gillian Sutherland, David Tovey, Saimina Virani, Rachael Wheatley, Kim Whitaker, Chris Williams, and Anita Woodcock.

Our special thanks to: Robert Watson, Liz Gooster and Sonja Jefferson. You three are an amazing team to work with, and it has been a true pleasure to work with you on this book. You have given us both the confidence to write the best book we can, while having fun along the way.

And finally our personal thanks:

Jo: I would like to thank Heather for her energy, vision and friendship in co-authoring this book. Throughout this project, Heather has consistently demonstrated that when you believe, anything and all things are possible; this book is the result. My deepest love and thanks to Win Mensah-Larbie: everyone should have a sister and friend like Win. I will never have enough words to express the importance of my valued friends who are always 'there for me', cheering me onwards and upwards.

Heather: I would like to thank Jo for joining me on the roller-coaster ride that has been this book. During this project, you truly brought a new meaning to the phrase 'have a life' and have helped keep me centred and grounded with your belief in the project. There are five people who are actively helping me create the life and career I want. My husband and two children are the reason I can smile in the morning and am motivated to create a legacy. Jon, my friend, business partner and rock – all I can say is thank you. Lisa, your support has been invaluable – and yes, every professional needs to have a Lisa in their life.

Overview and introduction

Sarah yawned, and decided to call it a day. She reflected on everything she had done during the day: up at the crack of dawn to attend a breakfast meeting, because 'it would be good for her profile', then client work, and somehow finding the time to finalize a proposal for a client. There never seemed to be enough hours in the day to hit her chargeable hours target and do everything else which was now expected of her. If only she won this new client, it might be just what she needed to prove to her partners that she really did have what it took to be a partner in the firm. The problem was that no one in her firm was actually able to tell her what she needed to do to be promoted to partner.

As she ran to catch the last train home, she remembered the last time she and her peers in the firm had gone for a few drinks after work. After the alcohol had loosened everyone's tongues a little, the topic of conversation naturally turned to firm gossip. Sarah pushed the unpleasant thought to the back of her mind that it was rumoured that Al in her team had been told he was on course to be the next partner in her department. It was so unfair; she'd given her life to that firm, made so many personal sacrifices, only to see Al waltz in and become the partners' favourite and make partner ahead of her. If only she knew what it was that the partners saw in Al that she didn't have – then she could do something positive to kick-start her career progression in the firm. Whenever she had asked her partners about how to get promoted to partner, she never seemed to get a consistent answer and it was all rather vague.

As Sarah collapsed in bed that night, her husband was already fast asleep. In her heart of hearts, she knew she needed to change her working hours. Time was ticking on, and if they were ever to start the family they both wanted, they needed to actually spend some quality time together. Ever since she had started as a trainee, she knew that she'd wanted to get to partner. However, she wanted the respect and financial reward which came with the title, but not to let it become her life.

Six hours later her alarm jerked her awake. As Sarah gulped down her essential first cup of coffee of the day, she wondered … *What if it could be different? What if I could make it to partner while still having a life outside work?*

Sadly, Sarah is not an isolated case. We have seen too many highly talented professionals like Sarah work themselves into the ground in their pursuit of partnership. Why is it that for every AI, there are so many Sarahs frustrated by their inability to progress to partner, and finding that they feel they have to sacrifice any chance of a life outside work to achieve their career goal? This is where the idea for this book came from. We've spent a large proportion of our working lives within professional services firms helping people demystify the process of getting to partner. This book has enabled us to achieve our vision by allowing us to make a positive difference to more people's careers and lives than we could have done on our own.

We both know that with the right guidance, choices and support it is possible to make partner and still have a life. We also know that this knowledge is very rarely written down and consequently hard for most professionals to access. Our experience has taught us that with the right early career decisions and an ever-present focus on long-term career and life ambitions, it becomes possible to achieve the seemingly impossible – how to make partner and still have a life. (If you have picked up this book and are thinking, 'It's too late for me now; I'm too long into my career within professional services,' don't worry – it is still possible to change things around.)

As you've considered this book, we know that you are one of the lucky ones. You are one of the very few people who have the only route map you will require for making it to the top in a professional services firm in the 21st century. By working through the material, you'll learn how to stand out, be in the right place at the right time, and build your kitbag of skills to overcome the many hurdles and reach the Holy Grail, making partner.

There are a variety of ways to become a partner. Unfortunately, as Sarah and her peers were finding out, the path to partnership is often shrouded by mystery, hearsay and conjecture. This book sheds light on the most effective and quickest routes. It highlights the skill set, qualities and attributes you will need, with practical techniques and tips for achieving success with your professional and personal goals.

The professions are renowned for expecting their staff to work long hours and give their heart, soul and life to the firm. The perception is that if you want to make partner, your life needs to become your work, regardless of your personal interests, hobbies or family circumstances. If you, like Sarah, know that you don't want to sacrifice all of these to make partner, then you've chosen the right book to show you how you can have it all.

Using research and interviews, this book provides practical techniques and tips for achieving professional and personal goals.

The book guides and teaches you:

- how to find out what it really takes to make partner in a professional services firm;
- how to decide what you really want for your career, and whether partnership is for you;
- how to identify your goals and create and implement your own career plan;
- the alternative routes you can take to become a partner;
- the core skills, qualities and attributes you will need to make the grade as partner, regardless of the size or type of firm;
- how to get noticed and marked as partnership potential;
- the importance of personal brand: how to build and develop your own successful profile and reputation;
- ways to quickly build up your own client base to support a successful career as a partner;
- how to make it to the top while still having a life outside work.

The book gives you the confidence, motivation and inspiration and all the information you will need to make partner.

Who is the book for?

This book is written for knowledge workers who are working 'in practice' within a partnership structure and sell their time for money. This includes lawyers, accountants, management consultants, architects, consulting engineers and surveyors.

While this book primarily caters to the needs of new entrants into the professions and experienced qualified professionals who have not yet reached partner, newly promoted partners and people responsible for talent management, leadership development and partner-level development will also find this book invaluable.

If you have recently joined a professional services firm and are starting out on your career as a professional adviser, this book will:

- provide you with a road map to enable you to make partner, without having to sell your soul or sacrifice what is important to you;

- help you take the right decision about what to specialize in;

- enable you to make the right early career choices which will provide a strong foundation for your future career progression;

- allow you to make an informed decision on whether partnership is right for you;

- assist you to devise an action plan for your career which will help you quickly make partner while still enjoying a better work–life balance;

- give you realistic and honest advice about how long it will take you to make partner;

- help you get the balance right between work and play.

If you are an experienced qualified professional who wants to make partner, this book will:

- answer the burning and often unanswered question: *What do I need to do to progress my career here?*;

- be an unbiased mentor who will show you how to overcome the many hurdles to becoming a successful partner;

- clearly show you what skills, attitudes and behaviours and experience you will need to demonstrate to rapidly progress to partner;

- give you the reassurance that you needn't sell your soul to become partner, while being realistic about what compromises you may need to take along the way.

If you are a newly promoted partner, you may be thinking, 'I don't need this book now, I've made it.' Before you put this book down, take a moment to consider whether you actually know what your promotion to partner really means. Many newly promoted partners sadly don't realize that making partner is not the end of their career ladder, just the start of another new ladder to climb. Typically, new partners will have 18–24 months to prove themselves to their fellow partners. Fail to make the grade as a new partner and you could be asked to leave the firm or even suffer the embarrassment of your career within the firm coming to an end by your being demoted back to director or senior associate. This book will help you, as a newly promoted partner, to understand the full extent of *what* it means to be a partner. It then helps you to identify *how* you will plug any gaps to help you flourish as a new partner.

If you are a managing partner or a senior leader who is responsible for talent development and succession planning within your firm, this book will:

- provide you with an overview of how you should approach the development of your talent pool;
- help you to create structured career pathways so that everyone knows and understands what they need to do if they want to become a partner at your firm;
- enable your firm to put in place a range of learning and skills development support that will aid your firm to build partners with the skills that your firm needs to be sustainable and profitable;
- help you to understand and think through what your firm must do to address your professional staff's demand for a better balance in their lives.

If you have picked up this book because you have been asked to help your own practice or advise a practice on leadership development, talent management and succession planning matters, you will find this book to be a jargon-free, rich source of advice. We are assuming that your firm knows that to ensure its long-term sustainability you need to think very carefully and probably differently about what skills, experiences, attitudes and behaviours your new junior partners will need to have.

Very often a firm, maybe similar to your own firm, will think about hiring expensive external consultants to advise on these matters, as these are seen to be the only source of advice available to help your firm identify how to grow and develop the partners of the future. This book helps firms like yours, without the need for large amounts of money to be spent on external consultants, to complete this exercise. At the moment, this book is the only widely available definitive guide to what makes a successful partner, both now and in the future. The book will become an invaluable, well-read and scribbled-on book for anyone responsible for talent management or succession planning within a professional practice.

Why is work–life balance becoming so important for professional services firms?

Until recently, most firms saw the demand for a better work–life balance as a gender-based, women's issue. However, we now know that this is a generation-based issue. The research shows that generations X and Y have a different work ethic from those who currently lead and manage professional services firms:

- They want to work hard and play hard.
- They don't want to spend their entire career working solely for one firm and can't imagine doing so – and they certainly don't want a career for life.
- They are not interested in deferred gratification.

Let's be clear: far from being work-shy, generations X and Y are focused and ambitious; however, they are unwilling to put the rest of their lives on hold for their career. So, if you want to attract, recruit and retain the brightest and best people to your firm, you must embrace this change and actively create a culture and working environment that values better work–life balance.

With widespread access to technology, which allows professionals and clients to be connected wherever they are, 24 hours a day, it is possible to meet the needs of both your clients and your professional staff. Can you really afford to let your brightest and most able people take their future elsewhere when you are in a position to make the changes which will ensure their longer-term commitment to your firm and clients? The answer: rather than blaming and writing people off, firms must introduce more flexible career paths.

How to use this book

This book is best read through from the start to the end, and then dipped into and out of as you progress your career in your firm. For this book to make a real difference to your career, don't ignore the exercises or questions it poses. Be brave, make a positive commitment now to your career and future happiness by making the time to answer the questions and complete the action points and exercises in each chapter. *Some of the techniques and processes will appeal to you more than others; however, we would encourage you to be curious, to keep an open mind, to have a go at using them. Some may not work for you, but until you have a go, you won't know.*

At the end of each chapter are:

- exercises for you to do to put into practice what you have just learnt;
- links and references to further resources.

The book is split into five discrete parts:

Part 1: Is partnership right for you?
The first part of the book helps you to decide whether to go for partnership or not. It lays out the options available to you in your career, whether you choose to go for partner or not. There is an honest appraisal of the merits of each career option and route to partner. Armed with this knowledge, you can take an informed decision on what is right for you and your future career.

Part 2: Building a firm foundation for partnership
The second part helps you build the essential foundations for partnership, by:

- identifying the attributes and behaviours of people who are seen to be partnership potential;
- demystifying how your firm works and how you fit into your firm's business model;
- helping you plan your career and set realistic milestones to reach partner;
- suggesting who you will require in your support team, who will guide you and champion you along the way;
- giving you the template to design and construct your network, which will be your biggest asset during your career progression;
- providing strategies and practical actions which will enable you to work productively and organize yourself so that you are able to deliver on your short- and long-term goals and objectives.

Part 3: Surviving the early years
Every partner, by the very nature of the professions, has to make it
through the early years of their career. Your role in the early years of your
career will be very different from your eventual role as a partner. This part
of the book explains:

– how your role will change as you progress up through the firm;

– how to keep your spirits and personal motivation high, even when the
  work gets tough or demotivating;

– how to keep your body running at peak performance to allow you to
  operate at your best in the workplace.

Part 4: How to build your own client portfolio and team
Every professional services firm is a business, run by its partners.
Each partner within a practice needs to be able to build up a client
portfolio, and a team to service the client portfolio. This part of the book
shows you how to do this by:

– giving practical advice on how to build your reputation so that you
  attract the right sort of clients to the practice;

– providing you with the skills, knowledge and behaviours to be able to
  win client work and build up your own client portfolio;

– offering you theories, practical tips and processes to enable you to
  lead, develop and manage others successfully.

Part 5: How to make it through your firm's partnership selection process
This final part of the book helps you make it through your firm's
partnership selection process and to set a solid foundation as a new
partner. It sheds light on the typically secretive processes that a
partnership takes when promoting people to the partnership.

It gives you practical advice on:

– what you can expect to happen in partnership assessment centres,
  and during tough panel-based interviews;

– how to write your own business case for promotion to the partnership;

– how to create your own personal business development plan to grow
  your client portfolio;

– how to successfully lay the foundations for the next part of your career –
  partnership.

We strongly encourage you to treat this book as your own personal guide, friend and mentor. It won't – and can't – do it for you, but we know that it will contain the right questions for you to answer to help you make and take the right decisions for you and your career. With that thought in mind we give you licence to scribble in the margins, fill it with sticky notes, highlight important phrases and paragraphs. Yes, make it *your* book and keep it with you; it's the only book you will need to help you make partner *and* still have a life.

And finally ...

You don't need to complete this journey alone. Both of us have played a significant part in many hundreds of partners achieving their lifetime career ambition, while still having a life outside work. We know that you can also accomplish this for yourself. Good luck on your journey and remember that we'd love to hear from you and be a real part of your support team.

Heather can be contacted easily via Twitter – @heathertowns or via e-mail, **heather@heathertownsend.co.uk**.

Jo can be contacted easily via e-mail – **jo@jolarbie.co.uk**.

For updates and downloads, also see our How to Make Partner blog at **http://www.howtomakepartner.com**.

01 What does being a partner in the 21st century actually mean?

TOPICS COVERED IN THIS CHAPTER:

- How the professional services firm is changing
- What it actually takes, mentally, physically and financially, to be a partner
- What makes a partnership environment different from a limited company
- The different types of partners

A partner needs to know their subject and be good at it because the expectation of the client is that someone at partner level has a certain amount of expertise. However, that is often not the defining characteristic – successful partners are generally people who are good at relationship building, both internally and externally.

AMBER MOORE, AMBER MOORE CONSULTING

This chapter is a scene-setter for the book and gives an honest, warts-and-all look at what being a partner really means in the 21st century.

Note: There is no one size fits all, both in terms of structure and culture for a professional services firm (PSF). This chapter aims to give you the *most likely* scenario for your firm.

The common characteristics of professional services firms are:

- The client is king: everything the firm delivers is driven by the client and is in service of the client. Client satisfaction is paramount.

- To meet the needs of clients, professional services firms are totally reliant on their skilled and motivated professional team.

- Professional services firms make money by selling their knowledge and expertise.

- The strength of a partner's position is based on their ability to win, serve and retain clients.

- The partners are 'player managers': they combine the roles of producing, delivering services and managing the firm. They value playing above managing: doing the work is much more interesting and fun to them than managing the firm.

- People become professionals because they want to practise what they have spent years learning and training to do. They want to practise accountancy, surveying, law, engineering, architecture, and consulting. Managing other professionals is rarely something which a newly qualified professional puts at the top of their list to do.

- Professional services firms are slow to change and, in our experience, often resist change. Despite the introduction of limited liability partnerships (LLP), the basic partnership model remains relatively unchanged.

What makes a partnership environment different from a limited company?

Ask any consultant and they will tell you that every company and industry thinks that they are unique. In their experience, very rarely is that the case. However, the professional services sector is one such industry that probably

TABLE 1.1   Differences between a partnership and a limited company

Partnership	Limited company
All owners of the business work in the business	Most owners of the business don't work in the business
Partners own the business	Shareholders own the business
Partners rather than directors are the senior decision makers in the business	Directors are the senior decision makers in the business
Decision making by committee	Decision making by role
Collegiate atmosphere	Corporate atmosphere
Partners are considered to be self-employed	Directors of business are employed by business
Loosely defined teams and structure	Typically clearly defined teams and structure
Managing partner and management board elected and appointed on the basis of their influence within the partnership	Managing director and board members appointed on their suitability to run the company

can lay claim to being unique. Most professional services firms (PSFs) adopt a partnership structure, as opposed to a corporate business structure. You may be thinking, 'So what? How does that make PSFs different?' Unlike most other businesses, the senior people, ie the partners responsible for delivering the firm's services, are also the firm's only shareholders. For example, if the firm has 20 partners, then there will be 20 people who feel that it is their right as owners of the business to have a say in most matters. In a limited company, those 20 shareholders would not have the same rights – which brings a very different dynamic to a partnership from that of a limited company.

The changing world of professional services firms

Go back only 30 years and the marketplace for professional services was very different from the present day. Those were the days when clients tended to remain with one professional adviser for life – and that was probably from the firm that their family or business had always used. When one partner retired, a senior level employee would get the 'tap, tap, tap' on the shoulder and be asked to join the partnership. The newly promoted partner would inherit the retiring partner's portfolio and normally fulfil the following criteria:

- be seen as a safe pair of 'technical' hands;
- be trustworthy, ie they were not going to run off with the partnership's or client's money;
- be a 'good chap';
- 'done their time' in the ranks.

> When I made partner, 30 years ago, it was in the days when clients stayed for life and paid what the work cost, without any quibbling.
>
> Peter Gillman, Managing Director, Price Bailey

Fast-forward to the present day and clients have become, in comparison, very price sensitive and happy to change their professional adviser if they think they can get better value and service with another firm. PSFs can no longer rely on clients staying for life, which has meant a fundamental change in the role of partner within a firm. Suddenly the role of partner has changed from someone who looked after a portfolio of inherited clients to someone who has to run a business while building and keeping a profitable client portfolio.

Technology has also changed the way that we do business, and the professions are no different. Communication technology, such as video conferencing, is also enabling firms to be able to extend their geographical reach and no longer be confined by their proximity to a client. It is becoming commonplace for firms to use virtually located teams to service clients' work. As a result partners and partnerships, to survive, have to be more technologically savvy and see technology-based solutions as core to the provision of a cost-effective service.

Over the last 30 years the world of business has become more and more global, and companies such as Amazon EU, who are headquartered in

Luxembourg but able to service their business all over Europe, are increasingly common. This has meant that clients now require their professional advisers to be able to handle all their local and global requirements across international borders. This has led to the rise in importance of the PSF's international network, whether as part of a global alliance, shared brand or shared legal entity. Even the very smallest firms will often be part of an international network, and use this as a point of differentiation to attract clients.

Increasingly firms, particularly accountancy firms, in their desire to drive down costs and operate more efficiently, are considering whether the partnership structure is the right structure for them. More firms are starting to adopt practices from the corporate world, such as:

- employing a chief executive officer (CEO) to run their firm for them, which frees partners to focus on finding and servicing clients;
- paying their partners a fixed 'salary' and giving them a bonus or 'dividend' dependent on the firm's and their individual performance;
- investigating bringing in outside investment and floating on the stock market;
- delegating key decision making to an executive or management board.

Over time, it remains to be seen whether the partnership structure will further 'corporatize' itself, or retain its unique collegiate culture and attributes.

What does it take to be a partner in a firm today?

> Partners now need to be business people and no longer technically brilliant.
> David Tovey, author of *Principled Selling*

A partnership is like any owner-managed business – just with more owners! Anyone who aspires to be a partner needs to realize that not only will they own the business they work in, but they need to think and act like a business owner.

As you read through this list of what it takes to be a partner in a PSF today you will probably note that there is no mention of the requirement for superior technical skills at the partner level in a firm. This is not a deliberate mistake or omission on our part. Our research for the book confirmed what we knew:

that being a partner is not just about your technical skills. To make partner relies on good technical skills coupled with excellent business acumen.

Client centric

Delivering great client service is a way of life for any successful PSF. This dedication to client service excellence starts from the top, ie the partners, and then permeates all through a firm. This means that any partner must be client-focused.

Work winner

> Successful partners are people who are good at relationship building, both internally and externally. They are really good at bringing business through the door.
>
> Amber Moore, Amber Moore Consulting

A partner in today's PSF lives and breathes by their ability to continually bring in profitable work. Today there is no place within a partnership for any partner who cannot bring in their own work to be serviced profitably by their team. Profit margins, particularly in times of global recession, remain under pressure and as a result, most if not all partnerships have taken action to deal with underperforming partners – including those who have not demonstrated a sufficient level of profit-generating activity.

Strategic player

As an owner of the firm, it is every partner's responsibility to identify and agree a motivating firm strategy, which will allow the partners to achieve their personal objectives. Note that we have used the words, 'personal objectives' rather than 'firm objectives'. This is because we are talking about a partnership, not a limited business with external shareholders. This means if the partners don't want to grow the firm, it can be difficult to make them do so.

Financial risk taker

Partners' incomes are linked to the performance of the firm, ie in lean years they may earn less than some of their employees. The press like to regularly inform us how many millions some of the partners are making in some of the biggest firms. What they don't tell us is how little some partners are making, and how much of their own money they may have to provide to stop their firm getting into financial difficulties.

Tough decision maker

Look around at the people in your office at the moment. If required, could you look people in the eye and tell them that you are shutting their office, and would you know what this would mean to each and every one of them, personally? While this is an exceptionally rare event, partners need to be able to take and implement tough decisions and courses of action. With the title of partner comes a responsibility to your employees to ensure the long-term health of the firm. This means that partners have to face tough decisions, such as making employees redundant.

Case study

Robert was looking at the senior partner and figured that the firm would need a replacement in a few years' time; however, Robert also realized that there were four other peers who were eyeing the same single vacancy. His response was to stay focused on strengthening his relationships in the partnership, in such a way they he kept one step ahead of his peers. Competition like this happens all the time.

Collaborator

In a partnership, all the partners have a stake in the business, which results in them being forced to work collaboratively – or at least maintain a facade that this is the case. Collaborative working means that every member of the partnership is bound to abide by a majority vote, regardless of how they personally feel about a matter. Sometimes if a partner does not agree with a majority vote their position can become untenable, and they have to resign from the partnership.

Working collaboratively within a partnership affords many benefits that many other business owners crave, such as having a team of people to learn from who also own a slice of the business.

Summary

A partnership has a very different feel and culture from a public or private limited company. This difference is driven by the fact that the partners, who are still very active within the practice, normally own the partnership. As a partner in a professional practice you have all the pleasures and pains of business ownership, while enjoying/suffering the collegiate and consultative culture of a partnership.

Action points

- Read the last three editions of your professional body's magazines. What future trends do you see emerging for your profession? What could that mean for you and your firm in the future?
- Speak to some partners within your firm. Find out what being a partner has meant to them mentally, physically and financially, and whether they are prepared to share this.

Further resources

Books

Dunn, P and Baker, R J (2003) *The Firm of the Future: A guide for accountants, lawyers and other professional services*, John Wiley & Sons, Hoboken, NJ

Ennico, C (2009) *The Partner Track:How to go from associate to partner at any law firm*, Kaplan Trade, New York

Lorsch, J W and Tierney, T J (2002) *Aligning the Stars*, Harvard Business School, Boston, MA

Maister, D (2003) *Managing the Professional Services Firm*, Simon & Schuster, London

Pipe, S (2011) *The UK's Best Accountancy Practices*, Added Value Solutions, UK

Susskind, R (2010) *The End of Lawyers? Rethinking the nature of legal services*, Oxford University Press, New York

Websites and blogs

Brian Inkster's The Time Blawg: the past, present and future practice of law – http://www.thetimeblawg.com

How to make partner blog – http://www.howtomakepartner.com

Matt Homann's the [non] billable hour – http://www.nonbillablehour.com

What do you want from your career and life?

TOPICS COVERED IN THIS CHAPTER:

- Understanding who you are and what makes you tick
- Identifying what fulfils you personally in your chosen career
- Identifying where your current career choices are at odds with your career and life goals

When one door closes, another opens; but we often look so long and so regretfully upon the closed door that we do not see the one which has opened for us.

ALEXANDER GRAHAM BELL

The purpose of this chapter is to help you understand more about who *you* are and what *you* want from your career and life. Are you doing what you love? Or do you feel that you are simply 'going through the motions' in a job that you find unsatisfying? One of the most important factors in enjoying your career is making sure that you are doing the work that you relish, and that you find what you are doing worthwhile. It is worth thinking about this carefully, because it only gets harder to motivate yourself if you are not passionate about your work. If you are going to get to partner and still be happy and fulfilled, inside and outside work, enjoying and being enthused about your work are essential.

I'm amazed by how few trainees, juniors, managers and associates can clearly answer the question, 'What do you want from your career and life?'

Jo Larbie

Recently, when Jo asked a group of new lawyers this question, their response was stunned silence. Finally, one of the group responded that it was 'too early to say'. The sad fact is that many professionals rarely spend time thinking about their careers from the beginning because they believe that their work is just that – work. This is surprising when you consider the time, money and effort it takes to graduate, find a position with a firm and then qualify. (Or, if you are in the legal profession, qualify and then find a position within a firm.)

On average in the UK, by the time you start your first paying job in a firm you will have student debts of £15,000 to £40,000 to repay.

You have brains in your head. You have feet in your shoes. You can steer yourself any direction you choose. You're on your own. And you know what you know. And YOU are the one who'll decide where to go …

Dr Seuss, *Oh, the Places You'll Go!*

Really understanding what you want from your career and life will make it easier for you to choose the best career directions, including whether or not you should go for partnership. In this chapter, we will help you to discover your answer to the question, 'What do you want from your career and life?' This will help you make the right career decisions, whether or not you decide to go for partnership.

Taking responsibility for your career

To be, or not to be, that is the question …

William Shakespeare, *Hamlet*

You may be wondering what taking responsibility for your own career has to do with making partner. To find out whether partnership is actually right for you, it's crucial for you to know what you want, or don't want; and how what you are doing relates to what you really want from your career. More importantly, if you don't actively build a career you love, the chances are you will not be fulfilled and not work at the peak of your ability – something you will need if you are going to achieve partnership in today's modern professional services firm. We have worked with numerous partners who are not passionate about their work, clients and their lives – it's just a job with onerous responsibilities, demands and pressures, albeit well paid (sometimes not even this).

In our experience, many professionals do not take responsibility for their careers because they believe that their career path is established. Their thinking is that basically if you do a reasonable job, stay out of trouble (ie don't annoy a client or partner), then career progression will take care of itself. Unfortunately, advancement within professional services firms no longer works that way. This is why taking responsibility for your career is a key theme of this book.

Being very honest with you, you are not at school now, so the only person responsible for creating the career and life you want is *you*. While your firm can help you to achieve your career aspirations, your firm is not responsible for your success. Only you can achieve the success you crave. If you are going to achieve the life you want, you will need to take charge of your role at each stage of your career. This means, for each job, regularly making time to set goals, planning to achieve these goals, and assessing progress against these goals.

You will know you are taking responsibility for your career when you:

- accept that you are in the driver's seat;
- have identified what you want to achieve, both inside and outside work;
- have established a plan, with actions and a time frame;
- are moving forward against the plan, checking progress at intervals and making adjustments if needed.

You, and only you, can drive your career forward.

If you are serious about making partner, take time now and again to work out how you see your career and life evolving – the things that you want to do and the goals that you want to achieve.

Who are you, and why does this matter?

> It is our choices, Harry, that show us what we truly are, far more than our abilities.
>
> J K Rowling, *Harry Potter and the Chamber of Secrets*

If you are going to craft the life you want to lead, then you need to firstly get to know yourself better, and most importantly, what makes you tick. Otherwise, how can you take informed decisions on what you want and need from your life inside and outside work?

Every human being has a unique identity, which is shaped by our:

- core values, which guide our behaviour at home and work;
- vision, ie what we want to achieve in our life;
- purpose, ie our reason for being.

See Diagram 2.1.

DIAGRAM 2.1 What forms your identity?

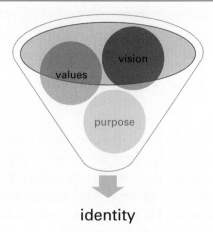

identity

Having a strong sense of your own identity is a powerful place from which you can direct your choices and make decisions that provide you with energy, enthusiasm and direction. There are no right or wrong answers to these questions, which you will continue asking throughout your career and life.

Exercise

To start to identify who you are, write down the answers to these questions:

- Think about a time when you felt most committed, passionate and motivated. What made you feel this way? Which of your talents were you using?

- Think about an example of when you were most sure of yourself and your decisions. What made you feel that way?

- What do you consider to be your greatest achievement? What aspects of that made it 'great' in your mind?

- What was the underlying drive in your decision to become a lawyer/accountant/architect/engineer/surveyor, etc?

- What did you think a lawyer/accountant/architect/engineer/surveyor would be doing, and what are you now actually doing? How big is the gap?

- What do you really want from your career and from life? To what extent do you have those 'balanced' to a level with which you are comfortable?

As we go through the rest of this chapter, the answers to these questions, will help you to uncover in more detail your own values, vision and purpose.

If your sole focus is currently doing the work and meeting your targets, don't worry. As we observed earlier, very few professionals have really thought about these vital questions. However, if you are going to build the career you want, it is essential that you take time to ask yourself these questions rather than continuing as you are. For most people finding out who they really are is a lifetime journey, so don't be concerned if it takes time before you can answer these questions; particularly if this is the first time that you have really thought about these things. Becoming aware of and understanding the things that excite and motivate you will help you to start seeing the things that you want to accomplish.

Your identity and the roles you play in life will change over time as you grow and develop. You will never stop learning about yourself. To help you understand yourself better, we would encourage you to 'try on different hats', until you discover your preferred roles. For example, Heather only discovered that she had a role as a writer when she tried her hand at blogging. Adopting this approach will also help you to make better decisions that are true to you. From knowing who you are, the important thing is to live true to that identity. Ensuring that your choices and decisions are aligned will help you to maintain a positive attitude when times are difficult.

Identifying your values – or how you want to live

Our values are the things that are important to us and define how we want to live and work, guiding our behaviour at home and work. Our values affect how we view our work and consequently our job satisfaction. Your values are the reason why you stick with a difficult assignment or decide to take a particular career path. For example, if you value financial reward, then you will probably be prepared to work hard in pursuit of your career goals.

Your values are personal to you, and in this section you will be drawing up a list of which ones are most important to you. Whether you realize it at a conscious or subconscious level, your values are informing both the important and unimportant decisions you take daily. For example, Sam is a partner in a small consultancy firm; her personal values are shown in Table 2.1.

TABLE 2.1   Sam's personal values

Value	How has this value impacted Sam's life and career to date?
Honesty and integrity	This means making commitments which can be kept, telling the truth, always owning up to mistakes, being able to explain decisions to colleagues. Sam struggled when she was employed by a large consultancy firm where she needed to be prepared to play a political game to advance her career. She left and joined a smaller consultancy firm as a partner, where she was measured on what she brought to the firm.

TABLE 2.1   *continued*

Value	How has this value impacted Sam's life and career to date?
Freedom	This means valuing automony and the ability to choose who she works with and what projects she gets involved with. Sam is at her most fulfilled now she has the freedom which comes from being a partner in a smaller firm.
Loyalty	This means having commitment, dedication and dependability, to her firm, friends, family and personal beliefs. For example, Sam has known many of her close friends since her university days, and been there for them during some tough personal times.
Challenge	This means enjoying personal adventure and seeking out opportunities to test herself. This explains why Sam enjoys the frequent travel which is expected in her role within a small consultancy firm.
Recognition	This means gaining the respect and acknowledgement of her peers, family and members of her firm. This need for recognition has been the driver behind Sam wanting to make partner ever since she started as a consultant.

If you can identify what it is you value, it will help in deciding whether or not making partner is right for you. Or what sort of firm you need to join to help you remain true to your values, while still making it to partner.

Completing the following exercise, taken from *Go Work on Your Career* (Gilbert, Frisby and Roberts, 2001), which will help you to identify and reaffirm the values that you hold:

Exercise

- Read the values which are in the left-hand column.
- Cross out anything which definitely doesn't apply to you.
- Identify those values which are significant to you by putting a tick in the column headed 'Significant'.
- Identify those values that are 'Most significant' to you in the second column.

TABLE 2.2 Your personal values

Personal values include:	Significant	Most significant
ACCOMPLISHMENT – attaining goals and a sense of achievement		
AFFECTION – love, caring and fondness		
BELONGING – participating with, being involved and including others		
CHALLENGE – adventure, new and exciting experience		
COMPETITIVENESS – striving to win, being the best		
CONTRIBUTION – assisting others and improving society		
CREATIVITY – being imaginative, inventive and original		
ECONOMIC SECURITY – having steady and adequate income		
FAME – being renowned, and having distinction		
FAMILY HAPPINESS – close relationship with family members		
FRIENDSHIP – close relationship with others		
FREEDOM – autonomy to choose own direction		
HONESTY AND INTEGRITY – standing up for your beliefs		
INDEPENDENCE – freedom, autonomy and liberty		
INNER HARMONY – being at peace with yourself and others		
LOYALTY – commitment, dedication and dependability		
ORDER – organized, structured and systematic		

TABLE 2.2   *continued*

Personal values include:	Significant	Most significant
PERSONAL DEVELOPMENT – learning and realizing your potential		
PLEASURE – fun, enjoyment and good time		
POWER – influence, importance and authority		
PROGRESSION – promotion and advancement		
RECOGNITION – gaining respect and acknowledgement		
SELF-BELIEF – having a belief in your own abilities, self-respect for who you are as an individual		
SPIRITUALITY – having faith, strong spiritual and/or religious beliefs		
TEAMWORK – collaboration and cooperation		
WEALTH – abundance and getting rich		
WELLBEING – physical and mental good health		
WISDOM – discovering knowledge, insight and enlightenment		

If there are other things you value, add them to the list.

If you find it difficult to decide which your most significant values are, think about why a value is significant to you. If your answer is that it is important 'just because', as opposed to a logical explanation, you can conclude that it is important as an end in itself. On the other hand, if the answer leads you to another value, for example, 'Fame is important because it will give me more power', the conclusion is that *power* is more important to you than *fame*, which is the means of you achieving *power*.

Now, review your answers and choose five *most significant* personal values.

Top five most significant personal values

1

2

3

4

5

Most people find that their values remain fairly constant throughout their life, although they may change after a life-changing event, for example a major illness or becoming a parent. Your vision, purpose and the environment you are in may change around you. Therefore, if you are serious about making partner and still having a life, be prepared to regularly check that your values are still aligned with your work and life.

The importance of your firm's values to you and your career

> We are not the sort of partnership which cares about partners having a shiny new car every year. If anything, we are suspicious of people like this.
>
> James, head of department, regional law firm

What does discovering your personal values have to do with whether or not you make partner in your firm? You need to check the alignment of your own values against the values of your employer. Being aware of your values will enable you to evaluate your career aspirations against your firm's values – the closer the match, the more likely you are to want to create a long-term career at the firm.

Freshfields Bruckhaus Deringer's (www.freshfields.com) values

Underpinning our firm and our work is a set of values and behaviours we strive towards:

- excellence in everything we do;
- outstanding teamwork;
- trusted relationships with our clients and our communities; and
- imagination.

The way we operate is characterized by a combination of openness, confidence, value and respect for people, a sense of humour and proportion, and an absence of hierarchy.

McKinsey & Company's values (www.mckinsey.com)

We are a values-driven organization. For us this means to always:

- Put the client's interest ahead of our own. This means we deliver more value than expected. It doesn't mean doing whatever the client asks.
- Behave as professionals. Uphold absolute integrity. Show respect to local custom and culture, as long as we don't compromise our integrity.
- Keep our client information confidential. We don't reveal sensitive information. We don't promote our own good work. We focus on making our clients successful.
- Tell the truth as we see it. We stay independent and able to disagree, regardless of the popularity of our views or their effect on our fees. We have the courage to invent and champion unconventional solutions to problems. We do this to help build internal support, get to real issues, and reach practical recommendations.
- Deliver the best of our firm to every client as cost effectively as we can. We expect our people to spend clients' and our firm's resources as if their own resources were at stake.

We operate as one firm. We maintain consistently high standards for service and people so that we can always bring the best team of minds from around the world – with the broadest range of industry and functional experience – to bear on every engagement.

We come to better answers in teams than as individuals. So we do not compete against each other. Instead, we share a structured problem-solving approach, where all opinions and options are considered, researched, and analysed carefully before recommendations are made.

We give each other tireless support. We are fiercely dedicated to developing and coaching one another and our clients. Ours is a firm of leaders who want the freedom to do what they think is right.

In the early stages of your career, it is relatively easy for you to outwardly accept your firm's values – to take things on trust. However, as you learn and discover more about your firm and partners, you will be in a position to better assess whether your firm actually lives its values or whether these values are only honoured in the breech. In fact, most firms' values are published on their intranet or the firm's external website. (See the Box on previous page for professional services firms' values as published on their website.)

When you have been working at your firm for some time, you can ask yourself if the partners' behaviour supports the firm's values – an important indicator of a firm's true values, which are often different from the 'official' firm values. If your personal values include having time for family and friends, is this a value shared by your firm? Does your firm have a long-hours culture, high billing targets and put partner profits ahead of every-thing else?

If you share your firm's values, then this may be the right firm in which to create the future that you want. If, however, you do not share these values, you should seriously consider whether this is the right firm in which to create the future that you want. Hard as it seems, you must trust your *feelings*. This is your career and life and you should not rely solely on your critical and analytical skills in deciding whether this is the right firm for you. If you decide to stay with your firm, you should be aware of your reasons for so doing.

Think about the following questions:

- How well do the values of your firm match your personal values?
- How passionate do you feel about the work that you do at your firm?
- How passionate do you feel about working at your firm?

What you value most in your life should be aligned with your career and where you work. This will make it easier for you to achieve your goals.

> Success without fulfilment is failure. To be both successful and fulfilled, we must be operating on all cylinders in all aspects of our lives.
>
> Antony Robbins

Identifying your vision – or what you want to achieve

Imagine you are a visitor at your retirement party. You see the people closest to you in your life take turns to address the party and talk about you and what you have achieved.

- Who would be talking about you, and what role would they have played in your life?
- How many people would get up to talk about you?
- What would they be saying about you?
- What part would you have played in their lives?
- What would you have achieved with them, with others or by yourself?

To do these questions justice, don't just answer them quickly. After all, your potential future happiness may depend on how seriously you take these questions. Make some time outside the normal hustle and bustle of your everyday life to consider the questions, write down your answers and then reflect on them. The more time you spend to build up as complete a picture as possible the easier it is to have a sense of your personal vision, ie:

- the personal and professional roles you want to play in your life;
- the key achievements you want to have outside and inside work.

For example, take Rakesh Shaunak, Managing Partner of MacIntyre Hudson LLP. His personal vision included the fact that he wanted to make partner by the time he was 30. When he realized that his current career progression within his firm was not going to facilitate this, he left and joined a firm who promised to support him to achieve his vision.

Balancing your career and life roles

So far, we have focused on what you want to achieve in your career. However, over our lives we play a number of different roles for different people in various situations. If you are going to make partner and still have a life, then you need to consider in your personal vision the roles you play inside and outside work. When life is busy, or all your time and energy are focused on completing a deal or project, it is all too easy to ignore the other important areas of your life. While making partner will take a significant amount of focus and effort from you, you cannot afford to ignore your other roles and responsibilities if you want to have a meaningful life.

Professional services firms are littered with partners who have devoted their lives to their careers only to find as they approach retirement that they don't have anything else in their lives.

Over our lives we play a number of different roles for different people in various situations – Table 2.3 shows the roles that Heather and Jo currently play in their lives.

TABLE 2.3   Life roles for Heather and Jo

Situation/arena	Roles
Family	Daughter Sister Wife Mother Auntie Godmother
Friends	Best friend Drinking buddy
Self	Gym member Cyclist Reader Writer School football team supporter
Work	Accounts Payable leader Boss Improvement facilitator Safety team member Mentor
Community	Neighbour Volunteer Committee member Churchgoer

Now let's think about you. What are your life roles? Using Table 2.4, brainstorm all the roles which you play in your life that are important to you. Do bear in mind that your roles and responsibilities will change over time.

TABLE 2.4   Your life roles

Areas of your life	Your roles
Family	
Friends	
Community	
Colleague	
Team member	
Work	
Hobbies and recreation	
Anything else?	

What have you learnt from completing this exercise?

Now that you have considered all the roles you want to play in the many facets of your life, it is time to consider some of the achievements you would like for each of your present and future roles. You may find using a template such as Table 2.5 helpful. This template can be downloaded at **www.howtomakepartner.com**

Only by having a good sense of your personal vision will you be able to determine whether you are on the right career trajectory to satisfy all the roles you want to play in your life. Very often it is this lack of personal vision which results in professionals letting their career progression drift or even stall.

TABLE 2.5 Template for desired achievements

Role	Timescale (years)								
	1	2	3	4	5	10	15	20	25
Family: *Parent*						Become a parent	Have 2 children		
Business			Be promoted to director	Have a portfolio worth £150k per year		Be asked to join the partnership			Start to reduce working commitments ready for retirement
Hobbies and Recreation: *Runner*	Run 5k	Run 10k	Run half marathon	Run full marathon					
Family: *Partner*					Be in a happy, long-term relationship				

Unlike your personal values, your personal vision will change as time goes on. For example, similarly to Sandra, ex-city corporate lawyer, you may find that the burning ambition which drove you to go for partner in your twenties may diminish in your thirties, very often this is because your role as a partner in a professional services firm becomes less important to you than your role as a parent.

The Wheel of Life

The Wheel of Life gives you a vivid visual picture of the way your life is at present, compared with the way that you would ideally like it to be. It is a great tool for you to regularly use to assess whether you are progressing in your career without sacrificing your quality of life outside work. This tool allows you to consider each area of your life in turn and assess where you currently are, and what's off balance. Equally important, the Wheel of Life can also help you to identify the areas where you need to pay more attention and prioritize. See Diagram 2.2.

DIAGRAM 2.2   The Wheel of Life

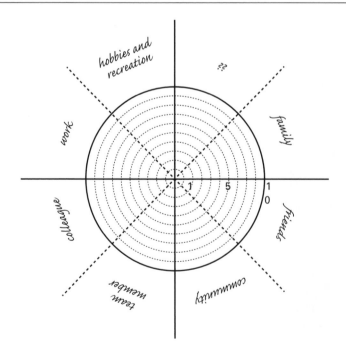

How to use the Wheel of Life

1 Write down each important area of your life on the Wheel of Life circle, one on each spoke of the wheel. We've suggested some generic areas – however, feel free to change the titles and choose your own.

2 Next think about each area in turn, and score yourself in each area on a scale of 1 (poor) to 10 (wonderful).

3 Join up the marks around the circle. In Diagram 2.3, you have someone who is over-investing in their life at work, compared to their life outside work. Does your life wheel look and feel balanced? What are the gaps? Do these areas of your life need immediate attention? Remember that gaps go both ways – like most people, there are almost certainly areas that are not getting as much attention as you would like. Equally, there may be areas where you are investing more time than you would ideally like. These are the areas which sap the energy and enthusiasm that may be better directed elsewhere.

4 Now, consider your ideal level in each area of your wheel – a balanced life doesn't mean getting 10 in each life area: some areas need more attention and focus than others, depending on where you are in your career and life. Like us, sometimes you will have to make compromises and tough choices because your time is limited; the really important thing is to decide your priorities and time you want to give to each area of your life. Once you have decided, plan your life around your roles and responsibilities. When you are planning your week ahead, ask yourself, 'What is the most important thing that I can do this week in each of my roles and responsibilities?'

> **Tip**
>
> Every six months, ideally before your annual or bi-annual performance review, take some time out to think about your personal vision. You may like to redo the Wheel of Life exercise to help you do this. Identify what changes you need to make in the next six months to help you achieve your personal vision.

DIAGRAM 2.3   A completed Wheel of Life

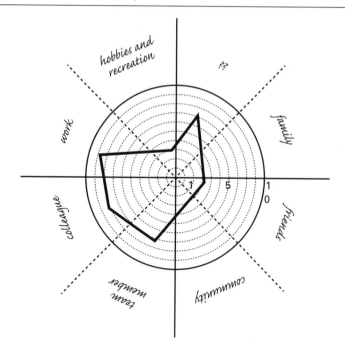

Identifying your purpose – or your reason for being

Now consider your answers to the following questions:

- How can I stand out and be different in my personal career?
- What difference do I want to make in my life at work?
- How can I make a positive difference to my firm and the people close to me?

The answers to these questions will help you understand your purpose, or 'your reason for being'. Your purpose helps you understand the reasons, and your personal motivation, for your specific vision for your life and career. When you identify your purpose, you will:

- be provided with more clarity about who you are, and who you want to be;
- have a career focus which is aligned with your personal vision;
- be energized and enthused when you are working towards your purpose.

Bringing together your vision with your purpose will ensure that your choices and decisions are aligned and true to who you are. This will also enable you to gain and retain your focus and momentum. As a result you will become increasingly clear about the following vital ingredients for your career within professional services:

- your talent – what you are really good at;
- what you love doing;
- what clients need and how you can help them;
- your development needs;
- what support you need from your firm.

In Chapter 7 you will be helped to write your own career plan, including your personal and career goals which you want to achieve. The values, vision and purpose for yourself which you have identified in this chapter will drive this career plan.

Summary

Being fully responsible for managing your life and your career will give you a wonderful feeling of empowerment. Remember that, hard though it may sound, you are personally responsible for building the career and life you want.

Your identity is made up of three elements:

- your values;
- your vision;
- your purpose.

If you are to successfully make partner and build the life you want both inside and outside work, your own values and vision need to be closely matched with your firm's values and vision.

Action points

- What inspired you to choose your profession?
- Complete the values exercise to identify your personal values.

- How many of your five 'most significant' personal values are present for you in your current job?

- Look at your firm's intranet or ask a partner about the values of your current firm. How well do they align with your personal values?

- Imagine you are attending your own retirement party. Who is there? What are they saying about you? How well does this match with your current career and life choices?

- What vision and purpose do you want to have?

- What gives you the greatest job satisfaction?

- In what areas would you like your job satisfaction to increase?

- What roles do you play in your life?

- Complete the Wheel of Life exercise for the areas of your life which are important to you now and in the future. What areas need more attention from you?

- Are you currently in the right firm to create the future which you want?

- Consider how your personal values have been formed. What is likely to influence you in the future? How will this impact on your career?

Further resources

Books

Gilbert, A, Frisby, N and Roberts, K (2001) *Go to Work on Your Career*, Go Mad Books, UK

Shindler, D (2011) *Learning to Leap: A guide to being more employable*, Hothive press, UK

Wilson, J and Blumenthal, I (2008) *Managing Brand You: 7 Steps to creating your most successful self*, Amacom, US

Websites and blogs

http://www.freshfields.com/aboutus/ourValues/
http://www.mckinsey.com/About_us/Our_Values
How to make partner – http://www.howtomakepartner.com

The four different routes to partnership

TOPICS COVERED IN THIS CHAPTER:

- The four different routes to partnership
- How the size of your firm will impact your journey through to partnership

Every professional services firm is different, which means there is no one-size-fits-all route to partnership. Your personal journey to partner will differ depending on the size of your firm, the opportunities that present themselves, as well as your own personal strengths. In this chapter we show a few of the diverse paths to making partner that others have taken. This will enable you to develop your own ideas on how to find and navigate the right road for you.

Differences between small firms and large firms

Every professional services firm (PSF) has its own distinct culture, infrastructure, processes and systems. As we have found many times, this is all part of the charm and the challenge of working within professional services. However, there are some generalizations we can make when comparing the route you will take to get to partner in a small firm or a large firm.

Formal talent management processes and systems

The large and increasingly the medium-size firms are likely to start formally assessing your potential to make partner if not from your first day, definitely from when you qualify. The partners, directors and sometimes managers in a large firm work to an annual timetable, driven by the firm's performance and development review (PDR) process, to routinely assess the potential of individual fee earners and their potential for making partner within the firm. Your perceived future potential will influence whether you are given more or fewer opportunities than your peers to acquire the experience and personal development that you need to accelerate your career progression.

In a small firm, talent management processes and systems are much more likely to be informal and, if they exist at all, less likely to be documented. Any talent management and development conversations are likely to happen primarily at partner-to-partner level with some input from the HR function. While the talent management and development processes are rarely documented in a small firm, there still will be an 'established' way of doing things which may differ depending on which partner you speak to within the firm.

Regardless of a firm's size, the majority of firms will only admit new partners to the partnership at the start of a firm's financial year. It then makes it easy for a firm to assess comparative performances of each partner across the financial year. However, some firms will also admit new partners at the halfway point of their financial year.

Assessment and development programmes at key career milestones

Large firms have the capacity to design and implement formal talent management development programmes and processes which focus on moving their people through a sequence of work-related experiences. The tasks/projects become more challenging as they groom potential partners to be business savvy. By contrast, small firms try to achieve the same in an informal manner.

As most small firms rarely have the resources to put in place formalized management processes and systems, you are highly unlikely to experience an assessment and development programme in a small firm after you reach associate or manager level.

Diversity of skill set

Where a firm has a large number of partners it will have more flexibility in terms of the skills and competencies required by each partner. As a result a large firm has the relative luxury that not all partners are required to go into the marketplace to generate their own client work. For example, some large firms have within their partnership a select and small number of highly respected technical specialists, who have a track record of delivering excellent client service and profitability. While such partners may lack the interpersonal skills and personality to build their own client base, their profile and reputation in the market make them highly marketable and the firm will do whatever is required to retain their expertise. Using their expertise, these partners generate money for the firm from referrals coming from other partners.

In a small firm, the size of the cake, ie profits to be generated and shared, is significantly smaller than in a large firm. This means that individual partners must be able to win more business from both existing and new clients, to contribute to the firm's revenue and profit. This is also required of the technical specialist partner – in a small firm each and every partner is responsible for bringing in business.

The four different routes to partnership

While each professional's route to partner is different, there are four main routes:

- The traditional route: This is where you work your way up from trainee to partner within the same firm.

- The lateral route: This is where you make partner by changing firm(s).

- The in-house route: This is where you leave private practice and go into industry (in-house), but return later to private practice, and either work your way up to partner or return as a partner.

- Going it alone: Rather than staying within an established professional practice and working your way up to partner, you leave to set up your own practice.

The traditional route

Twenty or 30 years ago, it was uncommon for established professionals to move between practices. If you look at the career paths of the older partners within your practice, you will find that there is a significant percentage who have grown up with the firm – 'man and boy' – having joined the firm usually straight from university as a trainee and made their way up to partner. Unless they have undertaken secondments along the way, they have no external work experience. It's now getting less common for partners to have only worked at one firm during their working life. For this route to partnership to be right for you, you need to be confident regarding the following criteria:

- Your personal values and those of your firm, are closely aligned.

- Your firm is able to meet your personal partnership ambitions in your chosen specialism, within your personal timetable.

- You feel that this is the 'right' firm, and you have established strong personal relationships within the firm.

Case study: Myfanwy Neville, BKL LLP

After university, Myfanwy decided to join BKL LLP, a small/medium London-based accountancy practice, rather than one of the big four, as she liked the personable, bright people that the practice was able to attract. Nine years later, Myfanwy was made up to partner. What has kept her at BKL, rather than moving to another firm, has been the quality of the people at the practice.

Case study: Peter Gillman, Price Bailey

Peter Gillman, Managing Director of Price Bailey, never had any ambitions to become a partner. However, his ethos was to never turn down an opportunity, and so he moved around the firm's offices as his career progressed upwards. Thirty years ago, he was offered the chance to join the partnership, after a partner in his office was convicted of fraud and left the practice.

The lateral route

The lateral route to partnership has become more common in recent years. Most firms expect that they will need to regularly augment their talent pool with experienced hires from outside the firm. This happens where the firm hasn't been able to develop their own talent in a particular specialism, or the firm chooses to bring in an experienced hire for strategic reasons, eg the experienced hire brings with them a valuable client portfolio.

You will need to seriously think about choosing this route to partnership if:

- your route to partnership within your firm is blocked by more senior members of your practice area who will make partner before you, and, in all probability, significantly slow your career progression;
- your personal values are clashing with the firm's values;
- you are not excited by the thought of spending the whole of your career with your current firm;
- you feel as if your face doesn't fit within your firm;
- you've had some personality conflicts within influential parts of the firm and believe that people will block your way;
- you feel as if you won't be able to achieve all your life goals if you make partner within your current firm;
- you are not excited and passionate about your firm's clients and likely future clients;
- your firm is experiencing financial difficulties and growth of the firm is looking very unlikely;
- your firm has many partners within your particular specialism, none of whom is likely to leave or retire in the short or medium term;
- you want variety, to experience work in more than one firm before making partner.

Janet Legrand, board member at DLA Piper LLP

Janet trained and qualified into the commercial litigation department at Lovells Hogan LLP. However, she felt that her career was not progressing fast enough, so she looked around for a firm that would allow her to achieve partnership faster. She joined a smaller firm, as a junior partner, which merged very shortly afterwards to become DLA Piper.

Rakesh Shaunak, senior partner at MacIntyre Hudson LLP

Rakesh wanted to make partner by the time he was 30. After qualification, he moved out to his firm's Beckenham office, with the view that he would take over from the partner in that office who was meant to be retiring soon. However, the firm's strategy changed and gaining partnership with his firm by the time Rakesh was 30 was looking less and less likely. So Rakesh looked around in the marketplace and interviewed with a few firms. He accepted a role with a newly merged firm, MacIntyre Hudson LLP, who delivered on their promise of making him partner before he was 30.

The in-house route

This is a less common route to partnership due to not having a client following, but one that brings many benefits, particularly the first-hand experience of being embedded in a client's business. Often you are recruited back into a professional services firm because of your now deep sector knowledge and the contacts you have built up while you were in industry.

The reasons for choosing this route are very similar to the lateral route to partner. However, you may like to consider this route if:

- you are not entirely convinced that you want a long-term career within a professional services firm;
- you want to be able to build up an in-depth knowledge of a particular sector and increase your network within the industry accordingly;
- you want to extend your commercial acumen.

James, partner at regional law firm

James trained and qualified as a commercial lawyer with his firm, but found that his career progression had started to lag behind his peers. As a result, he decided to leave private practice and take an in-house role in a national UK company. In his new role, James's confidence and self-belief soared. After four years in his role, an international company acquired his business. At this point, his old firm approached James with an offer of partnership, asking if he could persuade his international company to appoint the firm as their legal adviser. As a result, James was made an equity partner ahead of the people he had qualified with.

Going it alone

Instead of trying to make partner in an established partnership, you can start up your own practice. This is a very common route to partnership, and often people take this route after they have spent some time working outside in industry. If you want to be your own boss you have three different options:

- Buy into an established practice which is for sale.
- Buy a franchise.
- Start up your own practice from scratch.

Often senior members of the professions want to be in full control of their career.

> I wanted to stop being a bit player in someone else's story, and have the opportunity to write my own career story.
>
> Kim Whitaker, Kim Whitaker Legal Services

You may wish to consider this route if:

- you want the freedom and flexibility that being your own boss can bring;
- you are very entrepreneurial in your outlook, attitude to risk and reward;
- you feel stifled within an established practice;
- you want to run your own business;
- you want to practise as a professional, but weave your work commitments around your family or interests or hobbies;
- you have been made redundant and decide that this is an ideal opportunity to work for yourself.

Stuart Gould, turnaround specialist for SG Associates

Stuart trained and qualified as a turnaround specialist with KPMG LLP. He was pushing to make partner within KPMG LLP when he realized that he would have to sacrifice family time to do so. At this point, he moved to become a director at BDO LLP at their then new Cambridge office, with the promise of partnership if he built up the practice to a certain size, when the incumbent partner retired. However, the UK recession changed the strategy regarding Stuart's part of the business and he found himself surplus to requirements. At the time, few practices were in a position to take on a director with partnership ambitions in the next 12–24 months. Consequently, Stuart started up his own practice, doing what he did at BDO LLP and KPMG LLP but working for himself.

> ### Kim Whitaker, Kim Whitaker Legal Services
>
> After ten years of being in practice, and nearly ten years as the senior legal counsel, Kim knew she wanted to be able to write her own story rather than play a bit part in someone else's. A merger gave her the opportunity to set up her own practice. She initially worked for a virtual legal network before deciding the right thing for her personally was to be a sole practitioner.

> ### Dona Skaife, WBS Accountants
>
> Dona always knew that she wanted to run her own practice, and made her career choices accordingly. Dona moved into industry fairly early after qualification as she wanted to build up her commerciality before starting her own practice. After a couple of roles within industry, Dona started up WBS Accountants to be able to give her the flexibility to create a working life which worked around the requirements of her young family.

The three different types of partner

Partners typically split into three types:

- *Rainmakers*: These have a reputation for being very skilled at winning new work.
- *Leaders*: These are given specific leadership and managerial responsibilities for running part or all of the firm.
- *Technical specialists*: These have a deep level of technical expertise in a particular specialism, which is of strategic importance to the firm.

Most firms, regardless of their size, have now recognized that their partners need to be well-rounded individuals who can first and foremost develop their own client portfolio. Consequently, it is now extremely rare for a professional to make partner purely based on their technical expertise. Many firms have created a new job role to enable them to retain their prized technical specialists who do not have the capability to make partner.

Being a partner solely based on your technical expertise means that you will always be vulnerable – changes in the legal framework, marketplace or technology can wipe out the requirement for your technical expertise. For example, the recession after the 2008–09 UK property market crash caused a severe contraction in the business available to property specialists, such as corporate financiers, property lawyers and tax specialists. The senior and expensive property professionals who were weak business developers were the first people to lose their jobs in the recession.

Exercise: Which route for partnership is right for you?

- Gather together the results of your values comparison exercise and your Wheel of Life results, which you completed in Chapter 2. Read through these.

- Looking at the four routes to partnership, which route appeals to you and plays to your strengths and life aspirations?

- If your chosen route is to stay and work towards partnership within your current firm:
  - Schedule a meeting with your mentor or partner to discuss how you will achieve this.
  - In this meeting, talk about what is a realistic time frame to be able to make partner. Predicting the future in a firm is difficult, so be prepared for the time frame to be very loose.

- If your chosen route is outside your current firm, book some time with a career coach:
  - Discuss and agree key milestones for you to achieve.
  - With your partner, mentor or coach, identify a development plan to help you acquire the necessary knowledge, skills and behaviours to be successful on your chosen route.

As you read through the rest of this book, revisit this exercise as you go along.

Summary

You need to decide the best route for you, whether to stay at one firm throughout your career, or move firms and roles within industry. Your choice will be determined by how well your current firm is performing and whether it can accommodate your partnership ambitions within your preferred timescales.

Most firms have three types of partners; rainmakers, leaders and technical specialists. Over the last ten years it has become very rare for an individual to be made up to partner purely on the basis of their technical capabilities. However, most firms will still promote you up to partner if you are seen to be great at winning work, ie rainmaking.

Action points

- Ask your mentor or partner what route they took to become partner. What prompted them to take their chosen career choices?
- Interview some people who run their own business. Find out how they came to be running this business and the highlights and lowlights of being their own boss.
- Complete the Exercise: Which route for partnership is right for you?
- Find some blogs of professionals who have started up their own practice. After reading these blogs, are you inspired by their career path and accompanying lifestyle?

Further resources

Books

Ennico, C (2009) *The Partner Track: How to go from associate to partner in any law firm*, Kaplan Trade, US

Maister, D (2003) *Managing the Professional Services Firm*, Simon & Schuster, London

Mayson, S (1997) *Making Sense of Law Firms: Strategy, structure and ownership*, Blackstone Press Limited, US

Websites and blogs

Roll on Friday: News, views and gossip on law firms – http://www.rollonfriday.com/

The Big 4 – http://www.big4.com

Kim Whitaker Legal Services Blog – http://www.kimwhitaker.com

How to maker partner Blog – http://www.howtomakepartner.com

Is partnership for you? Making the right choices

04

TOPICS COVERED IN THIS CHAPTER ARE:

- Practical guidance to help you decide whether you want to go for partner
- What options are open to you if you decide not to go for partnership?
- The sacrifices you may need to make if you decide not to go for partnership

In the last chapter we asked you to think about what you want from your career. Despite what nearly every new entrant into the professions believes, partnership is not for everyone. In this chapter we look at the many different ways you can positively progress your career, without ending up in a partner role. Only by fully understanding all the career options open to you as a professional can you take an informed decision on whether going for partner is right for you.

Becoming a career manager

Case study: Louise

Louise joined a large consultancy firm after graduation. While Louise enjoyed the variety of the work, she was not excited about the prospect of becoming a partner. She really enjoyed the client work, and was quite content to stay at the manager role. When the recession hit, Louise was made redundant. With her large consultancy experience, Louise was able to pick up an interim contract with a smaller consultancy practice fairly quickly. Her role was made permanent, and she is currently enjoying her client work without feeling under any pressure to progress her career upwards in her new firm.

If you look at the hierarchical nature of professional services, not everyone is going to make it to the top of the pyramid. It's just not possible. Some professionals who realize that they either don't want to make partner or are not going to make partner choose to stay in professional practice. These people become known as career managers or career associates. Sometimes professionals fall into this position because they lose sight of their end career goals and 'drift' in career terms for a certain amount of time. But this isn't necessarily the case; increasingly people are consciously choosing to remain a career manager.

Positives

With the professional services world so focused on 'making partner' it can often be quite difficult to articulate the positives of staying as a career manager, ie someone without significant business development responsibility. However, throwing off the feeling that you are continually chasing career progression can sometimes be very liberating, if this is not what you want for your career and life. For example, if you are experiencing significant change in your life outside work, such as becoming a new parent, you will often welcome a less demanding time at work – whether temporarily or permanently. The great thing about pressing the pause button on your career's upward progression is to know that this is not a career dead end – you still have many career options left open to you. You can press the play button when you are ready and reignite your partnership ambitions at any time, or take a role outside professional services if you prefer. Staying as a career manager means you can focus more on the technical or managerial parts of the role rather than building up your own client portfolio. For many professionals, the technical aspects of their role are their key motivation for entering the professions; therefore being a career manager can mean playing to your personal strength, providing excellent client service and enjoying the personal satisfaction which comes with being able to do that.

Negatives

Becoming a career manager or career associate is often seen as a holding role, until you work out how to progress your career further. Many of the bigger professional services firms have (and apply vigorously) an 'up or out' policy; that is, you must progress up to the next level of seniority within a certain timescale or it will be made clear to you that your future lies outside the practice.

In many professional practices you can become very vulnerable as a career manager. Most firms hold on to their talent by dangling the promise of upwards progression within the firm. However, as most firms can only accommodate a finite number of people at senior grades, this means that if the existing professionals' careers are not moving forward, this has the effect of 'blocking' the career progression of more junior members. This is often referred to as 'bed-blocking' by partners. When bed-blocking exists in a firm, it effectively makes it more difficult for the firm to deliver, or can prevent it from delivering, on its promise to staff of upwards career progression – hence the existence of the 'up or out' policies. That said, the world of professional services firms is changing and many firms have recognized that there is an important and valuable contribution to be made by career managers (we will return to this later).

Moving out of professional services into industry: taking an in-house role

Case study: Mike Newton, Mace Group

Mike was a late entry into law and did his traineeship with Hammonds before qualifying into construction with Eversheds. While he enjoyed being in private practice, he got frustrated by seeing problems that were too late to fix easily and cheaply. He chose to go in-house to be nearer the commercial heart of an organization and enjoy a better work–life balance.

> It used to be a rarity to have really senior lawyers working in an in-house role, but now it would be rare to find a major company without senior general counsel.
> Frances Murphy, head of corporate at Slaughter and May
> (*The Lawyer*, 2012)

Many professional practices, particularly those with an aggressive 'up or out' policy, will often actively help their junior professionals get a role within industry – quite often, this may be within a client's organization. This is often a win–win for the practice and the client: the client gets a highly trained professional who knows their business already, while the professional practice keeps the relationship with the leaving employee positive as they have helped find them their next role, and also strengthens their web of influence within a client's business. Over time, this can also work to your advantage – as you progress to a senior in-house position, your former firm could be working for you.

Positives

For many the shift into working outside professional services will bring a similar level of salary to their previous role in practice, but with significantly less pressure and a shorter working week. The great thing about going into industry is it allows you to strengthen your business and commercial acumen – which is the reason why many firms support a secondment in a client's business, while not precluding a return to practice at a later date.

Industry also benefits from employing people with professional services experience. After all, they are gaining bright, able individuals who are not afraid of hard work. Even better, some other business has paid to train them up to a decent level of technical ability – which they can take advantage of.

In a recent survey by *The Lawyer*, 69 per cent of lawyers in practice would actively consider taking an in-house role in the future. Many professionals are seeing less and less of a divide between the quality of in-house roles and roles in practice.

Some individuals see a move into industry, whether rightly or wrongly, as the only way in which they can sustain a meaningful and intellectually challenging career with parenthood.

> I didn't want to have kids and never see them. It seemed like there were only two choices: either become a corporate lawyer and not see the kids; or see the kids and not be a corporate lawyer.
>
> Suzanne Dibble, ex-City corporate lawyer,
> founder of lawyers4mumpreneurs

Negatives

> You're more exposed and vulnerable in an in-house role. You're at the whim of the business, you can't hide behind the office and the proximity is more demanding.
>
> Sarah Ingwersen, specialist legal recruitment partner at
> Taylor Root (*The Lawyer*, 2012)

As a fee earner within a professional practice, you are core and central to the practice's success, even though it may not feel like it at the time. For those working in a large or medium-size firm this normally means that there are established career paths, a ready-made professional support network and abundant tailor-made learning, training and development opportunities for you. However, we know that this is not the case in all firms. It is worth bearing in mind that often when you move into industry you are taking on a role that supports the business's main function. We have found from personal experience that, as a result, the support functions within the business may have limited internal career progression options and promotion opportunities may be severely restricted; ie you have to wait for the person above or your boss to leave before you can be promoted. However, depending on the size of the company, you may find that your career options are vastly expanded, which may include leadership and management opportunities, and even international assignments.

Career change

Case study: John Stylianou, managing director of Actual People Limited

John became bored with accountancy, and when the opportunity arose he became involved in training and mentoring of trainees and accountants. This led him into leadership and managment development, as a learning and development manager within the profession. Though he was ever diligent and always accurate, a recession saw him displaced and he sought career advice. He chose to start his own business as an executive coach, working with PSFs. He has never been happier.

As schools and career advisers frequently point bright children to careers as lawyers, accountants, engineers, architects or surveyors, it's hardly surprising that there is often a large drop-out rate of professionals three to five years post qualification, as people realize that the career they have chosen isn't what they hoped it would be, and they hanker to do something else.

> I went to a small independent school which had a very narrow-minded career outlook, which was that if you were good at science you were going to be a doctor and if you weren't good at science you were going to be a lawyer.
> Melanie, lawyer

This drop-out rate is noticeable within the accountancy profession. In fact, nearly every accountancy firm anticipates and plans for losing a number of their juniors after qualification. You may be wondering why it's worse in accountancy rather than the other professions. The reality is this: many graduates enter the accountancy profession because it provides a well-paid job and three years of good-quality training, allowing them to gain a highly valued and respected professional qualification paid for by their employers. Equally important, this gives them three more years to decide what they really want to do in their career.

Positives

Deciding to embark on a career outside the professions gives you the freedom to identify and pursue the career you really want to have. This can be personally liberating and for many professionals it provides the *inner meaning* which was lacking in their first choice of career. In many cases, your early years in the professions can positively help you in the next phase of your career. For example, many professionals, in a similar position to John Stylianou, who have made career changes, remain working within the professional services sector, just not in the role they originally qualified to do.

Negatives

The earning potential as a professional is the reason why numerous people are attracted to the professions. However, it's this earning potential that often prevents people from making a career change out of the professions – where else can you earn the same level of money? This means that many professionals remain trapped in careers which they hate because they cannot afford to take a cut in income. Let us explain further. As a newly qualified lawyer or accountant within a mid-size London firm, you may earn £40k+ a year. Very often your lifestyle, financial responsibilities and outgoings adjust to this salary. This then makes it hard to take a significant pay cut or to take a couple of years out not earning anything while you are retraining. To be able to take a career change, most people need to plan and build their savings, which will then allow them to retrain.

Once you have retrained or travelled a way down your journey in your second career it may be very difficult, but not impossible, to go back into practice. This is because most professional practices will be concerned about your long-term commitment to the profession.

Is partnership for you?

In the last chapters we have looked at what it will take to become a partner in a professional services firm. The role of partner is not for everyone; for those for whom it is right there are huge rewards in terms of status, responsibility and very often significant financial gain. However, the journey to partnership is littered with people who have either not made the grade or made large personal sacrifices to get the word 'partner' on their business card only to find that it is not what they want from a career and life after all.

Have a look back at Chapter 2. Are your personal values, vision and purpose compatible with making partner within your current professional services firm? Or would another larger or smaller firm be a better fit for your career and life ambitions? Or would your career and life goals fit better in a career outside professional services? See Diagram 4.1.

DIAGRAM 4.1   Your career options

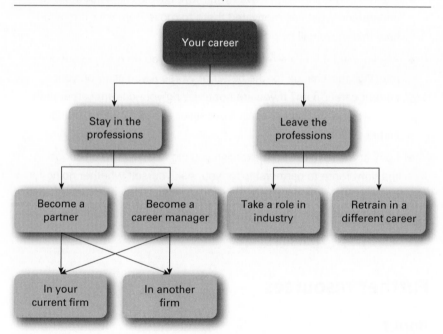

Summary

Only if you are fully aware of all the career options open to you are you able to take an informed decision on whether partnership is right for you. Despite what most trainees or juniors believe, not everyone is suited to the role of partner. The alternatives to making partner are:

- staying in a professional services firm and becoming a career manager or associate;
- moving out of the professions and into industry;
- retraining and choosing a different career.

Action points

- Next time you are at a dinner with your fellow professionals, ask them where they want their career to end, and why.
- The next time someone leaves your firm, have a chat with them to understand what has motivated them to move from your firm and how this move will help their career.
- Ask yourself if you are really enjoying what you do now in your current role. Will this change for the better or worse if you carry on your current career path? If you are not enjoying your current career path, then work with a career coach/counsellor to help you find the right career path for you.
- Look at the results of the exercise you did in Chapter 3 on choosing the right route to partnership for you. Ask yourself whether going for partnership is the right decision for you and your career. Will you still be able to achieve your career and life goals if you stay with your current firm and career path?

Further resources

Books

Bridges, W (2009) *Transitions: Making sense of life's changes*, Nicholas Brealey Publishing, London

Ennico, C (2009) *The Partner Track: How to go from associate to partner in any law firm*, Kaplan Trade, US

Finer, N and Nash, E (2011) *More to Life than Shoes: How to kick-start your career and change your life*, Hay House, London

Gilbert, A, Frisby, N and Roberts, K (2001) *Go to Work on Your Career*, Go Mad Books, UK

Shindler, D (2011) *Learning to Leap: A guide to being more employable*, Hothive press, UK

Websites and blogs

Roll on Friday: News, views and gossip on law firms – http://www.rollonfriday.com/

Career Shifters Blog — http://www.careershifters.org/blog

Position Ignition Career Blog – http://www.positionignition.com/blog

Jenny Blake's Life after college blog – http://www.lifeaftercollege.org/blog/

Articles

The Lawyer, Interior Designs article, 2 April 2012

The Lawyer, In-house attitudes report, 2012

05

How to become partnership potential

TOPICS COVERED IN THIS CHAPTER:

- What does partnership potential mean?
- What happens to those people formally or informally tagged as partnership potential?
- How do you get noticed and classed as partnership potential?

> *When you are seen to be partnership potential, your career is actively managed, your work load is constantly reviewed and balanced, and you are given the pick of the assignments.*

HEENA PATTNI, STRESS MANAGEMENT COACH AND EX-KPMG

So far in this part of the book we have looked at whether partnership is right for you. For some people, the route to partnership is a hard slog. However, there are often a select number of people who have a relatively easy route. These select few are often tagged by partners as 'partnership potential', meaning they may be given extra help, whether formally or informally, to make it to partner. In this chapter we explore what is meant by 'partnership potential' and how you, too, can be seen as partnership potential by your firm's partners.

What is partnership potential?

In identifying partnership potential, firms are looking for the individuals who have the highest *future* value to the firm: the fee earners whose performance is seen to be likely to be critical to the practice's future success. Every professional services firm (PSF) is, therefore, looking out for members of staff who have the future capability to progress through to a partner role. This process may happen either formally or informally, depending on how structured a firm is in its approach to talent development and management. For example, most large firms will have formal processes, including bi-annual performance reviews, quarterly evaluations and end-of-assignment assessments, in place to help them identify their most important fee earners. However, before you decide that you want to be seen as partnership potential, you should be aware that it can be both a blessing and a curse for your career within the firm. Of course, it's great for your career and visibility when you are doing well. The downside is that your failures will be more public and noticeable.

What is a star?

In addition to hearing people being referred to as having partnership potential, you may also hear the same people referred to as being 'stars' or having 'star' potential. Stars, who can be found at every level of a PSF, are defined in the following way by Jay Lorsch and Thomas Tierney in their book, *Aligning the Stars: How to succeed when professionals drive results*:

> Stars are people who have the highest future value for the firm, the individuals who will have the most impact on the business in the years ahead. Most, but not all, partner-level professionals are stars, as are potential partners and other exceptional performers who fulfil critical roles in the organization.
>
> J Lorsch and T Tierney

The importance of your market value

Can firms identify future partners early in their careers? The answer is, not with any degree of certainty – it's not an exact science. The new professional who after one year with the firm looks like a potential partner may be overtaken by a 'late developer' or they may decide to change career. A critical indicator used by firms in identifying those with partnership potential is their internal and external market value. Every professional, including you, has a perceived market value from their first day with a firm. Your *internal* market value is driven by the firm's ongoing need to decide whom to allocate to assignments, whereas your *external* market value is decided by clients and others outside the firm.

Your internal market value

In PSFs, professionals begin to compete with each other from day one in their career. While this may sound harsh, this competition is driven by the firm needing to sell as much of its professionals' time (utilization) and at as high a price as possible every year. The easier it is to sell a fee earner's time, the more in demand they are going to be. Hence, their internal market value is high. You may be familiar with the following scenario: partners are insisting that only a particular associate or manager can do the work, while another associate is left sitting around with little or no work to do. This is an example of the *internal* market demonstrating the two associates' perceived relative market value.

Most professionals understand the internal marketplace intuitively. In fact, in many firms, partners can tell within a year of new fee earners joining the firm who among them is in the top quartile and who is in the bottom.

Your external market value

Putting it very simply, your external market value is driven by how much you are in demand from your clients or other advisers acting on behalf of your client. Very often your market value can significantly increase by, usually unprompted, favourable client feedback; which then leads to you undertaking more assignments for that client.

How to be perceived as having partnership potential

Based on our years of experience in working with professional services, and our research, we have identified five characteristics that enable firms to identify the individual's future partnership potential.

These are:

- commitment to the firm, its vision and its clients;
- commerciality;

- leadership and management;
- emotional intelligence;
- 'thinking' skills.

Our purpose in setting out these characteristics is to help you to understand what your partners are looking for when they perceive someone to be partnership potential. All too often, in our experience, associates and managers have limited information regarding what their firm and partners are looking for and as a result, they rely on word of mouth, which can be both misleading and sometimes totally wrong.

Unfortunately there are no hard and fast rules for which of these characteristics are seen to be more important in your firm. The only way for you to find this out is to ask the partners in your firm what they are looking for in deciding that someone has partnership potential. While one firm may place more emphasis on some of these characteristics, typically your firm will expect you to acquire and demonstrate, if you are to be selected as partnership potential, *all* of these characteristics in the early years of your career.

Commitment to the firm, its vision and its clients

> The first thing which happens after you are made up to a partner is you are given a P45.
> Darryn Hedges, divisional business director, Addleshaw Goddard LLP

When you become a partner, you stop being an employee and actually own a slice of the business. As any business owner will tell you, the very nature of running your own business means you have to be 100 per cent committed to making your business a success. This means that most business owners, whether or not they are a partner in a PSF, do not have a nine-to-five type of job. As a consequence, partners are looking for the next generation of partners to already show that they are totally committed to helping make their firm a success.

This commitment tends to manifest itself in five ways:

1 responsiveness to clients' requirements;
2 commitment to the firm's vision;
3 openness to responsibility and opportunities;
4 taking initiative and regularly going the extra mile;
5 trustworthiness and reliability.

1. Responsiveness to clients' requirements

Ultimately, a PSF lives or dies by how well it services its clients; which means that any fee earner who wants to have a long and enjoyable career within a PSF, must be passionate about their clients and the work they do for them.

Typically, partners will be looking for people who are totally committed to the firm's clients to be demonstrating:

- they understand their client's needs;
- they take pride in delivering a great service for their clients;
- they can empathize with their clients.

2. Commitment to the firm's vision

Partners are looking for people who at an early stage in their career are actively participating in helping the firm achieve its vision. As partners are responsible for the future sustainability of the firm, it makes sense that they are looking for people who are also committed to making this happen. It may only be small things, such as speaking up in a meeting on firm-wide proposed changes, but this can help you to be seen as 'committed' and someone the partners want to nurture for the future.

3. Openness to responsibility and opportunities

> Within our new crop of graduates at Accenture, there were basically two types of people we had. There were those who were indignant that they would need to travel because it would impact their personal lives. And there were those who jumped head first into the travel and embraced it. Since a successful consultancy relies on going where the work is, this was a critical test of which ones were going to make partner.
>
> Antoinette Oglethorpe, leadership consultant and coach

One of the ways in which partners assess someone's commitment to the firm and its clients is seeing how open they are to responsibility and opportunities.

Peter Gillman, Managing Director of Price Bailey LLP, unusually for a partner, openly admits he never had any ambitions to become a partner. When he was promoted to partner, 30 years ago, technical competence drove the partnership selection process; ie can we trust you to sign off a file? However, he always had an ethos of never turning down any opportunity. As a result he took on a range of roles within the firm in the different Price Bailey offices, which opened doors for him to be promoted eventually to partner.

If you want to be identified as partnership potential, you have to be prepared to embrace the opportunities that may come your way. This may involve a secondment in a client's business after qualification, regularly attending a networking group for young professionals, or you could volunteer to be a departmental representative for a firm-wide initiative.

Tip

One of the ways of raising your profile with the people who can accelerate your career is to volunteer to be on cross-firm projects and committees, eg the firm's social committee.

This openness to opportunities will help you gain early responsibility during your career with a firm. It may only be organizing the social stuff. Or it could be taking on the responsibility for the marketing plan for your part of the practice. It's this willingness to get involved – particularly on cross-firm projects or events – which will help build your profile in the firm so you get noticed and potentially considered to be 'one to watch for the future'.

4. Taking initiative and going the extra mile

An important thing for trainees (and in fact, anyone at any stage of their careers) to remember is to take ownership of their work. It's very easy when you're a junior, senior or sometimes even a manager to think that someone else above you will sort out a problem.

Myfanwy Neville, partner at
Berg Krapow Lewis LLP

With the many calls on senior people's time, the less they have to help you to complete the task they have delegated to you, the easier it is for them to ask for you to work on their clients. Understandably, when you are very junior in a firm, you are not expected to be the finished article and a certain amount of close supervision is expected. However, the more times that you can find the answers to your questions yourself and not get other people to solve your problems for you, the more likely it is that you will begin to gain a reputation for being a 'self-starter'. Being labelled as a self-starter will significantly increase your internal market value within your firm. Ask any partner what types of people they want working with their clients. The likely answer is that someone who is a 'self-starter' will feature high on their list.

5. Trustworthy and reliable

One of the many reasons why graduates are attracted to the professions is the opportunities that many are given to do real mentally stretching work on interesting clients. However, before you will be let loose on the really juicy and challenging assignments, which will build your profile with the right people in the firm, you have to be seen to be committed and trusted to regularly deliver error-free work of a high standard. No one is going to give sensitive or difficult assignments to those in the firm who have a question mark over their competence, reliability or trustworthiness.

Commerciality

> Any professional services firm is composed of three main functions: marketing, manufacturing and management.
>
> Rakesh Shaunak, managing partner of MacIntyre Hudson LLP

The long-term health of any PSF is firmly rooted in its ability to market itself and win new business. This means that any partner within a practice is routinely expected to spot and exploit commercial opportunities to ultimately benefit the whole firm, not just their area of the practice. It also means that when partners are looking for people with partnership potential, they are looking for those fee earners who are keen to become involved in the firm's business development activities, and have a 'nose' for identifying potential work-winning opportunities both with existing clients and in the marketplace as a whole. Therefore, if you are going to progress in your firm, understanding your firm's business and how it makes money is essential knowledge that you must acquire early in your career. See Chapter 9 for more information on how your firm makes money.

Your ability to make partner relies heavily on you building and maintaining a loyal client following. This means increasingly clients are expecting their professional adviser to be more than just a technical specialist; you must be able to utilize your commerciality to benefit your clients. In fact, in the mind of a client a professional's technical ability is a given. What they really want from their adviser is someone who can:

- understand what makes their business tick;
- identify opportunities to help the business;
- tailor their advice to the client's business circumstances.

However, not every professional is able to demonstrate these abilities – which is why when a partner spots these abilities in a junior member of staff they sit up and take notice of that individual and their career.

Leadership and management

Unless you are a sole practitioner, you will always have responsibility to lead, develop and manage others. It's common for a professional to have responsibility for others very early on in their career. For example, recently qualified accountants will be expected to manage the junior members of the team on a client's site, while the supervisor or manager for the job will be based out of the firm's office. Being a successful partner is not just about your ability to lead and manage others, but also how well you are able to self-lead and self-manage. After all, when you get to partner, you nominally become your own boss.

Partners will typically be looking for people who do four things:

1 Drive their career.
2 Commit to achieving outstanding results.
3 Build, lead and develop a team and the people within it.
4 Work well within a team.

1. Drive their career

> I remember when I was a trainee I went out with the managing partner and told him that I was going to be managing partner by the time I was 30!
>
> James, partner

No one else is going to drive your career forward – it has to come from you. Long gone are the days when, as Peter Gillman, Managing Director of Price Bailey experienced 30 years ago when he was asked to join the partnership, you would experience a tap on the shoulder from the partners inviting you to become a partner of the practice.

As Jonathan found on his way to becoming a partner at a high street law firm, he was only able to move his career progression on by having direct conversations with the partners in his practice about what he needed to do to be promoted to partner. So ask yourself this question. How many influential partners and directors in your part of your practice know about your career aspirations? If your answer is 'none or not many', then you probably have some work to do to drive forward your career.

2. Commit to achieving outstanding results

Striving for mediocrity within a PSF is normally a recipe for disaster. Clients want their professional adviser to be fully committed to helping them solve their problems and meet all expectations set. Assignment managers want the fee earners on their assignments to be a safe pair of hands who they can rely on to do the tasks assigned to them. Think about the last time a client said they would e-mail or phone you and didn't. How did it make you feel about the client? Now imagine that it was the other way around – how damaging is this to your relationship with the client?

Partners know that one of the ways to keep and build a loyal client base is to consistently meet or exceed clients' expectations. Therefore, when assessing who has the potential to be a partner of the firm, partners will be looking for employees who share this ethos of delivering outstanding results for clients.

3. Build, lead and develop a team and the people within it

Most pieces of client work involve a team of professionals working on it. These teams are often quickly brought together for a piece of work, and then rapidly disbanded when the engagement is finished. Consequently, firms need good team players who can quickly build a high-performing team. If from an early stage you show an aptitude to knit together and lead a team, the partners in your firm will notice you for the right reasons. In Chapter 19, we look at the skills required to be able to do this.

> Eventually, I learnt the truth. You don't make people want to spend time with you because they feel good about *you*. You do it by making them feel good about *themselves* when they are with you.
>
> David Maister

4. Work well within a team

Like any business owner, partners running a professional practice generally want to have a profitable and happy firm. Their life is much easier if their employees get on with each other. Let's face it: staffing issues can be difficult and time consuming, preventing partners from getting on with the stuff they love – working with clients and winning new clients. So, if you are going to be picked out as partnership potential, then you need to personally:

- develop and maintain a happy and 'can do' attitude;
- encourage openness and cooperative working;
- develop mutually supportive relationships;
- communicate openly and honestly with others.

5. Emotional intelligence

Daniel Goleman found that the qualities normally associated with leadership – such as intelligence, toughness, determination and vision – are required for success, but they are not enough. Truly effective leaders are also distinguished by a high degree of emotional intelligence, which includes self-awareness, self-regulation, motivation, empathy and social skill. Consequently you will find that many firms, similar to BDO LLP, will assess potential partners for emotional intelligence.

The six signs of emotional intelligence, which partners will notice when thinking about someone's partnership potential, include:

1 maturity;
2 resilience;
3 'fit' socially;
4 likeability, approachability, enthusiasm;
5 self-confidence;
6 communicate well.

1. Maturity

> When I was at Accenture, the new graduates who stood out were self-assured without being arrogant.
>
> Antoinette Oglethorpe,
> Leadership Consultant and Coach

Most new trainees into a professional services firm have joined straight from university. Understandably a firm is not looking for their trainees to be the final product at this early stage in their careers. However, the people who stand out at this early stage are the ones who have a level of maturity and self-confidence without being arrogant, that many young professionals take a few years to acquire.

2. Resilience

We've often heard many professionals joke that their job would be easy if they didn't have any clients! The very nature of the PSF's business model, which relies on selling time for a high fee level, means that daily pressure is part and parcel of life as a professional adviser. If you are not under pressure because you have too much work on your plate, you are under pressure to find more work. Inevitably because business in professional services firms is ultimately 'won' or 'lost', there will always be setbacks and disappointments. This could be:

- managing a bad debt when a client has cash flow problems;
- missing out on a great piece of client work which you were sure was a done deal;
- having to redo a piece of work because a client has changed their mind.

This means that partners are looking for their successors to be resilient and thrive on working under pressure.

3. 'Fit' socially

How you 'fit' into a firm is more than just getting on with everyone, ie how likeable you are, and being passionate about your work. It is also about how your values 'fit' with the firm's values. For example, if you have a driven personality and want to get on with things quickly, then you need to be in a firm that is dynamic and takes decisions quickly.

If you are feeling that you will need to 'sell your soul' or 'dumb down' your personality to fit in at your firm, then this is a strong indication that this may not be the right firm for you. In Chapter 2 we explored the importance of choosing a firm where your values are closely aligned with the firm's values.

4. Likeability, approachability and enthusiasm

> For young accountants looking to climb the career ladder, my advice would be simply to work hard and be enthusiastic. Having a 'can do' attitude is vital. It's not easy to get excited about ticking off audit schedules, but if you do it with gusto, you're more likely to be rewarded with more exciting things to do later on because people like working with you.
>
> Myfanwy Neville, partner at Berg Krapow Lewis LLP

As employers, we can testify that it is a joy to work with people who are enthusiastic about what they do. This enthusiasm and passion for their work is infectious. It's much easier to invest in an employee's career if they are enthusiastic and passionate about their work.

> I've aimed to cultivate a reputation for being a nice guy in the office. I think everybody likes me, but I've tried really hard to be liked.
>
> Jonathan, partner

While we are not asking you to be someone you are not, your aim is to be approachable and to make people feel comfortable around you in the office. It's not the easiest thing to do. However, if you cultivate a reputation as a nice person to be around and work with, it will help you stand out from your peers, and clients will also ask for you to work on their jobs. While this may seem obvious to you, what may not be so obvious is that in many firms all the partners will have to sign off your promotion to partner. This means that if you are serious about getting to partner within your current firm, that you can't afford to badly offend people or, worse, create enemies within your firm.

> Being seen as partnership potential boils down to two things: one is working bloody hard at being good at what you do, and the other is getting on with the right people.
>
> Raj, partner in consultancy firm

5. Self-confidence

From a very early stage in many professionals' careers they are often required to work, unsupervised, with very senior individuals within a business. Occasionally, such as when a team is on a client's site, you may be unsupported by a more experienced member of the firm. It goes without saying that your credibility as a professional is often demonstrated by your self-confidence in how you conduct yourself with clients and the advice you give to them; which means your self-confidence is one of the yardsticks that partners use to assess your partnership potential. When your firm knows that you are 'safe' to be left alone with clients, it not only signals that you have the potential to run your own client portfolio, but it will significantly increase your internal market value within your firm.

This self-confidence will manifest itself in different ways; for example:

- speaking up for your own views, and if necessary being able to justify decisions with evidence;
- proactively seeking feedback on your performance from clients and peers;
- knowing when it is appropriate to consult others for advice and guidance;
- inspiring others with confidence.

6. Communicate well

Speaking frankly, great results and teams are a result of good communication. On the flip side, most difficult situations are normally caused by poor communication. If you ask anyone about who they really rate, they will mention how good a listener or communicator they are. Your ability to communicate will be a fundamental driver of how well your career progresses in professional services.

When partners are looking for someone with partnership potential, they are typically looking for someone who:

- listens attentively and shows that they have listened;
- can explain complex points and technical matters clearly, accurately and simply, so that these are understood by clients;
- can convince, persuade, reassure and negotiate when appropriate.

In Chapter 12, we look in detail at the communication skills you will need if you are going to make partner.

Thinking skills

It's no accident that PSFs aim to hire the brightest graduates. The biggest asset any PSF has is the minds of their people. Early in your career, your thinking skills may be tested by having to analyse complex data and make recommendations based on your findings. The delight of dealing with clients means that regardless of where you are in your career, you will always need to think on your feet. Later on in your career, you will need to be able to spot opportunities for your clients and the firm. If there is one certainty in your life as a professional, it is the requirement to utilize your thinking skills on a daily basis.

While many people associate the professions with dry technical-type work, very often this is not the case. For example, creativity is almost always required to:

- find a solution for a client which works for everyone;
- identify new profitable service offerings for the firm;
- meet all deadlines when everyone is already working flat out;
- identify and exploit loopholes in regulations.

Exercise: How strong is your partnership potential?

For each of these statements, score yourself between 0 and 4, where: 0 = strongly disagree; 1 = disagree; 2 = neither agree or disagree; 3 = agree; 4 = strongly agree.

1 I take great pride in delivering an excellent service for my clients.

2 I am actively seeking ways for the firm to achieve its vision, goals and objectives.

3 I am open to any opportunity which comes my way.

4 I am well known, for positive reasons, across the firm.

5 I have a reputation for being trustworthy and reliable.

6 I regularly receive feedback that my clients, team and supervisors value my ability to take the initiative and go the extra mile for my clients and the firm.

7 I am good at spotting ways in which we can provide a greater service to my clients.

8 I know what motivates my clients.

9 The partners in my part of the practice know what I want to achieve with my career.

10 I always meet and often exceed my clients' expectations.

11 People within the teams I manage say I am a good team leader.

12 I have developed many strong and mutually supportive relationships across the firm and in teams I have worked with.

13 I bounce back quickly from setbacks.

14 I like socializing with people from my firm.

15 I am enthusiastic about who I work with and what I work on.

16 I am seen to be mature and self-confident by clients and partners in the firm.

17 I routinely ask for ways I can improve.

18 I often receive feedback about how well I communciate with others.

19 If necessary I can influence others positively to my point of view or way of thinking.

20 I'm good at finding solutions to clients' problems.

21 I have suggested ideas to partners in the firm about new services the firm could offer.

22 I am able to explain complex technical advice in simple, easy-to-understand language for clients and junior members of staff.

23 I am a good listener.

24 I inspire others with confidence.

Take a look at your answers – if you are answering mainly 3s and 4s, then it's likely that someone at your firm has already noticed your potential.

If you have some 0s, 1s or 2s, then these are areas where you will have to pay some attention. Do set up a conversation with your counselling/line/staff manager and/or mentor to discuss the areas which you scored yourself low on.

Summary

Every professional practice is looking out for members of staff who have the future capability to progress through to a partner role, and ultimately be their successors. Very often when a member of the firm is seen to be either a 'star' or partnership potential they will be given both informal and formal help to rise through the ranks to partner.

Typically when someone is seen to have partnership potential they will have a high perceived external and internal market value; ie both clients and assignment managers will want them to work on their work.

To be seen as partnership potential typically means you are displaying all of these five competencies and characteristics more than your peers:

- commitment to the firm, its vision and its clients;
- commerciality;
- leadership and management;
- emotional intelligence;
- thinking skills.

Action points

- Ask your department head what they look for when considering who will be the firm's next generation of partners.
- Ask the person who does your performance review, eg your supervisor, counselling manager/partner, what the three things are that you need to address to help you be promoted to the next level.
- Ask for an opportunity to do a secondment within a client's organization or a different department within your firm.
- Next time you find yourself complaining about a client assignment, stop yourself and think about what is positive about the assignment.
- Get into the habit, after each piece of client work is finished, of always asking your supervisor, assignment manager or partner what you did well and what you could improve for the next piece of work.
- Ask to 'bag carry' for a more senior member of your department when they go to client meetings and prospective client meetings.
- Talk to your partner or head of practice and find out about the firm's vision, strategy and plans for the next three to five years. Ask how you can play your part in delivering that plan and vision.
- Next time you come to the end of an assignment, ask both the client and other people working on it to give you some feedback about your performance and personal impact.

Further resources

Books

Ennico, C (2009) *The Partner Track: How to go from associate to partner in any law firm*, Kaplan Trade, US

Frankel, L (2004) *Nice Girls Don't Get the Corner Office: 101 unconscious mistakes women make that sabotage their careers*, Little, Brown and Company, New York

Goleman, D (1996) *Emotional Intelligence: Why it can matter more than IQ*, 1996, Bloomsbury Publishing, London

Goleman, D (1998) 'What makes a great leader', *Harvard Business Review*

Lorsch, J W and Tierney, T J (2002) *Aligning the Stars*, Harvard Business School

Mayson, S (1997) *Making Sense of Law Firms: Strategy, structure and ownership*, Blackstone Press Limited, US

Websites and blogs

How to make partner and still have a life – http://www.howtomakepartner.com
Legal Cheek – http://www.legalcheek.com
Harvard Business Review – http://www.hbs.org

How to develop yourself on the route to partnership

06

TOPICS COVERED IN THIS CHAPTER:

- How people learn and develop new skills
- The importance of playing to your strengths
- How we identify gaps in our skill base
- How to keep your knowledge up-to-date

If you wish to achieve worthwhile things in your personal and career life, you must become a worthwhile person in your own self-development.

BRIAN TRACEY

In this chapter we explore how you can build and develop both your technical and non-technical knowledge and skills needed for your journey to partnership. We also look at what you can do to improve your self-awareness and insight to increase your self-knowledge and improve relationships with colleagues and those you manage.

How we learn and develop new skills and behaviours

Kolb's Learning Styles

Everyone learns in different ways, however, according to Kolb's learning styles model, a person only learns effectively when they complete the learning cycle. According to our individual learning preference we will start and finish the learning cycle at different points. If you know your preferred learning style it can speed up the transfer of skills and knowledge.

There are four main learning styles:

- *Activitists*: who learn by doing, whether by themselves or with others;
- *Reflectors*: who learn from activities that allow them to watch, think and review;
- *Theorists*: who think problems through in a step-by-step manner;
- *Pragmatists*: who apply their new learnings to actual practice to see it they work.

DIAGRAM 6.1   Kolb's learning styles

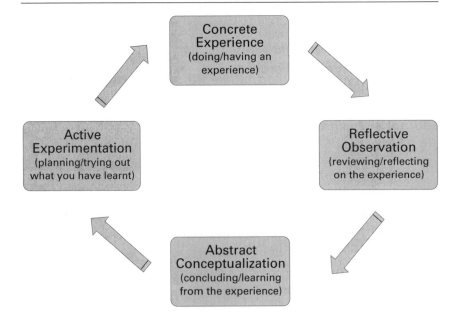

If you are interested in understanding what your own learning style prefer-
ence is, then you can complete the Honey and Mumford Learning Styles
Questionnaire, which can be bought from **http://www.peterhoney.com/** or
Amazon.

Most people when they identify that they need to acquire new skills and
knowledge tend to instantly think about completing some classroom-based
training. This is not the only development option available to you, and often
the most ineffective option you can pick. Robert Brinkerhoff discovered that
70 per cent of everyone on a training course will have a go at implementing
what they learnt, but give up when it gets tough. In fact, less than 15 per cent
successfully implement what they learnt!

Here are the development options available to you to expand your skills and
knowledge:

- coaching (see later in this chapter);
- mentoring (see Chapter 8);
- on-the-job training;
- self-study, eg reading, internet research;
- observation, eg bag-carrying for a more senior member of the team;
- studying for a qualification;
- professional development options provided by your institute;
- writing articles and presenting and seminars;
- project work.

Stages of your development

As you learn a new skill or behaviour, you go through 4 levels of increasing
competence until you reach full competence. By recognizing your stage of
development, you can identify what you still need to do to fully master the
skill or behaviour.

Unconscious incompetence

Think about when you first started to learn to drive a car. You were
probably very enthusiastic about driving and thinking 'how hard
can it be to learn to drive'. This stage is characterized by enthusiasm and
often unrealistic expectations of how easy it will be to gain the new skill.

TABLE 6.1   Differences between the learning styles

	Activist	Reflector	Theorist	Pragmatist
Strengths	1. Flexible and open-minded	1. Careful, thorough and methodical	1. Rational and objective	1. Keen to test things out in practice
	2. Happy to have a go	2. Good at listening to others	2. Disciplined approach	2. Practical and realistic
	3. Happy to try new things	3. Thoughtful	3. Logical thinkers	3. Process-driven
	4. Low resistance to change		4. Good at asking probing questions	
Weaknesses	1. Tendency to act without thinking	1. Tendency to hold back from direct participation	1. Out-of-the-box thinking	1. Not very interested in theory
	2. Poor planners	2. Not assertive	2. Intolerant of anything subjective or intuitive	2. Tendency to be task- rather than people-orientated
	3. Get bored with repetition	3. Slow to make up their minds		3. Impatient with waffle
Most appropriate learning solutions	1. Learning on the job	1. Work-shadowing and bag carrying	1. Self-study	1. Projects
	2. Coaching	2. Group Discussions	2. Coaching	2. Coaching
	3. Tutor-led courses and workshops	3. Coaching	3. Group Discussions	3. Projects
	4. Tasks	4. Self-study	4. Projects	4. On-the-job training

Conscious incompetence

At this stage you have started to learn the new skill and realize just how much you don't know or need to learn. Very often, this stage can be demotivating. Going back to the example of learning to drive: for most of us we were in a state of conscious incompetence for our first few lessons.

Conscious competence

After a while we do start to learn the new skills and implement them. However, because they are so new to us it takes a conscious effort to use them. For example, when you learnt to drive you used phrases like *mirror, signal, manoeuvre* to remind you of what you needed to do every time you changed lane in traffic.

Unconscious competence

With practice, you get so good at a new skill that it becomes second nature and you no longer need to think about doing the skill.
You just do it. As an experienced driver you no longer have to think about *mirror, signal, manoeuvre* to change lanes, you just do it on autopilot.

An investment in knowledge always pays the best interest.

Benjamin Franklin

Coaching

Coaching is about unlocking a person's potential to maximize their own performance. It is one of the most effective ways of developing your skills and behaviours.

Coaching can be divided into three main areas:

Executive coaching: Where an external coach is brought in, either by the firm or the individual, to help the, typically senior, individual to reach a higher level of performance.

Internal coaching: Where a manager within the firm takes on the role of coach to their staff using everyday work situations as a vehicle for learning.

Life coaching: Where an individual seeks assistance from an external coach to develop coping strategies around life issues; common examples are stress associated with major family illnesses and communication issues within the family. Difficulties outside work can impact on a person's work performance. It is beyond the scope of this book to address this type of coaching, however the authors strongly suggest you seek a Life Coach if you are involved in domestic difficulties.

Coaching provides benefits by:

- helping people achieve sustainable levels of performance, particularly leadership capability;
- improving people's interpersonal skills and correcting blind spots in their behaviour towards others;
- providing focus and accountability;
- increasing knowledge transfer for high performers and exceptional managers;
- turning around under-performance;
- developing higher-performing project or cross-firm teams;
- helping people play to their strengths;
- offering an impartial sounding-board for ideas and opinions;
- reducing stress levels;
- helping the coachee become self-sufficient.

Internal and executive coaching provide excellent opportunities for building and developing the core skills required to become a successful partner, and you should refer to Chapters 8, 19 and 21 for more on this topic.

The importance of playing to your strengths

There is no such thing as the 'perfect' individual. We all have strengths and weakness. Very often our strengths can become over-played and become a weakness for us. For example, Simon gained a reputation for having a great eye for detail and was often given work to check because of this. However, he often found it hard to complete the jobs he was given within the time allowed, because of his thirst for detail and his tendency to make sure the details were absolutely correct. When you become aware of your natural strengths and talents you can improve your performance by choosing work that plays to these strengths, and team members who complement these.

Case study: Abi

Abi started her career in tax compliance, and while she took pride in her work she wasn't thriving and developing as quickly as her peers. She found the day-to-day work of checking and entering numbers into schedules and tax computation software to be boring and 'not her thing'. She longed for more interaction with the client, so she requested a move into tax investigations. She soon found that the variety and the problem-solving element of the tax investigations work really suited her personality and natural preferences. Her aptitude and enthusiasm for the different type of work started to shine through, and her career took off from this point.

If you are interested in identifying your strengths, we recommend that you read *Now, Discover Your Strengths: How to develop your talents and those of the people you manage*, by Marcus Buckingham and Donald Clifton. The book gives you access to Gallop's Strength Finder 2.0 Tool, which gives you a very useful report on your natural strengths.

How to identify gaps in your skill base

Before you can build your technical and non-technical knowledge, skills and behaviours you have to be able to identify where you have gaps in your knowledge. Sometimes these gaps are very obvious to you and people around you, other times you will use tools such as 360-degree feedback exercises, assessment and development centres, psychometric tools and competency frameworks to identify your gaps.

The tools and questionnaires that we showcase only highlight the possible gaps for an individual. It still falls to you the individual to take action to close the gaps.

360-degree feedback

This is a management tool to improve individual's self-awareness and collaboration between teams. It can either be delivered formally or informally. Using a comprehensive set of questions, the individual gets performance and effectiveness ratings from trusted people above them, below them and their peers (hence '360-degrees'). Typically the survey is done using software and the results are collated into a formal report. The feedback is particularly useful as input into your career action plan. If the 360-degree feedback is administered as part of your firm's HR practices, you can expect to receive a formal report that is shared with you and your manager. Very often, 360-degree feedback will be used to write personal development plans, such as your career action plan, (see Chapter 7) to enable improved personal, team and firm-wide performance.

Gathering feedback from colleagues has many advantages. In addition to receiving valuable feedback from your appraiser, it's also extremely important to know what peers and employees think. Receiving 360-degree feedback is more comprehensive and less prone to individual bias, since there are multiple perspectives. For example, a manager who may have thought that his boss was just being picky about his communication skills will begin to take it seriously when everyone around him is also suggesting that he needs improvement in that area.

Assessment and Development Centres

Large and some mid-size firms use Assessment and Development Centres (ADCs) to assess and evaluate their employees on their *non-technical skills* (see Chapter 20 for more information on partner promotion assessment centres). Typically, firms will use ADCs to assess an individual's potential to transition to the next stage in their career. An ADC is a highly participative event, which is designed to explore an individual's performance against the firm's competency framework. After an ADC you will build jointly with your firm a career action plan to help you achieve your career Goals. See Chapter 7 for an example of a career action plan.

Benefits of an ADC typically include:

- helping you (and your firm) get a clearer 'fix' on the match between your career aspirations and current performance;
- assisting you to define and clarify your career objectives;
- encouraging you to take greater responsibility for management of your career and for developing your performance;
- providing realistic insights into your career choices and identifying further development experiences needed for you to fulfill your potential.

If your firm invites you to attend an ADC, go. It is normally a very positive endorsement of your future career with the firm. The clear feedback that you will receive on your strengths and development needs will be invaluable in helping you to shape your future career path.

Psychometric tools

During your career, it is highly probable that you will complete one or more psychometric tests as:

- part of a recruitment process;
- preparation before attending an ADC;
- part of a leadership and management development programme;
- part of a team building programme;
- a diagnostic test when beginning to work with a coach.

This section provides a brief guide to some of the psychometric tools that are often used within professional services. These tools are standardized questionnaires, in which you are asked to indicate your typical or preferred ways of thinking, behaving and reacting to people or situations. They typically give an indication of your personal motivation, preferences and behavioural traits. The results from any psychometric tools will feed directly into planning your career.

There are quite a few personality questionnaires on the market and your firm will select those it wants to use. The most widely used are:

Myers Briggs Type Indicator (MBTI)
MBTI is a very common psychometric test used in professional services. By categorizing people into types based on their response to standardized multiple-choice questions, the MBTI test gives people insight into who they are and the work environment in which they might operate best. MBTI is designed to promote understanding yourself and others; and understanding and managing different relationships.

Insights Discovery
Insights use a four-colour model to understand an individual's unique preferences. These preferences are based on an individual's response in an online questionnaire. The output is a personal profile report, which identifies strengths, weaknesses, communications styles, and value to a team. Each personal report includes suggestions to support learning and development across a range of areas.

Emotional Intelligence tools (also known as EQ)

Emotional intelligence is seen to be a good indicator of future leadership capability, which is why it is often used within a firm's ADCs. There are several Emotional Intelligence tools on the market place. They all typically focus on helping individuals identify their strengths in coping with stress and pressure, their personal interaction style with others and in team situations.

Competency frameworks

Many firms have defined what it takes to be successful in each role and each level of the firm. This data is often put together in a 'competency framework'. If your firm has one, it is a very useful exercise to compare your current and next level of technical and non-technical knowledge and skills with where your firm requires you to be.

How to keep your knowledge up-to-date

Nothing ever stays the same in the world of professional services. The changing business environment, the speed of change and access to the internet mean that current products, services and capabilities cannot guarantee a firm or individual's future business success. The only sources of long-term competitive advantage, for you and your firm, are the capacity to learn and to apply new knowledge and skills. Your future career progression is reliant on you taking a disciplined approach to your self-development, rather than leaving it to chance or the rare moments of less activity.

Here are our tips for keeping your knowledge and skills up-to-date:

- always capture promptly, and share, what you have learnt winning or completing a piece of work;
- have a filing system, ideally online, for you to keep (and refer back to) interesting and relevant articles and documents;
- combine business development activities, eg networking at a conference, with opportunities to learn;
- identify the thought leaders in your specialist area, read their articles/ blog, buy their books and attend their workshops, tele-seminars, webinars and seminars;

- subscribe to the journal or magazine for your specialist area;

- volunteer to be an early tester of new and emerging technology;

- create time in your diary every month to acquire new knowledge relevant to your specialism.

Summary

To progress your career to partner you will need to learn and apply daily new skills, knowledge and behaviours. Your personal and professional develop-ment is not something that should be left to chance, but woven into the way you do business. Everyone has a personal preference on how they choose to learn, but everyone needs to go around the learning cycle before they can reach a state of unconscious competence, ie a fully-developed skill or behaviour.

You may find that your firm uses tools such as assessment and development centres, 360-degree feedback, psychometric tools and competency frameworks to help you measure the gaps in your skills and knowledge. All insights gained from assessments should lead to action which you record in your career action plan (see Chapter 7).

Action points

- Obtain a copy of Honey and Mumford's Learning Styles Questionnaire to determine your preferred learning style. What have you learnt about yourself, and how will you use this knowledge to improve your effectiveness?

- Ask your mentor, partner or manager what tools your firm has or uses to help people identify their development requirements. Then get permission to participate in these tools and act on your findings.

- Ask for feedback on your performance at work from the people you work for, your peers and the people who work for you. An easy way to do this is to ask them for one thing you do well and one specific thing that you need to improve. Encourage them to be honest. Remember to listen to the feedback and take steps to improve your performance based on the feedback.

Further resources

Books

Briggs-Myers, I and Myers, P (1995) *Gifts Differing: Understanding personality type*, Davies-Black Publishing, Mountain View, CA

Brinkerhoff, R (2003) *The Success Case Method – Find out quickly what's working and what's not*, Berrett-Koehler, San Francisco, CA

Buckingham, M and Clifton, D (2005) *Now, Discover Your Strengths: How to develop your talents and those of the people you manage*, Pocket Books, London

Kolb, D (1984) *Experiential learning: Experience as the source of learning and development*, Prentice Hall, Upper Saddle River, NJ

Websites

Honey and Mumford Learning Questionnaire – http://www.peterhoney.com/
Hire your own executive coach – http://www.howtomakepartner.com

Creating and writing your own career action plan

07

TOPICS COVERED IN THIS CHAPTER:

- Why set goals?
- How to get started planning your career
- How to break your big career goals into smaller milestones
- How to set yourself goals and objectives
- What needs to go into your career action plan
- The importance of gaining feedback from others

> *Developing the plan is actually laying out the sequence of events that have to happen for you to achieve your goal.*

GEORGE L MORRISEY

In this chapter we are going to take the roles you identified for your life from Chapter 2 and help you decide the top priorities for these roles. Then we'll break them down into milestones, establish objectives with measures and finally set up weekly planners to help you keep focused on a day-to-day basis on your career plan.

Why set goals?

Athletes, partners and other people who are driving themselves forward for success use goal setting to establish a future focus, then the milestones along the way give them short-term motivation. Having clarity about goals allows you to decide whether something is, or is not, a priority, ie do you need to invest time in this?

Goal setting will focus your acquisition of knowledge and help you to organize your time and resources so that you can make the most of your career and life. By setting sharp, clearly defined goals, you can measure your achievements of those goals, and you will make progress in what may have previously felt like a long pointless grind. Your self-confidence will also improve as you achieve your goals.

We have worked with professionals who worry about whether partners and colleagues will see them as 'pushy' if they set goals and are open about their career aspirations. Actually, telling other people about your goals is an excellent way of committing yourself to action.

The difference between goals, milestones and objectives

Goals: These are what you want to achieve in the future, and are focused on your life inside or outside work.

Milestones: These are sub-goals, which if achieved will help you realize your goals.

Objectives: These are the specific, measurable actions you will do to accomplish your milestones.

How to get started

The road to hell is paved with good intentions.

British proverb

Don't confuse good intentions with action. Sometimes we find that professionals delay writing a career action plan until they have reached a certain point in their career; eg 'After I have made manager I will plan how I get to partner.' In our experience, there will never be a right time to get started. If you are serious about making partner and having a life, the time to take action is now. Merely saying you want something won't make it happen!

> The journey of a thousand miles starts with one single step.
>
> Lao Tzu, Chinese philosopher

Take a look back at Chapter 2, and refresh your memory on:

- the roles you want to play in your life;
- what you want to achieve in these roles;
- your preferred route to partnership.

We are now going to help you write a career action plan for the next five to ten years. We strongly encourage you to include the roles and achievements you want outside work. Otherwise the risk is you focus all your energy on your career, at the expense of the life you want to live outside work. (See Chapter 16 for more details on why this balance is important.)

Identifying your priorities

You've now identified a number of goals for your life inside and outside work. Sometimes having many goals can overwhelm you and stop you from achieving any of them because you don't have the time to invest in any of them properly. Giving each of your goals a priority level can help you focus on what matters most to you.

To help you identify your priority levels for your goals, it's crucial to check how motivated you are to achieve each goal. The more inspiring a goal, the more likely it will keep you moving forward even on the days when you feel like giving up. A great way of helping you identify your motivators is to ask yourself a series of 'Why' questions:

> *1st Why question: 'Why is this goal important to me?'*
>
> *2nd Why question: 'Why is the answer to the 1st question important to me?'*
>
> *3rd Why question: 'Why is the answer to the 2nd question important to me?'*
>
> *...and so on...*

Carry on asking yourself these Why questions until you reach one of two points:

- an answer similar to 'just because'; or
- Well, it's not really important to me.

When you have reached the 'just because' answer, you will have normally uncovered a key driver or motivator for you. If you reach the 'Well, it's not really important to me', it's very likely that you've identified a goal which your family, friends or others have given to you. Let's look at a worked example:

Mohammed identified his goals, which included becoming the firm's top expert on environmental audits for housing developers, and getting an MBA. He then asked himself the Why questions:

Q. Why is it important that I become the firm's top expert on environmental audits for housing developers?

A. Because I enjoy carrying out environmental audits and these are becoming high-profile pieces of work for the firm.

Q. Why is it important for me to be doing high-profile pieces of work for the firm?

A. Because these are bringing me to the attention of key partners in the firm, and helping me hit my chargeable hours target.

Q. Why is it important for me to be hitting my targets and be noticed by key partners in the firm?

A. So that I am seen to be one of the firm's stars and future partners.

Q. Why is it important for me to seen seen as a future partner?

A. Because I want to be a partner in my firm.

Q. Why is it important for me to a partner in my firm?

A. Because I want the status and influence which come with being a partner.

Q. Why is it important for me to have status and influence?

A. Just because ...

Mohammed then repeated the same exercise but for his goal of getting an MBA:

Q. Why is it important for me to have an MBA?

A. Because it's a great commercial qualification to have.

Q. Why is it important for me to have a great commercial qualification?

A. I'm not sure, but my parents are telling me that it will be good for my career.

Notice that in the first example, Mohammed quickly uncovered a *personal* driver towards a goal. In the second example, he was honest with himself and found that his motivator was *external*. It is very important when planning life's goals to understand that we can only truly be passionate about things when they come from within ourselves.

Exercise: Determine the priority levels of your goals

For each of the goals you have identified, ask yourself the 'Why is this goal important to me' question, and repeat Why questions until you come to an end.

Based on your answers to each of the Why questions, rank your goals in priority order.

Now take a look at your goals ranked by priority. Are there any goals that you can remove from your list because they are not important enough to motivate you?

With your remaining goals, ask yourself, 'If I were to share this with other people, what would I tell them to convince them that it is a worthwhile goal?'

Identifying your milestones

Most of us find big goals very daunting. It's only when we break them down into smaller more achievable goals – milestones – that we find the motivation to start working towards our big goals.

There are many different ways of chunking down large goals into smaller milestones, and we encourage you to use a process that works for you. We are now going to describe an exercise that we use with our clients, to help them identify their milestones.

To help yourself identify your milestones, give yourself a quiet 30 minutes and the space to think by removing distractions from around you. For each of your goals you now need to break them up into milestones and attach a time frame to each milestone. For simplicity's sake, let's assume that you are going to use one-month, three-month, one-year, two-year and five-year milestones. Taking each goal and its milestones in turn, what will you need to have accomplished within each time frame if you are going to achieve your goal?

You may find it helpful to write these down using a spreadsheet, calendar or Gantt chart. Let's go back to our previous example with Mohammed. He decided to ditch his goal of getting an MBA because he wasn't passionate about gaining this qualification. However, becoming the firm's top expert for environmental audits for housing developers was something that he was passionate about. Mohammed identified the milestones shown in Table 7.1 he would want to achieve to accomplish this goal:

TABLE 7.1

Time frame	Milestone(s)
1 month	Gained agreement from head of environmental consulting to be my mentor
3 months	Started to write articles for the firm's blog on advice for property developers on what environmental factors they need to consider before buying land for development
	Be on a project team completing an environmental audit for a property developer
1 year	Have attended at least two pitches for environmental audit work that the firm is trying to win
	Have sat down with all the partners in the environmental consulting part of the firm to find out more about them and their major property developer clients
2 years	Have gained permission to do a short 3-month secondment with one of the firm's property developer clients
5 years	At least 70% of my chargeable time is spent on environmental audit work for property developers

We've used a milestone planner to record all of Mohammed's high-priority career and life goals, and the milestones to achieve each goal. See Diagram 7.1.

Exercise: Identify your milestones

For each of the goals which you have identified in the previous exercise, identify and write down the milestones you want to have achieved by one month, three months, one year, two years and five years from now. Use a template similar to the milestone planner in Diagram 7.1. This template can be downloaded at www.howtomakepartner.com

DIAGRAM 7.1 Mohammed's milestone planner

Milestone Planner			
	Work	**Family**	**Hobbies**
5–10 year Goals	1. Become the firm's top expert on environmental audits for housing developers 2. Make partner	1. Get married and start a family	1. Keep myself fit and healthy
1 month Milestones	• Gained agreement from head of environmental consulting to be my mentor	• Go out at least once a fortnight for a 'date' with my partner	• Swim at least 1,000m once a week
3 months Milestones	• Started to write articles for the firm's blog on advice for property developers on what environmental factors they need to consider before buying land for development • Be on a project team completing an environmental audit for a property developer	• Maintain the fortnightly 'date' night with my partner • Organize time off so that we have 2 weeks holiday together this year	• Maintain my weekly swimming trips and increase my distance to 1,500m per visit
1 year Milestones	• Have attended at least two pitches for environmental audit work that the firm is trying to win • Have sat down with all the partners in the environmental consulting part of the firm to find out more about them and their major property developer clients	• Maintain the fortnightly 'date' night with my partner • Plan in at least 2 weeks of holidays together	• Maintain my weekly swimming trips • Start yoga classes at weekends with my partner
2 years Milestones	• Have gained permission to do a short 3 month secondment with one of the firm's property developer clients	• Get married to my partner	• Maintain my weekly swimming trips • Do at least 60 mins of yoga a week
5 years Milestones	• At least 70% of my chargeable time is spent on environmental audit work for property developers	• Have started a family • Work at least 1 day from home	• Maintain my weekly swimming trips and yoga sessions

Creating objectives from your milestones

Now that you have identified your milestones to enable you to achieve your career and life goals, it is time to turn them into specific, measurable, shorter-term objectives, which identify *what* you need to do to achieve your milestones within the desired time frame.

Some tips on effective objective setting:

- Write each of your objectives as a single sentence, containing what you want to do to achieve your milestones.
- Write them down and share them with other people.
- Review them every three months.
- Make sure you include a time frame, eg weekly or 'by this date'.
- Check that they are realistic and measurable.

Let's go back to the milestones which Mohammed had identifed that he needed to accomplish on his way to becoming the firm's top expert on environmental audits for property developers. Considering Mohammed's goal to become the top expert in environmental audits for property developers, he worked down the list of one-month, three-months and one-year milestones, expanding each one into specific, time-framed objectives, eg:

- By 5 December have had a meeting with the head of environmental consulting to ask him to be my mentor.
- In preparation for my meeting with the head of environmental consulting, I will have completed the following action points:
  - Identified three reasons why I want him as my mentor and how the firm and his department will benefit from the relationship.
  - Asked my performance manager to speak to him about becoming my mentor.
  - Ascertained what time commitment I want from him as my mentor.
- By 31 January I will have identified what blogs and articles our competitors are writing for property developers to help them when considering environmental factors before buying land to develop.
- By 14 February I will have brainstormed six different titles of articles I can write for the firm's blog and written at least one of these articles.

Exercise: Identify your objectives

For each of the goals which you have identified in the previous exercise, brainstorm what you could do in the next 12 months to achieve your one-month, three-month and one-year milestones. Now look at what you could do, and what you *will* do, to complete your milestones in the next 12 months. Write down these as your objectives. These will form the basis of your career action plan.

Writing your own career action plan

Now that you have identified your career and life goals, milestones and one-year objectives to achieve these goals, it's time to put them down into a formal career action plan. Remember you need to focus on both your career and life goals if you are going to make partner *and* still have a life outside work.

The first step in the process is to take each of your milestones you want to achieve in the coming year, for all the roles important to you, and create an action plan for each of these roles. You may like to use your firm's standard career action plan forms, or something like the career action plan which we have completed for Mohammed's career goal to become the firm's top expert on environmental audits for housing developers. You can download a blank career action plan at **www.howtomakepartner.com**. See Diagram 7.2.

As a rough guide you should allow about three hours, including thinking time, to complete your career action plan for all of your goals.

Exercise: Complete your career action plan

Write a career action plan for each of your goals you have identified for the roles you wish to play in your life.

DIAGRAM 7.2   Mohammed's career action plan

Career Action Plan			
Role	Work	5–10 year Goal	Become the firm's top expert on environmental audits for housing developers
Time frame	Milestones		Objectives

1 month	• Gained agreement from head of environmental consulting to be my mentor		• By 5 Dec, have had a meeting with the head of environmental consulting to ask him to be my mentor
			• In preparation for my meeting with the head of environmental consulting, I will have completed the following action points:
			  – Identified 3 reasons why I want him as my mentor and how the firm and his department will benefit from the relationship
			  – Asked my performance manager to speak to him about becoming my mentor
			  – Ascertained what time commitment I want from him as my mentor

3 months	• Started to write articles for the firm's blog on advice for property developers on what environmental factors they need to consider before buying land for development • Be on a project team completing an environmental audit for a property developer		• By 31 Jan, I will have identified what blogs and articles our competitors are writing for property developers to help them when considering environmental factors before buying land to develop • By 14 Feb, I will have brainstormed 6 different titles of articles I can write for the firm's blog and written at least one of these articles • Attended the firm's seminar for property developers on 12 Jan
1 year	• Have attended at least two pitches for environmental audit work that the firm is trying to win		• By 20 March, I will have gained permission from my mentor to bag-carry for him on his next pitch to property developers • By 20 March, I will have sat down with my mentor and started to map out my career path within the firm, with a view to me specializing in environmental audits for property consultants

To keep your focus on both what has to be achieved within your day job and your career action plan, you may wish to use a weekly planner. Any weekly planner that you build for yourself must allow you to differentiate day-job tasks and career action plan tasks. You may like to use a similar weekly planner to the one we have filled in here, by way of an example, for Mohammed. You can download this weekly planner at **www.howtomakepartner.com**. See Diagram 7.3.

DIAGRAM 7.3 Mohammed's weekly planner

WEEKLY PLANNER	Week no: 47	From: 30 November			To: 6 December		
Mon	Tues	Wed	Thurs	Fri	Sat	Sun	
Business development, networking, people management and client service actions to complete							
Work on report for HGR audit	Work on report for HGR audit	Finish report for HGR audit	1:2:1 with my performance mgr	Planning meeting for ABC audit			
Career action plan tasks to complete							
	GAB meeting to ask him to be my mentor	• Write up notes from meeting with GAB • Book time in with GAB's PA for mentor kick-start meeting	Research blogs for property developers on environmental issues	Date night with my partner		Go swimming in am	
Any other actions to complete							
Departmental monthly meeting			Complete self-appraisal form for HGR project work	Submit weekly timesheet			

Your 3 Critical Results this Week – What You *Must* Achieve this Week	Done
Meeting with GAB to ask him to be my mentor	
Evening out with my partner for our fortnightly date night	
Finish report on likely polluters for HGR audit	

Objectives for the month (taken from career action plan)	Done
Agree on date night with partner for fortnight before Christmas	Yes
Complete report for HGR audit within timescale allocated in the budget	To do this week
Schedule time in my weekly planner for my weekly swim	Yes
Attend meeting with head of environmental consulting, GAB, to request that he becomes my mentor	Scheduled meeting

Exercise: Using a weekly planner

Fill in a weekly planner, for your next four weeks, planning in when you will complete your client work and your one-month objectives from your career action plan.

As you work through this book, you should record any specific actions you want to take to further your career action plan. Finally, a plan is only as good as the last time you looked at it and took action. Make sure you review your career action plan, milestones and objectives every month. This is the only way that you will make sure that your career will fit in with the way you want to live your life.

The importance of gaining feedback from others

It is important that you are honest with yourself about your performance and suitability for your future proposed career. It may sound slightly extreme, but it's no good working away at your career plan to become a partner at your current firm if you are consistently under-performing in your current role. You can only plan a realistic career path for yourself, if you actively and regularly seek out from others, feedback on your performance and your proposed career action plan.

Summary

Goal setting is important for progessing your career and life. Breaking your goals down into smaller, more manageable milestones will make these more achievable. Progress will be more visible when you identify milestones and objectives to achieve these goals.

Your career action plan will help you make the vital distinction between what you do and what you hope to accomplish on your journey to making partner. Using your plan you can see where you're going, reflect on the lessons learnt and fine-tune your approach, taking additional actions in order to hit your career and life goals.

Action points

- Write down the roles you want to play in your life; what you want to achieve in these roles: your preferred route to partnership.

- Complete the Why question exercise to flush out the important goals for you to achieve in each of these roles.

- Complete the exercises described in this chapter to identify your key milestones to achieve the career and life goals you have identified for yourself. Then identify objectives for the next 12 months to enable you to achieve your one-year milestones.

- Write your own career action plan to help you achieve these milestones.

- Each week use the weekly planner to maintain your focus on both your day-to-day work and your career action plan.

Further resources

Books

Covey, S (2004) *The Seven Habits of Highly Effective People*, Simon & Schuster, New York

Tracy, B (2004) *Eat that Frog: Get more of the important things done today*, Berrett-Koehler Publishers, CA

Websites and blogs

Free career action plan templates at **http://www.howtomakepartner.com**

08 | Building your support team

TOPICS COVERED IN THIS CHAPTER:

- Who do you need in your support team?
- What do mentors do?
- How to get maximum value from your relationship with your mentor?

"Making partner is not a do-it-alone project! Every potential partner needs a mentor and a champion."

ANITA WOODCOCK, AW CONSULTANTS

Everyone we interviewed for this book spoke about the need to have a support team to help achieve your ambition of making partner. Your support team is composed of people who are drawn from your personal, professional and family networks. All the members of your support team have an important role to play in helping your achieve your career and life goals. However, as a minimum you must have a mentor on the team. All throughout your career you will need influential partners in your firm who will look after your interests in partnership reviews regarding your perceived potential and current performance. Almost always, these advocates for you and your career will already be supporting you in a formal or informal mentoring capacity. In this chapter, we provide the information that you need to build the right support team around you, in particular helping you find the right mentor.

Why do you need a support team?

The commitment to go for partner while still having a life outside work is a very serious intent – and at times will be all-consuming. As you will have already seen in this book, this isn't something you can achieve in isolation. This is why you need a support team. They will be at your side throughout your journey to get to partner. For example, they:

- allow you to see the wood for the trees;
- buck you up when your commitment and motivation to achieve your career and life goals take a dip;
- help you celebrate your successes;
- commiserate with you when you hit bumps in the road;
- provide contingency plans for your life in and out of work.

Who should be in your support team?

Everyone's support team will be different. However, we suggest that an effective support team will have people playing five different types of roles.

Mentor: Having someone in your firm who is more experienced and can act as a sounding board and provide objective guidance and feedback is essential if you are going to make partner.

Executive or career coach: There are many benefits to having your own coach who is independent from your firm, although your firm may be paying for their time. Your own coach helps you to take time out from the hurly-burly of your work life to focus on what really matters to you. They will also work with you in acquiring the key skills and knowledge required to make partner.

Family: Having a supportive and happy home life is important if you are to become a well-rounded individual who is properly equipped to handle the stresses and strains which are part and parcel of the everyday life of a professional adviser.

Friends inside work: You are going to be at work for a significant part of your working life. Therefore, if you are going to 'fit in' (see Chapter 10) and enjoy your time at work, then you need to have friends at work.

Friends outside work: Good friends unconnected to your work life give you the opportunity to truly let your hair down, relax and let off steam outside work. It is important not to let your friendships outside work slide, as you never know when you may need them.

The crucial role of a mentor

Every athlete who aspires to win a medal at the Olympic Games has a coach; and when they win a medal, the first person they thank is their coach. We will state quite simply that in the professional services sector, a mentor is essential and is the equivalent of the athlete's 'coach'. The right person will guide you through the maze to partner level, assisting you to grow and develop. Where your university and professional qualifications involved studying to gain technical knowledge, that knowledge is only half of the journey towards partnership. Your mentor will provide you with business and social opportunities, which help you mature into the partner role.

When mentoring works well, it provides mentees with an ally in the firm and a further reason to stay the course. Within professional firms, a mentor is normally a partner, and can 'champion' and speak up in support of a mentee as appropriate. That said, we have known mentees to also have external mentors particularly where the skills and guidance that they require are unavailable within their firms.

Sometimes you may have the support of an informal mentor without realizing it. Toni Hunter, partner at George Hay Chartered Accountants, with the benefit of hindsight, became aware that she had an unofficial mentor championing her career progression. However, rather than leave this to chance, in this chapter you will learn how to proactively find the right mentor, and reap the rewards of the relationship.

The difference between a coach and a mentor

Coaching is a way of using everyday work situations as a vehicle for learning. It is about unlocking an individual's potential to maximize their own performance, and about helping them to learn rather than teaching them. There are two main forms of coaching: either helping the learner to change behaviours or to acquire new skills. It is performance-oriented, job-focused and task-related, and tends to concentrate on personal development in the short term.

A mentor is a trusted adviser, usually someone more experienced or in a more senior role, who acts as a sounding board and helps the mentee to find their own direction. It focuses on long-term career development and personal growth. The flow of learning is two-way, as the mentor also benefits from gaining a different perspective. The relationship often develops into a strong, long-term friendship.

The two approaches do, however, overlap in many ways, and should be regarded as complementary rather than mutually exclusive. Your mentor may be a skilled coach, and you may find times when you want to tap into the benefit of your coach's experience. Normally you will find that most professionals have a mentor who is internal to their firm and a coach who is external to their firm.

Mentoring and diversity

Mentoring is often used as a means of increasing diversity in organizations, helping female employees and those from black and ethnic minorities to break through into senior management roles. One of the commonly stated benefits of mentoring is that it gives individuals greater access to senior management and influential figures within the organization, increasing the individual's exposure and visibility, and so enhances their career prospects. It also introduces individuals to the power structures and information networks within a firm, and can provide an insight into the 'hidden' or unwritten aspects of a firm's culture.

Recent survey results presented by David Clutterbuck showed that a comparatively large proportion of women found that mentor relationships had been beneficial in their rise to the upper ranks of organizations. Reasons given were that they felt that having a mentor improved their self-esteem and confidence to seek advancement. Most women also felt that they became more visible to top management as a result of their participation in the schemes.

What do mentors do?

Mentors can play a wide range of roles. Some of the most common roles are:

- Role model, providing an example from which the mentee can learn and emulate.

- Coach, helping a mentee to acquire new skills and abilities.
- Career counsellor, listening and helping a mentee work out solutions to their career problems.
- Networker, helping a mentee develop the connections they need to gain experience, get a job, promotion and so on.
- Facilitator, helping to set and achieve goals.
- Critical friend, telling the mentee the uncomfortable truth that only a true friend can.
- Sounding board, giving the mentee the chance to try out ideas and approaches in a safe environment.

This is a two-way relationship. A mentor provides informal support to improve your development, which benefits not only you but also the mentor and the organization. The focus is on supporting and progressing your career to partner level.

For the relationship to work most effectively, the mentee needs to be open and honest when working with their mentor. Normally, a mentor has no direct line management responsibility for their mentees.

What to look for in a mentor

Choosing a mentor within the firm can be a great way of getting an ally for yourself and what you do. When a mentor agrees to take on a mentee they will (if the relationship works) invest emotionally in you and your career success. This means that they will automatically start to speak for you in meetings and make sure you are considered for the opportunities that you need to shine and expand your capabilities.

We don't recommend picking just anyone as your mentor within the firm. Your mentor must be someone who is already influential within the partner group in your practice area, or if this option is not available to you, someone who is seen as an up-and-coming star of the firm or department. There is no point in having someone fight your corner who isn't listened to by other partners! As well as the influence that your mentor can exert on your behalf, you also need to select someone whom you respect and like. If there is no positive chemistry between the two of you, it will be difficult for your mentor to emotionally invest in helping you succeed in the practice.

Sometimes by the very nature of who has taken you under their wing – particularly if they are a very prominent partner in the practice – you will be seen as a contender and one to watch for the future.

If you work in a firm that allows mentees to choose their mentor, use the box below to find the right mentor for you.

An effective mentor is:

- a partner;
- a good role model, respected within the firm and by you;
- an open-minded and good listener;
- a strong coach, with a willingness to help the mentee grow;
- a person who challenges the mentee.

What should you expect from a mentoring relationship?

Your relationship with your mentor is personal to you and your mentor. Before you embark on your relationship you need to set expectations regarding what you want from the relationship. These expectations, from both sides of the relationship, ideally need to be written down and referred to over time to see whether you and your mentor are meeting these expectations.

Regardless of your individual requirements for your mentor, you should, as a minimum, ask for and expect the following from your mentor:

- They will get to know you at a deep enough level that they give you (almost) unconditional support, and champion your cause.
- They will assist you to lift up your head out of the detail, to see the bigger picture as you develop.
- They will be an inspiring role model.
- They won't provide you with all the answers, but help you to solve your own problems.
- They will be a supportive but critical friend who will provide timely critical feedback which is constructive.

Unconditional support from your 'champion'

It's a great feeling to know that someone at the partnership table is looking out for you and your career. When you and your mentor's relationship is strong this is what will naturally start to happen.

At the point where a highly influential partner deems that you have partnership potential, they will normally be working behind the scenes to champion you and your career. As Toni Hunter discovered, it only became apparent over time that she had an advocate within the partner group. Whenever she did anything well, her 'champion' would report this back to the other partners, as well as being her eyes and ears regarding what the partners were thinking about her. Often, by having a mentor, you will have greater exposure to opportunities which help build your skills and knowledge, for example going on secondment to a client.

Helper to see the bigger picture

When you are in the day-to-day grind of a difficult long assignment or project, it can often be hard to see the bigger picture, and easy to lose sight of why you signed up to the job in the first place. This is where spending some time with your mentor can help. Sometimes, all you need is a restorative pep talk with your mentor to help reignite your passion for the job, and the focus you need on your professional and career development. You should expect your mentor to never be happy with the status quo, and to always challenge you to continuously improve and perform. This improved performance should lead to more of the type of assignments, deals and projects which will enable you to demonstrate your partnership potential.

An inspiring role model

A mentor is someone whom you choose (or have chosen for you), who has been there, done that and got the scars to prove it. It's the chance to learn from the experience of your mentor which helps you to accelerate your own development. However, if you are to gain the most from the relationship, you must look up to your mentor as a role model. Whether you realize it or not, as your relationship strengthens, you will start to emulate your mentor's behaviours. Do not underestimate the importance of being mentored by a partner who sets high standards, produces first-class professional advice, excellent service and walks the talk.

> **Tip**
>
> If your mentor fails to measure up to your standards or the personal chemistry is not there, then find another mentor to work with.

A problem solver

You should expect your mentor to help you deal with existing and potential problems, and confront issues that you may be avoiding. After all, part of your reason for having a mentor is to tap into their wisdom. Equally, if you have a trusting relationship with your mentor, you should feel confident about approaching your mentor for support when a problem arises. Don't expect your mentor to always know what is going on in your world – mentors are busy people!

A supportive but critical friend

You should expect your mentor to provide you with positive and supportive feedback. When you successfully complete an assignment or project a good mentor will acknowledge and praise your achievement. Ideally this acknowledgment will be both privately to you and publically to other partners – after all, this is your champion!

> **Tip**
>
> Positive feedback is a great motivator and encourages you to 'go the extra mile' for the firm and its clients. Remember to ask your mentor to provide you with positive and supportive feedback.

In turn, you should expect your mentor to provide constructive criticism if something has not gone so well. The focus should be on learning from the experience and how to improve next time around.

> **Tip**
>
> Every time someone says to you, 'You did a good job', smile and thank them. Then ask if they can give you just one tip to help you improve.

You should build a trusting relationship with your mentor. Often in the professional services environment, associates and managers are unsure whom they can trust, but trust is a two-way relationship and unless you take the risk of opening up and being honest with your mentor, you are unlikely to fully benefit. When the relationship works well, your mentor can provide a 'safety valve' by being the person to whom you can express your frustrations and feelings, as well as your ambitions. Building and developing a trusting relationship with your mentor will take time, and they will not happen unless you both put in time and effort.

Others may approach the mentor if they are unhappy or concerned about a mentee's performance or their failure to deliver. While a mentor may 'protect their mentee's back' by dealing with the problem at the time, a good mentor will discuss the difficulty with the mentee at an appropriate time.

How to get the most from your mentor

A strong mentoring relationship provides you with an ally in the firm. However, mentors themselves face many challenges. Although mentoring is usually an optional role in most professional services firms, it can impose considerable time demands on the mentor, eg one to two hours per month. This is unchargeable time, for which they may not always receive credit. Consequently, the easier and more rewarding you are to work with, the greater the likelihood that your mentor will want to spend quality time with you.

To get the most out of your relationship with your mentor, we suggest you do the following before, during and after you meet with them:

Before

- Prepare thoroughly for any sessions with your mentor and be ready to put forward your own views and ideas.

During

- Be realistic about what you can achieve when agreeing action items with your mentor.
- Be prepared to listen to and evaluate new ideas, consider uncomfortable questions, and accept critical feedback; but be prepared to challenge (with facts) your mentor if you do not agree.
- Be honest with yourself about your strengths and weaknesses.
- Be honest with your mentor – say if things are not working.

- Get to know your mentor as a person; after all, this is a two-way relationship. Be interested in your mentor as a person.
- Write down your action points as the meeting progresses.
- Finally, give your mentor feedback – we all like to know whether our advice and guidance are hitting the mark. Given the multiple demands on your mentor's time, they will want to know that their time with you is well spent and that they are making a valuable contribution.

After

- Make every effort to progress and complete the actions you have agreed to do. Your mentor will want to help you if you are motivated, enthusiastic and do what you say you will do.
- Make clear notes of what was covered, how the session went, what you got from it and any follow-up action points for you.
  Think carefully how you can apply what you learnt from the session.
- Diarize any actions.
- Agree the date of the next session and make sure that it is in both your diaries.
- Review and refine your objectives between meetings, noting any progress made and problems or opportunities that you would like to raise for the next session.

Summary

Having your own support team who help and cheer you along the way is vital if you are going to make partner and still have a life. Probably the most important member of that team is your mentor.

Every partner can point to someone who has acted either in an official or unofficial capacity, as a mentor, to help them achieve their career ambitions.

A good mentor will play many roles for you, but ultimately will be someone whom you respect and like. They will help you solve problems – sometimes by enabling you to see the bigger picture. The right person will emotionally want you to succeed, so they will voluntarily champion your cause within the partnership. A great mentor will be good at helping you hold a mirror up to yourself, and if necessary gently letting you know a few home truths.

With the many calls on a good or popular mentor's time, the easier and more rewarding you are to work with, the stronger the likelihood that your mentor will invest their own time, emotions and resource in your future success.

Action points

- Identify an influential partner or director within your practice whom you have a good rapport with, and ask them to be your mentor. Make sure you present a case on what you want, what you are commiting to in your career, and why you have chosen that person to be your mentor.

- Look for role models, within and outside your firm, who are recognized leaders in their field; do some research to find out how they have achieved their success: what can you learn from their experience, and how can this help your own career?

- Look around you. Who is in your support team? Who is missing from the team? What action could you take today to build stronger relationships between you and your support team?

- Draw a diagram showing the members of your support team. Make a few notes under each name reminding you of what their strengths are in their support role.

- Get into the habit, after each piece of client work is finished, of always asking your supervisor, assignment manager or partner what you did well and what you could improve for the next piece of work.

Further resources

Books

Gilbert, A, Frisby, N and Roberts, K (2001) *Go to Work on Your Career*, Go MAD Books, UK

Kay, D and Hinds, R (2004) *A Practical Guide to Mentoring: Play an active and worthwhile part in the development of others, and improve your own skills in the process*, How to Books Ltd, Oxford

Websites and blogs

How to make partner – http://www.howtomakepartner.com

How your firm makes money

TOPICS COVERED IN THIS CHAPTER:

- How firms typically make money and profit
- What financial terms you need to know about
- How a firm finances itself
- How to build your financial knowledge
- How you can help your firm become more profitable

> *Partners need to understand the financials, the markets in which their firm operates, the services it is able to provide, the experts in particular fields.*

GILLIAN SUTHERLAND, GLOBAL BUSINESS DEVELOPMENT DIRECTOR, DAVIS LANGDON, AN AECOM COMPANY

In the previous chapter, we identified the skills, knowledge, behaviours and attitudes sought by firms in prospective partners. In this chapter, we look more closely at what you need to learn and know about the way your firm makes money so that you can demonstrate over time to your partners that you are a suitable candidate for future partnership at your firm. All partners are required to pay for their equity share by investing a sum of capital at the point they are admitted to the partnership. Like any financial investment you make, it seems prudent to understand the risks and rewards of doing this.

> Potential partners are interested in the firm's business as a whole and how the firm makes money and grows.
>
> Toni Hunter, partner, George Hay Chartered Accountants

In vetting potential partners (see Chapter 20) most if not all firms' promotion criteria will assess and evaluate the depth of candidates' knowledge and understanding of the firm's business, particularly how it makes its money and profit. This means that you must get to grips with this early in your career. Having a reputation for poor time recording, failing to complete your time records and losing the firm money will not endear you to your partners and colleagues.

Unlike other types of organizations, professional services firms sell time and expertise – not tangible, physical products like a CD. For example, in a manufacturing business, once a product has been designed, mass production can create units 24/7 on machinery monitored by low-paid workers. Manufacturing managers emphasize the importance of standardization, quality and productivity in their teams.

But how does this compare with, for example, an accountancy practice? While managers still stress quality and productivity, they can't mass produce their services. Their profitability comes from face time, or billing hours with clients, all of whom have different needs and demands. If the team don't meet with clients or work on specific projects, they don't earn money for the firm.

Building your understanding of your firm's financial performance

> If you don't hit the numbers, you are not going to end up a partner.
>
> Partner, global firm

Time and time again, people we interviewed in our research for this book highlighted the crucial importance of understanding your firm's financials, including:

- how fees charged to clients are calculated;
- knowing how much the client is being charged and then making sure that you deliver to that budget;

- how much profit is being made on each client assignment;
- being able to plan work, manage the cost of service delivery and always generate the required level of profit;
- understanding the relationship between profit and cash, and managing staff to ensure timely receipt of cash from clients;
- why delegating work down to suitably qualified lower-level staff is the best way to make profit from work assignments;
- being able to talk to clients about fees, and if necessary chasing them for unpaid bills.

Earning fees is without doubt the most important contribution you can make to your firm in the early years of your career. However, as a senior associate or director who wants to make partner, your job is to understand the key financial performance issues facing your firm, and your role in achieving those performance measures. You may already be responsible for supervising a small team, deciding who has the skills and ability to take on a matter or, weighing up if an assignment can be done more economically at a junior level. But do you know what drives financial performance in your firm? Is it clear what reports, tools and practices you should be using in order to deliver a profitable job? Your goal is to obtain sufficient information to enable you to contribute to the business more effectively at the appropriate level.

Your answers to the above questions will vary depending on your firm's approach to communicating and sharing their financial information. Some firms circulate weekly or monthly information packs to all partners and non-partners which is then reviewed in team and discussed in one-to-one meetings; in others, financial information is regarded as highly confidential and distributed to partners only.

It is not our purpose to teach you everything that you need to know about professional services firms' finance. However, before making a start on building your understanding of how your firm makes money and profit, you will need to ensure that you are familiar with terms and metrics used by firms. Most professional services firms use a fairly standard set of financial metrics to track, measure and manage the financial performance of the business.

Common financial terms used in a professional services firm

WIP or work in progress: This refers to work that is being completed for clients, but not yet billed or invoiced.

Chargeable or billable work, expenses, time or hours: These are blocks of time, expenses or pieces of work that the firm can charge clients for.

Non-chargeable or non-billable work, expenses, time or hours, sometimes called firm time: These are blocks of time or pieces of work, such as marketing, internal working groups or committees, recruitment, networking and training, which the firm cannot charge clients for.

Chargeout rate: This is the rate at which fee earners' time is charged out to clients (see below).

Lock-up: This is the amount of cash still 'locked up in the firm', because either the firm has not yet billed the client for the work, ie WIP, or the client hasn't yet paid their bill. Lock-up is often broken down into WIP lock-up, where the client hasn't yet been billed, and debtor lock-up, where the client hasn't yet paid their bill.

Payment terms: This is how many days the client needs to pay its bill after the work has been delivered.

Utilization: Each fee earner is normally given a target for the amount of hours or days (depending on the firm's financial model), that they need to bill to clients. If a fee earner is fully utilized, they will have used all their available chargeable hours on billable client work.

Realization or recovery: This is a measure of how many billable hours the firm records which it actually charges out to the client. It is typically expressed as a percentage.

Gearing or leverage: This is a term that represents the ratio of partners to fee earners within a firm or practice area. Typically, but not always, the higher the gearing the more profits generated per partner.

Profit and loss (P&L) statement: It represents over a period of time how much money the firm has made or lost during that time. The firm's annual accounts will include a P&L statement for the financial year.

Balance sheet: This is a snapshot of a firm's financial position at any one point in time. It includes the firm's assets (what it owns), its liabilities (what it owes to other people) and its net worth. The firm's annual accounts will include a balance sheet for the firm's financial position at the end of its financial year.

How does the firm make money and profit?

> Potential partners need to have a consistent track record of fee earning and profitability. I don't think anybody will get to partner without having an outstanding financial track record.
>
> Alan Pannett, Chief Executive, Fresh Professional Development Ltd

In *Managing the Professional Service Firm*, David Maister compares the professional services organization to a medieval craftsman's shop. Today, just as in the Middle Ages, there are *apprentices* (junior managers or trainees and interns), *journeymen* (mid-level managers or experienced professionals), and *master craftsmen* (equity partners or senior management). Some people call these levels the *grinders*, *minders* and *finders* of a firm respectively. In Chapter 14, we look in more detail at how your role changes as you move from being an apprentice to a master craftsman.

Most firms use what is known as a leveraging system to maximize profitability. When clients hire a firm, they generally do so because of that firm's reputation and the skill of their high-profile fee earners. But clients don't necessarily get the first-hand expertise of the senior managers and high-profile fee earners. It's the lower-paid junior members of the firm who frequently perform most of the hands-on work. Clients then meet for a limited time with the higher-paid senior managers, who oversee quality and offer advice. This allows the firm to charge a high fee to clients, and still retain a high profit margin.

Charge-out rate

Every client-facing employee will be given a charge-out rate by their firm. Their charge-out rate is what the firm charges its clients for their time. This then allows the firm to recover the individual's total salary costs, fixed costs such as office rents, and contribute to firm profit. Your charge-out rate is normally determined by your salary and how much clients are prepared to pay for your time.

A charge-out rate also reflects the experience and salary of the professional performing the service. Clients are charged more for the time of someone with many years of experience and greater technical knowledge than someone with less. Partners, based on their expertise and years of experience, may be ten times more expensive than a trainee or an inexperienced professional. Some firms simply set their rates as a multiple of salary; for example, all fee earners are often budgeted at three times their annual salary.

The key factors considered by firms when deciding on charge-out rates include:

- the type of work;

- the person's level of expertise, eg partners, senior associate, associates, managers, qualifieds, trainees;

- what clients will pay for individual fee earners;

- the costs incurred by fee earners;

- the value of the work to the client;

- the market for the firm's services;

- the rates charged by the firm's competitors;

- the potential lifetime value of a client, ie the potential fees a client may pay while they are still a client of the firm.

Fixed fees versus 'time on the clock'

Regardless of the size of your firm, your firm will either charge a client a fixed fee, eg 'We will complete your audit for £20k', or fees based on the time spent by the fee earners. Sometimes you will hear about a 'capped fee' arrangement, where the work is still charged by time on the clock, but capped at a certain amount. The marketplace for professional services is such that clients are typically looking to have a level of certainty for the fees they will pay, which means that more and more clients are requesting fixed fees or capped fees arrangements from their professional advisers.

Financing the firm

Understanding the finance of any business is crucial if you are going to be any good at running it. Potential partners are often judged on their financial performance and being able to demonstrate a clear grasp of what matters will set you apart from the rest.

Amber Moore, Amber Moore Consulting

Every firm will need access to a source of funding above and beyond what they receive in payments from clients, both for the day-to-day expenses of running the firm and long-term planned expenditure. This is because most firms typically ask for some or all of the payment from their client after the work has been delivered. This results in a delay between the fee earners doing the work and the firm getting paid. Even though many firms will bill their clients monthly while the work is being completed, there still will be a delay between doing the work and being paid for the work. This results in a firm's available cash in the bank rising and falling as clients pay their bills and the firm pays its bills. The funding used to plug this gap is normally called working capital.

Common sources of funding for a firm, both for working capital and investment in the firm's future:

Capital introduced by partners: Typically this happens at the start-up of a firm or when a new partner is admitted to the partnership. Sometimes if the partnership is facing a hole in their finances, there may be a 'cash call' to the partners, where they all contribute additional capital to the firm.

Bank loans: These are normally paid back over the long term and used to fund capital items (eg IT equipment, office refits) and to ensure that there is sufficient working capital to keep the practice going.

Long-term overdrafts: Overdrafts are typically used to smooth cash flow fluctuations in the business, such as unpaid bills. The interest charged on a long-term overdraft is normally significantly higher than a bank loan.

Retained profits: Only part of the firm profits is paid to partners. The remaining profits are retained and used to meet the costs of maintaining and developing the practice. Usually profits are retained because they have not yet been converted into cash because they are 'invested' in lock-up (see below).

In order to minimize the amount of working capital needed to keep the firm solvent, it is vital that a firm efficiently bills its clients and makes sure its clients pay promptly. Many partners and senior managers hate talking about money to clients, but the reality is that a vital part of their role is to make sure their clients pay their bills correctly and on time.

Why is time recording so important?

Most professional services firms make their fee earners complete a time-sheet, documenting how they have spent their time. Most firms will normally allocate a job number for a piece of client work. Any time spent on a piece of client work will be recorded under the assignment's job number on the fee earner's timesheet. Having a true and accurate time record allows firms to:

- correctly bill clients for the time spent on a job;
- be confident that their quotes for fixed-fee pieces of work are profitable;
- manage a client's expectations on how long a piece of work will take and approximately how much it will cost them.

Common problems that impact profitability in a professional services firm

> All successful partners need to have the ability to acquire and service work profitably.
>
> Jamie Pennington, Managing Director, Pennington Hennessy

There are many factors that affect the profitability of a professional services firm. Five of the most common factors are:

- poor utilization;
- poor realization or recovery;
- poor financial management;
- high levels of lock-up;
- too high fixed costs.

Poor utilization

Ideally, each fee earner should bill their targeted hours each month and year. However, in reality, utilization levels are often under 100 per cent for the following reasons:

- *Insufficient work*: There is not enough work to go around, or the work which is available is low-quality work. Sometimes a firm's work is seasonal, and the client work to be serviced comes in peaks and troughs.
- *Partners or senior managers not delegating work down*: For a firm to gain the most profits from a piece of work, the best person to do the work is the person who is technically able but has the lowest charge-out rate. This relies on the ability and willingness of senior members of the firm being prepared to delegate the work downwards. When work is light on the ground or a member of the firm is worried about achieving their personal chargeable time targets, there is a temptation to hang onto work rather than delegate it downwards.

- *Memory lapses*: If fee earners do not have the discipline to record their time at the time they spent it, very often the firm ends up recording less time on the clock for a piece of work than it actually took. This can result in a firm undercharging for current work, but often underquoting for future work. When a firm offers to quote a fixed fee for a piece of client work, it is vital that they know realistically how long a similar piece of work has taken them to complete.

- *Moral editing*: This is where a fee earner decides not to bill all the time they spent on a piece of client work. This could be because they are under pressure to complete a job to the fee agreed to the client for the piece of work. Or they may undercharge their time because of inefficiencies or mistakes made within the firm.

- *Too many fee earners*: It's always a delicate balance having the right number of fee earners in a firm. Too many and some will be underemployed at times. Too little and the firm may end up paying expensive overtime rates to fee earners or their ability to deliver a great client service may suffer.

- *Clients who won't accept that their work will be delegated*: Sometimes clients have a fixed idea of who they want to work with, and who will actually be trusted to handle their affairs. This can potentially lead to underutilized team members, and unprofitable work for the firm.

Poor realization or recovery

One firm Heather worked with targeted its fee earners to bill five hours' chargeable time a day, but budgeted to recover only 50 per cent of the time it recorded on the clock. This is an extreme example, and most firms will expect to recover 85 to 95 per cent of their time recorded on clients' work.

- *Deliberate underpricing*: This is where the firm or an individual will deliberately undercharge or discount their fees to secure the client. This is a tactic very often used within firms where the firm is able to recoup the money it has lost by upselling highly profitable services to the client. Sometimes a fee earner will underprice to secure a new piece of work, when they know they have to hit revenue targets, even if the work will not be profitable. Sometimes a fee earner underquotes for the work because they don't have the nerve to charge for the true value of the work.

● *Poor quality, performance or relationship management.* Despite a firm's best intentions, sometimes things go wrong. This could be a relationship within a client not being handled well or a more junior member of the team not being supervised correctly. As a result the firm may write off some fees either voluntarily or in discussion with the client.

Poor financial management

As already stated, it is important that fee earners in a firm are good at issuing invoices promptly and making sure the client pays up in good time. In effect, until a client has paid their bill, the firm are financing the client at no risk to the client, while the firm may have to pay bank interest on its borrowings or overdraft. Other forms of poor financial management that can adversely impact a firm's profits are:

● poor credit control leading to bad debts;

● agreed billing arrangements with long payment terms for the client;

● partners or fee earners are slow to invoice their clients, leading to high WIP balances;

● poor negotiation with suppliers on fees;

● unrealistic budgeting, which results in the firm overspending against what they are actually able to earn.

High levels of lock-up

Our fee earners are given targets to achieve for their lock-up. A high lock-up means they are probably not billing frequently enough, or delivering a great client service.

Toni Hunter, partner, George Hay Chartered Accountants

It is not uncommon for firms to have a high level of lock-up. Sometimes it is due to process or project management problems; ie not getting the bills out quickly enough and checking that they have been paid. However, it can be because partners and senior managers are avoiding talking about fees with their clients, which often results in fee write-offs for the firm.

Too high fixed costs

As a rule of thumb, the lower a firm's fixed costs, the more profitable they will be. However, the less support or non-fee earning resources available to the fee earners, the greater the likelihood that there will need to be more charge-able time from the fee earners spent on non-chargeable activities, such as financial administration, reception, training, marketing. It is always a tricky balance getting the right level of support for the fee earners to help run the firm. Very often a firm is vulnerable to having too high fixed costs when there is a contraction in the economy, such as happened in the UK in 2008, or the firm loses a large client.

Taking steps to build your financial knowledge

Really good partners bill quickly and promptly and, because they understand the finances, they manage their lock-up and debt too.

Amber Moore, Amber Moore Consulting

You now need to think about the people within your firm who can help you to develop and broaden your understanding. Your finance team is always a good place to start. Discuss this with your colleagues as well – if a number of you are interested, compile a list of things that you would like to know, send it in advance to the member of the finance team with whom you are meeting. In our experience, this could result in the finance team putting together short firm-wide or department or team-based finance workshops, and production of a financial information pack with explanatory notes.

In recent years, more firms have started to organize both internal and external financial training sessions for professional staff. Make sure that you attend, particularly as quite often partners will also attend to talk about how the firm actually manages its financial controls and performance.

Ask your partners and mentors about what drives financial performance at your firm. Begin by asking questions about the following:

- the firm's financial performance;
- how to minimize lock-up;
- clients' expectations on fees;
- how to maximize the profitability of an assignment;
- how you in your role can help improve the firm's financial performance.

The time and effort that you invest in understanding your firm's finances and financial performance will pay off when you make your pitch for partnership because you will be better equipped to contribute to your department's and the firm's profitability. Remember that partners are continually looking for people who show potential for partnership by demonstrating financial and commercial acumen.

We will return to this topic in Chapter 20, when we discuss how to prepare your business plan for your promotion to partner.

Summary

As a potential partner, you need to be able to demonstrate a sound understanding of how your firm makes money and profit. This means you need to understand the role you play in:

- increasing your personal and team's utilization;
- being proactive with conversations about fees with clients to increase the recovery or realization on a client assignment;
- billing promptly to reduce lock-up and work in progress.

As most firms experience a delay in doing the work and getting paid for the work, they rely on other sources of financing to keep the firm's cash flow healthy and to help pay for large planned expenditure. New partners are required to invest a sum of capital into the firm when they join the partnership.

Action points

- Find out what financial information your partners make readily available, such as an annual report. Request to see a copy regularly and read it.
- Have a conversation with your partner, or member of the finance team, to find out about how you can help your bit of the practice become more profitable for the firm.
- Ask your partners and mentor about what drives financial performance in your firm.
- Look at your own WIP and lock-up for your clients. What three small things can you do to reduce them?
- Attend any internal or external financial training sessions offered by your firm.
- Find out which parts of your firm are the most profitable.

Further resources

Books

Haigh, J (2011) *The FT Guide to Finance for Non Financial Managers: The numbers game and how to win it*, Financial Times Publishing, London

Maister, D (2003) *Managing the Professional Service Firm*, Simon & Schuster, London

Scott, M C (2001) *The Professional Service Firm: The manager's guide to maximising profit and value*, John Wiley & Sons, Chichester

10 How to be seen as 'one of the club'

TOPICS COVERED IN THIS CHAPTER:

- What is a firm's culture and why it is important for you and your career?
- How to avoid career-limiting conversations and be politically savvy
- How to be seen as a member of the club

> *So I watched my step. There are a million little rules to obey; I knew none of them.*

MICHAEL LEWIS, AUTHOR OF *LIAR'S POKER*

In the last chapter we discussed how your firm makes money and profit. However, if you are going to get to partner you need to be seen as 'one of the club', which means you need to fit in. Fitting in is more than just doing or saying the right thing, ie avoiding career-limiting conversations; it's being seen as someone who really embodies the brand, core values and culture of the firm. In this chapter we help you navigate and survive the politics of your firm so that you are seen as inside rather than outside the club.

The firm's culture – warts and all

In Chapter 2, you were asked to think about your *personal* values and now you will need to refer to them as you consider your *firm's* culture. Put simply, *culture is the way we do things around here*. Culture and values (the moral compass which directs and guides the firm) bind a firm together in service to its clients and its vision.

> It comes down to little things – every firm is different but if your face isn't fitting it doesn't matter if you are a great lawyer. It doesn't matter if you are bringing in lots of clients, but if you are not 'one of the club' it's never going to happen.
>
> Jonny, partner

Each firm has a distinct character, look and feel, which are shaped by the people who work there, its history, external and internal relationships, clients, and the market it serves. Together all these things define your firm's identity. From your viewpoint, you need to feel, not just know, that you are working in the 'right' environment for you – if you are comfortable in your practice and your partners are comfortable with you, you are more likely to 'fit in', thrive and perform well. When you consider how much time you spend and will spend in the office, you must respect what your firm stands for, like and be liked by your partners and your colleagues.

Case study

When Jo joined a global accountancy firm, she attended a new hires' induction week. One hundred and twenty senior new employees were flown to the firm's learning and development centre in Illinois, USA. They spent most of the week being told stories about the firm's history, philosophy and values as well as receiving information about processes and systems. The attendees met all the leaders of the firm face to face. This made a powerful impression on everyone. They learnt a lot about the way things got done around the firm, and why things were done in particular ways. The programme gave the new employees a jump-start to really getting embedded in the firm's culture and core values.

Why is this important? Your firm cherishes and seeks to preserve its unique identity, culture and core values, and this affects every aspect of how it does business. Therefore, it will be looking for its future partners to be committed to these. Anyone who doesn't fit in, or isn't seen as 'one of us', is unlikely to be considered as a future partner for the firm.

Exercise

To see how well you fit into your firm, answer these questions:

- How would you describe your firm's culture, both written and unwritten?
- How well do your personal values match the firm's culture? If there is a mismatch, how seriously does it challenge you?
- Do you feel proud when you tell people which firm you work for?
- What is the gap (rate on a scale of 1 to 10) between your personal values and your firm's values and culture?
- In what ways, other than financial, does your firm reward good behaviour?
- Do you enjoy relaxing with the people around you?
- Are you happy spending time with your colleagues in work and out of work?
- Do you feel 'included' at work?
- Do you have role models and people you respect within your firm at partner level?

How to navigate and survive the firm's politics

> Successful partners are diplomats, but honest, open and fair.
>
> Patrick Raggett, PJR Consulting,
> ex-partner City law firm

Like any business, professional services firms are complex systems of egos, constituencies, issues and rivalries. Even the best-managed firm has partners with strong egos, sensitivities, and empire protectors. People who are politically savvy accept and deal with it by considering the impact of what they say and do on others. This should not be confused with being 'political', which is a polite term for not being trusted or lacking substance. In a firm, being politically savvy means that you can work with others and get things done in the maze with a minimum of noise, without triggering unnecessary negative reaction from your partners.

> Successful potential partners are committed to understanding the rules of the game and develop strong networks across the firm.
> Suzanne Lines, Director,
> Abamentis Limited

Political mistakes come in a variety of shapes and sizes. Such as:

- saying the wrong thing, either because of ignorance or because you couldn't help yourself;
- creating rivalries, conflict or tension with influential people in the firm;
- acting inappropriately with clients, introducers or firm members.

You need to accept and be aware of the politics within your firm and learn how to deal with it when it comes your way. Here are our tips for navigating and surviving the politics within the professional services environment.

Identify the movers and shakers in your firm. Who are the highly influential people in your firm? They may not be a partner or have an imposing job title. Who are the gatekeepers who control the flow of resources, information and decisions? Who are the guides and the helpers? If you don't already know, find out who they and get to know them. Be aware of anyone in the firm who has a reputation for 'throwing their toys out of the pram' if they are not consulted or involved. Remember that everyone has a mixed bag of behaviours, and to keep any 'labels' you have for people in your firm to yourself.

Tip

Find out who are the real movers and shakers in your firm by asking the personal assistants, as they always know these things.

Prepare before speaking with senior management. Senior management are notorious for being incredibly time poor. They often appreciate being

informed face to face. Be prepared with what you want to say
to them and don't waste their time; if they have given you
ten minutes then keep to time or, better still, finish ahead of time.

Tip

Before you want something from senior management, spend some time with a tough critic, to hone your ideas and arguments.

Be careful when dealing with influential partners. Very often these
partners have large egos and can be very sensitive, often because
they are managing highly tense situations behind the scenes. As
a consequence, there is a lot of room for making statements or acting
in ways that could be seen as showing poor political judgement.
There isn't usually a second chance to make a good first impression
with these people in your firm. You have been warned!

Tip

Before you go to see an influential partner, prepare by listing all your worst fears and what bad things you think might happen. Then mentally practise how you would recover if any of these things actually happened.

Always be prepared to be flexible when spending time with a partner.
Very often your time together may be cut short or postponed because
a client requires their input. Don't moan about this – it's par for the course
within a professional services firm. Have a contingency plan if this
happens, and be prepared to summarize your key points and conclusions
and send a written follow-up.

Exercise self-control before saying what is on your mind. Often
people get themselves into political trouble by being too candid
and annoying influential people, or by having too little candour, which is
seen as holding back due to fearfulness or lacking guts. While saying what

you want to say and to hell with the consequences may make you feel good, it would fail the political savvy test. You need to weigh up each situation on the candour scale. Are the right people here? Is this really the best time to speak my mind? Should I let someone else start before I pitch in? Did the speaker who asked for candour really mean it, or could this be a career-limiting conversation?

Tip

Let others speak first and follow their lead before you say what's on your mind.

Avoid gossiping or supplying information to the firm's grapevine. In a firm, people quickly find out what you have said about them, and that includes gossip. It can be very easy to get burnt by sharing private views with others in the wrong setting and with the wrong people.
If you choose to gossip and pass on stories, it *may* limit your career.
If you choose not to gossip, it *won't* limit your career.

Tip

Before you share some information, think about:

- Why am I sharing this?

- Does it create or solve a problem?

- Do people really need to know this?

- If I choose to *not* tell anyone, will the firm be any worse off?

- Am I name-dropping?

- Have I labelled facts as facts and opinions as opinions?

- Will this be considered grassing, gossiping or cutting down another person or group?

- In the worst case, how could this person use this information so that it could reflect badly on me?

Avoid sexist or politically incorrect humour. Times have changed drastically and humour that was seen as positive a few years ago is now politically unacceptable. The rules are simple. Any humour that hurts others, demeans others, or makes fun of the difficulties others face is out. What's left? You can tell clean jokes, make fun of yourself, tell funny stories and laugh with others.

Treat everyone as individuals, and with respect. The magic and complexity of life are that people are different. Everyone, particularly partners, requires special consideration and treatment. What may work with one person may annoy another, so you need to learn to read people. Relationships which work in a firm are ones where there is mutual respect – both for each other and, particularly in a professional partnership, for what each other has achieved.

Learn to read non-verbal body language. Very often the first sign of trouble will be seen in someone's body language, rather than what they are actually saying. When you are in meetings or talking with people, tune into their body language as well as what they are actually saying.

Non-verbal signals that not all is going well:

- changes in body posture, especially turning away;
- crossed arms;
- staring;
- withdrawal of eye contact;
- doodling on the notepad;
- looking out the window;
- drumming fingers;
- frowning;
- glancing at the clock or their watch.

> **Tip**
>
> When you sense that a conversation is going wrong, or there is tension in the air, pause, take a deep breath and ask how people are feeling.

Be cautious about initial or rigid assessment of people. You may do a reasonable job trying to read a person and form an initial judgement, but it may be wrong or it could change over time.

Have a kitbag of tools and tactics to help you get things done. Whatever its culture, as discussed earlier, every firm has its own ways of doing things and when it comes to getting things done there are a multitude of ways you can do it. For example, you could try the direct approach, or you could speak to your mentor and get them to test the water on your behalf first. Some of these tactics are more effective and acceptable than others. Some people get into trouble because they treat all situations as the same. Do your research about the most effective ways to get things done appropriately. People who are politically savvy pick their time, pace, style, tone and tactics based upon an evaluation of what would work best in each situation. We all have a number of ways in which we can behave if we want to. It's the one-trick ponies that get into political trouble because they don't adjust what they say and do for each audience.

Avoid being too black and white. Being too black and white often leaves you very little room to manoeuvre and extreme views can very often switch other people off. These may be the very people you need to influence or befriend. To avoid being seen this way, where possible, make the business case first. Be more tentative than you actually want to be, so others have room to get comfortable and negotiate and bargain.

> **Tip**
>
> In the collegiate environment of a professional services firm, it's important that you allow people the opportunity to preserve their position, save face and feel as if they have won something – however small that may be.

Join 'the club'

Many firms still choose their partners on the basis of 'more people like us'.
Amber Moore, Amber Moore Consulting

To succeed in any firm, you need to be seen as a member of 'the club' and the influential groups within that club. In our experience, professionals who are 'loners' greatly reduce their chances of making partner if for no other reason than the fact that they haven't raised their profile and the partners don't know who they are. However hard you work, keeping your head down will not help you to make partner. Unfair as it is, it is those people who have invested in being seen as 'one of us' who are more likely to make partner, regardless of how hard they have worked or how brilliant they are technically.

It is possible to build your profile for the wrong reasons such as hanging around with the 'wrong' people. Spending time with the firm's 'problem child' can often tarnish your reputation by association. In some firms, spending more time with secretaries and support staff rather than the fee-earning staff will not enhance your career prospects. This is not to say that you should not build and develop your relationship with them, particularly as they can provide you with invaluable support and guidance. However, you need to communicate where you see your career direction by associating with the firm's 'stars' and 'winners'.

Tip

A great way of increasing your profile is to get work from highly influential partners.

You may not want to go to the firm's social events, but these are a great opportunity to informally mingle with the influential partners and decision makers. Do look for opportunities to become involved in high-profile firm-wide activities, such as graduate recruitment. These, as well as helping build your profile, provide an ideal opportunity for you meet and work with colleagues from across the firm whom you would not normally meet.

Case study: Simon and his car

Simon, who drove a black turbo sports sedan, took a new job at a consulting engineering firm. The partners made it quite clear that he was to change over to a mid-range Ford family car because they didn't want clients seeing them being rich or extravagant. So that's what he did. Twelve months later his firm was taken over by a larger organization, and the culture was different. So Simon went and bought a Mercedes, and all the other partners made similar upgrades!

You can be prevented from advancing in a firm for a whole lot of never openly discussed reasons. Not all of these reasons are legal. If you feel you are being sidelined, we advise you to seek professional help.

Summary

Your firm is looking to preserve its identity, culture and values. In doing so, it will look for future partners who are committed to preserving these for the future. Your career progression relies on you fitting in.

To avoid career-limiting conversations you need to be politically savvy. This relies on preparing before you speak with senior people, and treating everyone in the business with respect.

Communicate your career direction within your firm by spending time with the people who are either where you want to be, or can help you get there.

Action points

- Look on the firm's website and ask one of the longest-serving partners about the history and culture of the firm, particularly about how the culture may have changed after a merger with another firm. Listen for things which are being held dearly by the firm, and ask yourself whether these match things you value.
- Spend some time with the support staff in your firm, and ask their opinion of who are the movers and shakers in the firm.

- Ask some of the influential people in your firm to share with you how they go about getting things done in the firm.
- In the next meeting you attend, look at the body language of the participants. Who is really leading the meeting? Who is bored? Who is keen to make things happen?
- Observe someone in your firm who has a reputation for being very diplomatic. What do they do well to earn this reputation?
- Aim to have a monthly lunch, coffee or breakfast with someone in your firm who is seen to be more influential than you are.
- Volunteer to help with a cross-firm project which will bring you into contact with more senior people in your firm, such as graduate recruitment, induction programmes, internal firm training courses.
- Do attend the next social event planned for your team, department, intake or firm.

Further resources

Books

Ennico, C (2009) *The Partner Track: How to go from associate to partner in any law firm*, Kaplan Trade, US

Lewis, M (2006) *Liar's Poker*, Hodder & Stoughton, UK

Lorsch, J W and Tierney, T J (2002) *Aligning the Stars: How to succeed when professionals drive results*, Harvard Business School Press, US

Websites and blogs

How to make partner – http://www.howtomakepartner.com

How to find the time to fit it all in

11

TOPICS COVERED IN THIS CHAPTER:

- The challenge of having to do it all
- How to adopt the right mindset to organize your time effectively and have a life outside work
- The importance of being assertive
- How to make time for the 'right' stuff
- How to stop distractions and interruptions, such as phone calls and e-mails, from limiting your daily productivity
- How to stop meetings wasting your time
- How to delegate effectively

In the last two chapters you learnt how your firm works and how you can use this knowledge to help you make a successful bid for partnership. Professional services firms make money by selling their time. Therefore, if you are going to achieve partnership while still maintaining a meaningful life outside work, you need to be able to manage and use your time effectively in the interests of clients, your firm and your career. This chapter provides a framework that will help you to develop habits and behaviours to enable you to be highly productive when you are at work.

The challenge of having to do it all

Lack of direction, not lack of time, is the problem. We all have 24-hour days.
Zig Ziglar

As your career progresses, the one thing you can be sure of is that the multiple demands on your time both at work and in your personal life will grow exponentially. As a non-partner, your primary focus is on client service and working with your partners to deliver to the clients' satisfaction. As you get more senior you will be expected to actively take part in day-to-day management of the firm. This could include supervision of individuals, management of a team, carrying out performance reviews, coaching, mentoring, and becoming a member of various firm-wide working groups. As if this wasn't enough, when you make partner, you will become an owner of the firm. This brings with it not only partnership responsibilities but also the responsibility of building and developing the business, which is going to keep you, your team, department and the firm profitable for the future.

In our experience, the professionals who do this best are those who learnt early in their careers how to systematically plan, set goals, prioritize and manage their time efficiently. There are no 'quick fixes'. If you want to have a successful career and life you need to learn how to do this from your first day in your firm.

Adopt the right mindset to be productive

Wander into any bookshop and you will see a whole shelf of books all promising to help you become the most highly organized person you could ever want to be. Look at your in-house training menu and time management will always feature. So, why is time management such a problem for many professionals? Very simply, it doesn't matter how many books you read or how many techniques you know, if you don't have the right mindset then you may as well have not read these books or attended the numerous courses available on time management.

All great achievements require time.
David J Schwartz

After delivering many time management courses over the years, it has become very apparent to us that you have to 'choose' to be organized. It's amazing how many people can get their work done on time when they have a powerful reason to leave the office on time. Have you noticed how those people who have to get home at a certain time – often to pick up children – seem to be able to get much more done during the day and still leave on time?

To help you get into the right mindset to be more efficient and effective while at work, consider these questions:

- What would I, and the people around me, gain by me being more organized?
- What am I missing out on – both in work and outside work – by not managing my time more effectively?
- How many projects, new client work and business development opportunities am I missing by not managing my time more effectively?
- How would my performance or career progression improve if I were able to do more work in less time?

Why you need to be assertive

> If you had been asked to draft four agreements before you went home that night, you did as you were asked.
>
> Kim Whitaker, commercial lawyer

Even the most organized person can come a cropper if they can't say no to requests from others. However, when a partner or client makes a request of you, it's often very difficult to say no. In fact, many professionals believe (whether rational or not) that they can't say no to a partner or client. Whenever we have run a programme on time management, this is a scenario which always comes up as difficult for people to deal with. This is where adopting an assertive mindset comes in.

So what do we mean by assertiveness?

Ken and Kate Back in their book *Assertiveness at work: A practical guide for handling awkward situations* define assertion as:

- standing up for your own rights in such a way that you do not violate another person's rights;
- expressing your needs, wants, opinions, feelings and beliefs in direct, honest ways.

There is a scale of assertiveness, which runs from passive at the left up to aggressive on the right, and assertive sits in the middle. Aggressive is when you totally disrespect the other person's feelings and needs. Passive is when you totally downplay your own feelings and needs. Assertive is where you balance your feelings, needs and requirements with the other person's feelings, needs and requirements.

Let's illustrate this by an example. It's 16:30 on a Friday and you are tidying up your desk ready to head off to drinks with your friends. A client rings up with an urgent request for some work to be done by the end of the day. The aggressive and career-limiting response in this scenario is to say no outright to the client's request. The passive response – and often the one most professionals feel they need to say – is, 'Yes, I'll meet your request and stay late until the work is done.'

So what's the happy medium and assertive response? Very simply, handling this assertively requires finding out more about the request, what needs to be done and actually how urgent it is, and find a way which gets the work done to the client's timetable, while not compromising your plans for the evening. In reality, unless you are in the midst of a time-critical deal – such as a merger – most client requests, which apparently need to be done by close of business Friday, can actually be completed on Monday.

If you are going to achieve the work–life balance which is important to you, then you will need to learn to be assertive – otherwise you are always going to find that the 'life' part of balance never quite seems to happen for you. See the Wheel of Life (Chapter 2) for more on creating balance in your career and life.

On the how to make partner website (**http://www.howtomakepartner.com**) there is a quick diagnostic questionnaire which you can complete to see how assertive your behaviour is at work.

Setting and managing expectations

> Lack of planning on your part does not constitute an emergency on my part.
>
> Anon

Far too often, we find that others hijack our own plans and priorities. Very often this is due to expectations not being set – normally with clients and people within our team. How much easier would it be for professionals generally if the client actually did what they said they were going to do? How many times have you been involved in a project where the timeline for a project has slipped because the client hasn't delivered on their commitments – but the client is still adamant that the original delivery date for the project still stands?

If you get into the habit of behaving assertively by setting and managing expectations, it can help prevent many of the 'urgent' calls on your time. You can use formal planning documents, regular governance calls, or simple 'I need this by because…' type of statements to help you proactively manage expectations. See Chapter 12 for more details on different influencing techniques.

How to make sure you make time for the 'right' stuff

Regardless of the demands on your time, if you are going to get to partner and still have a life, you need to know what is important to you – both inside and outside work. We all naturally tend, whether consciously or subconsciously, to prioritize what is important to us. When you know what is important to you, you are more likely to make it happen, and also turn down opportunities or requests which distract you from what you need to achieve.

It's interesting that every time we interviewed partners, they all said that for an individual to get to partnership takes dedication and focus. To be focused means you need to know your goals and what you want to achieve in the short, medium and long term. (For help to identify your goals, reread Chapter 2 and Chapter 7.) If you have these goals and road maps of what you want to achieve in your life, you are then able to evaluate each opportunity against these – 'Will they help me achieve them or not?' You can then turn down the opportunities that will distract you from achieving your goals.

How to use your diary to plan for success

> Most people don't plan to fail; they fail to plan.
>
> John L Beckley

There is an urban myth that a professor was delivering a lecture to a crowded lecture theatre. He produced a pint glass and filled it with rocks. He then asked the class *Is the glass full?* The class said *yes*. He then produced some pebbles and added those to the glass. He then asked the class *Is the glass full?* The class said *yes.* He then produced some sand and filled the glass with them. He then asked the class *Is the glass full?* The class said *yes.* He finally poured water into the glass and asked *Is the glass full?* The class said *yes.*

If you apply this story to your diary, the rocks are the big things that will help you achieve in your job and progress your career, eg training courses, new business meetings with clients, time with your mentor. The pebbles are the normal day-job stuff like client work, meetings with your team and direct reports. The sand is the small bits and pieces, such as your expense form, tweeting, reading blogs and articles, which tend not to be very important or particularly urgent. The water is the distractions, such as chatting at the coffee machine, spending time on Facebook. The takeaway from this story is that if you let it, you can always fill your diary with water, sand and pebbles but then there is no room for the big stuff, ie the rocks. If you plan the rocks into your diary, then you are more likely to achieve your big goals and progress your career, while still achieving your ideal work–life balance.

A useful way to help you make sure that the rocks get into your diary is to use a technique called a default diary. This is where you have a standard daily, weekly, monthly, quarterly routine, which is timetabled permanently into your diary. This makes sure that the important but often non-urgent stuff happens. For example, your quarterly lunch with your mentor and the daily quick meeting with your team where you discuss current caseloads. Many successful professionals will have one day in the week where they leave it free of client meetings – often working at home for this day, to minimize interruptions from the office. This then gives them time in the week to either actually do the client work or focus on important work such as business development campaigns. The weekly planner template used in Chapter 7 will help you start to utilize a default calendar. See Diagram 11.1.

Know what is important and urgent

Without doubt, you could quickly write down at least five things that you need to do now. The key to managing your time effectively is prioritizing what is (or isn't) important and urgent for you. Stephen Covey, in his book *The Seven Habits of Highly Effective People*, identified the importance-versus-urgency matrix. Every task you do can be categorized in terms of its importance and its urgency, and plotted into a two-by-two matrix. See Diagram 11.2.

DIAGRAM 11.1 Example of a default calendar

GMT+00	Mon 23/4	Tue 24/4	Wed 25/4	Thu 26/4	Fri 27/4
					Work from home – no
07:00					
08:00		08:00 – 09:00 Networking time	08:00 – 09:00 Networking time	08:00 – 09:00 Networking time	
09:00	09:00 – 10:30 Time with team – agreeing on weeks priorities	09:00 – 17:00 Client work	09:00 – 17:00 Client work	09:00 – 11:00 Follow up sales calls	09:00 – 11:00 Personal admin time
10:00	10:30 – 17:00 Client work				
11:00				11:30 – 14:30 Lunch out with client/prospect/ team member	11:00 – 14:00 Catch time with clients on current projects
12:00					
13:00					
14:00					14:00 – 15:00 Blog/article writing time
15:00					15:00 – 16:00 Personal career review time
16:00				16:00 – 17:00 Weekly team meeting	16:00 – 17:30 End the week & prepare to do list for next week
17:00					

DIAGRAM 11.2 Stephen Covey's importance-versus-urgency matrix

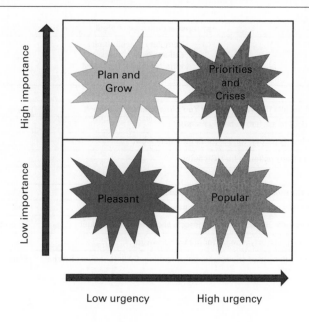

Priorities and crises – Do it

These are tasks with high importance and high urgency. Client work, pitches and staffing problems tend to go in this box. To help you make sure that you complete your 'priorities and crises', identify up to three critical results which you must achieve by the end of the week.

Plan these into your weekly planner. See Diagram 11.3.

DIAGRAM 11.3   *Weekly planner, with critical results identified for the week*

WEEKLY PLANNER	Week no: 47	From: 30 November			To: 6 December		
Mon	Tues	Wed	Thurs	Fri	Sat	Sun	
Business development, networking, people management and client service actions to complete							
Work on report for HGR audit	Work on report for HGR audit	Finish report for HGR audit	1:2:1 with my performance mgr	Planning meeting for ABC audit			
Career action plan tasks to complete							
	GAB meeting to ask him to be my mentor	• Write up notes from meeting with GAB • Book time in with GAB's PA for mentor kick-start meeting	Research blogs for property developers on environmental issues	Date night with my partner		Go swimming in am	
Any other actions to complete							
Departmental monthly meeting			Complete self-appraisal form for HGR project work	Submit weekly timesheet			

Your 3 Critical Results this Week – What You *Must* Achieve this Week	Done
Meeting with GAB to ask him to be my mentor	
Evening out with my partner for our fortnightly date night	
Finish report on likely polluters for HGR audit	

Objectives for the month (taken from career action plan)	Done
Agree on date night with partner for fortnight before Christmas	Yes
Complete report for HGR audit within timescale allocated in the budget	To do this week
Schedule time in my weekly planner for my weekly swim	Yes
Attend meeting with head of environmental consulting, GAB, to request that he becomes my mentor	Scheduled meeting

Plan and grow – Defer it, but plan it in your diary
These are non-urgent tasks, but highly important tasks for your future career, such as going to a face-to-face networking event, following up on new client leads, meeting a client team after the audit has been signed off for the year, reviewing how the case went with the team on the case, doing a performance review with a member of your team, etc.
The non-urgent tasks, which help your achieve your long-term career goals, generally go in this box.

Pleasant – Dump it
These are tasks with low importance and low urgency. These include chatting at the coffee machine and gossiping with your friends at work, reading your trade magazine, etc.

Popular – Delay or delegate it
These are those tasks with low importance and high urgency. Very often the urgency is actually only perceived to be high. For example, these tasks include checking e-mail, voicemail, social media accounts and returning calls.

It is worth noting that some tasks if left may increase in importance and urgency. For example, filing your paperwork may not seem urgent or important at the time – but when you have a huge pile of paperwork on your desk and can't find a vital piece of client documentation, and your partner starts talking about the firm's tidy-desk policy, suddenly ignoring the filing seems to be a bad move on your part.

The way to apply Covey's matrix is to use it as a mental guide to help you identify what your priorities are, ie your critical results for the week, based on your personal goals. Ideally, you should be focusing your time and energy on tasks in the *Plan and Grow* and *Priorities and Crises* sections.

How to stop procrastinating

Regardless of how focused and determined you are, no one is immune to procrastination. It is something that we all do, and stops us delivering on our priorities. Very often if you find yourself spending too much time in the *Pleasant* or *Popular* boxes of Covey's matrix it is a sign that you are procrastinating on the important tasks. Here are eight ways in which you can minimize the amount of time you spend procrastinating:

1 *Break the task up*
 Break the task up into smaller pieces. When the task is smaller and seemingly more manageable, you are more likely to get on and do it. Remember, how do you eat an elephant? One bite at a time...

2 *Give yourself milestones*
 Similar to breaking the task up into smaller pieces, set yourself milestones on the way to completion. Reward yourself when you achieve a milestone, for example, time for a cup of tea and a biscuit.

3 *Have a To Do list, eg your weekly planner*
 Write down all your tasks and things to do. When you have completed them, then scrub them off the list. As you see your progress building it will give you the momentum to finish the list. Your weekly planner needs to contain your three or four critical results which you must achieve that week.

4 *Set deadlines*
 Whether they are real or artificial deadlines, set them. You will be amazed how a deadline can give you the stimulus to complete a task. Use your weekly planner to write down your deadlines for the week.

5 *Get the difficult stuff out of the way first*
 Brian Tracy in his great book *Eat that Frog: Get more of the important things done today* talks about a concept called frog eating. His philosophy is if the worst thing you can do is to eat a frog, then everything else becomes easier. The 'frog' is the large and important task which you have been procrastinating over. Very simply, if you do the difficult stuff when you are at your most alert and energetic, often at the start of the day, then you will gain the momentum to get the rest done.

6 *Avoid perfection*
 Aim for 80/20 or 90/10, as total perfection is rarely needed in business. Aiming for perfection (and knowing you cannot achieve it) is a factor in procrastinating. Perfection is a major obstacle to consistently achieving high levels of personal productivity.

7 *Delegate or outsource*
 If you know what you don't like doing and what tasks you tend to procrastinate over, then (if possible) delegate or outsource those tasks. Procrastinating over certain types of tasks often suggests that this is not a personal strength or there is a lack of personal motivation to complete the task.

8 *Use power hours*

Power hours are where you allocate an hour into your diary to 'power' through your To Do list. You need to turn off all distractions and make sure you are not interrupted during the hour. Power hours are a great time to focus on clearing down your e-mails or doing client follow-up calls. Heather schedules two power 'half hours' daily into her calendar. This is when she tackles her e-mails, next steps, phone calls and social media updates.

Conquering distractions

Despite our best intentions, there are always a multitude of distractions which, if not managed, can cause even the most organized professional to become unproductive.

Paperwork

Paperwork is part of every professional adviser's life. It needs to be proactively managed, otherwise it can waste our time. For example, how distracting is paperwork sitting on your desk? How much time have you spent recently searching for a document which didn't get filed away properly?

Follow this simple process (FART) to make sure your paperwork is handled efficiently and effectively.

File it: Don't make the mistake of filing your paperwork into your in and out trays – all this does is create trays of unfiled paperwork. After you have read the paper (and if it needs to be kept), file it. Put a discard date on papers that will outlive their usefulness and clutter up your files.

Act on it: If you can, deal with it there and then. Anything which will take you less than five minutes to deal with, do it now – otherwise schedule time in your weekly planner to deal with the task.

Refer it: Keep some files for people who you deal with or meet on a regular basis. Keep these files handy, and when you next see them, (instead of contacting them separately for each individual item), take care of all the items in their folder in one go.

Throw it away: Take a look at your non-client-specific files. How much of this paperwork do you actually need to look at again? Or are you printing and filing it 'just in case'? Do you really need to print it out? Would an electronic copy suffice? If you have an assistant, how about delegating your filing to them, as well as the sorting, screening and disposal of mail? Be ruthless with your paperwork: unless you can think of a valid reason to print out or keep a piece of paperwork, then recycle or shred it.

Minimize any interruptions

Anyone in an open-plan office will testify to interruptions – be they by people stopping by or phone calls. These can seriously affect your productivity. Ideally, you need to have a strategy to assess each interruption and deal with it, eg:

- If it's urgent, deal with it straight away.
- If the interruption is unnecessary, stop it or avoid it – try standing up as the person comes in so that they can't sit down; or leave the area yourself.
- If the interruption is untimely, reschedule it.

Stopping e-mail taking over your day

E-mail is one of the biggest sources of inefficiency in the workplace. How many of us would be able to get so much more done if we weren't constantly bombarded with e-mail? Here are seven ways in which you can minimize the amount of time you spend on e-mail:

1 *Set times of the day when you will look at and deal with your e-mail.*
   Outside these times, switch off your smartphone, e-mail and e-mail notifications – plus any social media notifications. Then decide when you will dedicate blocks of time during the day for dealing with your e-mail. Eg 11:00–11:30, 15:30–16:00. If you use public transport to get to work and can access your e-mail on a mobile device, you may find this is an ideal time to screen and action e-mails.

2 *Set up e-mail rules.*
   Mail rules are great for auto-sorting out your mail before it arrives in your inbox. For example, you can set up a folder for each of your regular e-mails, such as monthly recurring invoices or regular reports for which you are on the distribution list. Then set up the rule that puts the e-mail into the right folder – for example, a monthly recurring invoice could go into a folder called 'invoices to process'. You can even

put follow-up flags on these rules, so that, for example, any e-mail from your most important client is flagged to be dealt with by you that day.

3 *Unsubscribe to newsletters.*
Unless you read the newsletter, unsubscribe to it.

4 *Action, file or delete immediately.*
Double or even triple handling e-mail is what leads to personal inefficiency. Have as your mantra that you will only touch an e-mail once. Either process the e-mail immediately or schedule time in your weekly planner when you will process the e-mail.

5 *Set limits on amount in your inbox.*
Get into the personal discipline of never letting your inbox get more than a page full of e-mails in at the end of the day. There is nothing worse than an important client e-mail getting lost in a mass of e-mails.

6 *Use flags to follow up important e-mails.*
Use the follow-up flags. If you have an e-mail to action, mark it with a dated follow-up flag. Then file it! In the morning, you can then sort all your e-mails by flags, and you will get a list of the most urgent e-mails to be actioned.

7 *Number your most important folders.*
If you give your folders a number, eg '1 – Clients', your most frequently accessed folders will be at the top of your folder list, regardless of where they would come in true alphabetical order.

Dealing with phone calls

Phone calls, like e-mail, can interrupt your day. As with e-mails, there are ways in which you can lower the amount of interruptions you get from the phone. Here are three such ways:

1 *Switch to voicemail or divert to a secretary.*
If you need to focus on a task, then switch your phone to voicemail or transfer to your secretary. If you use techniques such as 'power hours' (see above in this chapter), this is the time to switch off your phone.

2 *Save up your phone calls so you do them in chunks of time.*
Similar to having dedicated times to process your e-mail, then dedicate times in your weekly planner to doing your phone calls and returning calls.

3 *Tell people when you are available to be contacted.*
   If you can train your clients and network to phone you at times which work for you, then you can minimize the amount of time you are disturbed by the phone. If you leave a message on your voicemail (or even bottom of e-mail) of the times when you are around, you may find you receive fewer interruptions by phone.

Stopping meetings wasting your time

Back-to-back meetings won't get the job done.
Jo Larbie

Most of us have at one time or another said that if we didn't have as many meetings we could probably get more done in half the time. Unfortunately, the very nature of professional services means that client, supplier, team and staff meetings are intertwined in the fabric of how business is done.

The first stage in using meetings effectively is to evaluate whether you need a meeting or whether you need to attend. In a business that makes money by selling time, you also need to add up the cost of inviting people to a meeting and multiply this by the length of the meeting. Now that you know the true cost of bringing people together, do you still need to have a meeting or is there a more cost-efficient way to deal with items on the agenda?

Consider these options before scheduling potentially expensive meetings:

- video conferencing or a conference call;
- seeing people personally – management by walking about (MBWA);
- circulating a memorandum or sending an e-mail;
- working instead of meeting;
- sending a representative instead of attending yourself;
- reviewing at regular intervals whether the meetings that are held are still necessary and in that format;
- attending meetings only for the time required to make your contribution.

It is a truism that any meeting or agenda item will expand to take all the time allotted to it. Aim to keep the agenda items short and punchy. Consider

TABLE 11.1 Effective meeting dos and don'ts

Do	Don't
Use an agenda	Leave the agenda to chance
Give everyone a chance to speak	Produce the agenda at the meeting
Circulate the agenda in advance	Let someone dominate the meeting
Ask people at the meeting what they want to get out of the meeting	
Ask people how they thought the meeting went at the end of the meeting	

whether using a meeting facilitator would help to keep the meeting to time and the discussions on topic. See Table. 11.1.

Delegation

> If it can be delegated, it must be. Never work on something that someone less experienced than you can do – your career will be on hold and you'll become more and more obsolete with each passing day.
>
> David Maister

In Chapter 9, we explored how profits are eroded in a professional services firm. Very often, the biggest 'profit leak' is when professionals hang onto work which could be completed by a more junior and cheaper member of the team. However, this is only one of the many reasons why it pays to delegate. For example, if you *can't* or *won't* delegate, then you will never free up the time to take on roles and responsibilities, which you will be required to demonstrate to be considered for promotion to the next level, especially from director to partner.

Delegation isn't something that comes to a professional adviser naturally. Most of us are hard-wired to want to do the best job possible on a piece of work, particularly when the stakes are high. If we have to delegate tasks down to other more junior members of the team, very often we are worried that the quality of the work will slip, so we keep it all to ourselves.

Commonly the way a firm rewards performance can stop delegation happening. When the workload is light and there is pressure to achieve targets, many professionals hang onto work rather than delegating so that they still hit their financial targets. Do not follow their example, as you will limit your career progression.

If we don't have competent people to delegate to, then very often we will take the view that it's quicker and simpler to keep the work rather than delegate it down. How many times have you heard the remark 'By the time I've briefed someone else, I could have already done the work'? However, if staff don't get the chance to pick up the requisite skills, they will never develop them. This can lead to demotivation among the junior ranks of a firm as they don't feel that they are learning. What may be routine and boring for you may be a very interesting and stretching task/assignment for a more junior member of the team.

Here are five ways of minimizing risks when delegating:

1 *Identify the risks.*
   When delegating a responsibility for the first time – or if the stakes have risen considerably – do an analysis of where the risks are. That way, you can put in place an action plan and structure to minimize the risks.

2 *Monitor the risks.*
   When you know where the high risks are, you are then in a position to monitor those areas. For example, if you delegate the management of a budget and cost centre, until the budget holder is completely up to speed you will want regular updates on the spend going through this account.

3 *Use management by exception.*
   After you have agreed a plan of action with the person you are delegating the responsibility to, ask them to update you if anything doesn't go to plan. This way you will be involved if anything deviates from the ideal plan. You can then help to develop contingency plans as necessary.

4 *Build in controls.*
   There are several controls that you can build into a project or responsibility – for example, spend or budget limit, project milestones, key performance indicators. Have the person that you delegate to provide regular feedback and reports on progress to date; agree this when you give them the task.

5 *Have a contingency plan.*

Despite your and others' best intentions, sometimes stuff doesn't go to plan. However, we know from our days in practice that it always pays to have a contingency plan in place.

Summary

Time is the professionals' most valuable commodity and in order to manage time, you need to record, monitor and assess how you are using it. If you want to demonstrate your eligibility for promotion to partnership, effective management of your time will demonstrate your professionalism to your partners. You have to choose to be organized and use time management tools and techniques such as weekly planners and default diaries.

Assertive behaviour means that you stand up for your own rights in a way that does not violate another person's rights. If you are going to balance both your life and work, you will need to adopt assertive behaviours.

Delegation is a key skill for every professional to learn. In a partnership, your future career progression – as well as the firm's profitability – heavily relies on your ability to delegate successfully to others. Doing it well shows that you understand the importance of leverage, and that you are commercial in managing your emerging practice.

Action points

- At the beginning of each week, ask yourself, 'What are the three critical results that I must achieve this week that will make a difference to my career and my department's performance?' These are your critical results, and you need to work out how you are going to achieve them.

- Use your firm's time-recording system to review how much time you are spending on your key roles and responsibilities. Can you see a pattern emerging? Are you investing time on the things that will help and progress your career goals?

- Find someone in your firm who is better at time management than you are. Watch what they do and compare it against what you typically do. Focus on doing more of the things they do.

- Start using your weekly planner.

- Attend time management or assertiveness training.

- Have a go at doing a power hour – how much more work did you manage to get done by minimizing any interruptions?

- Introduce a default diary into your calendar, and train yourself to only check your e-mails at dedicated points during the day.

- Look at your big career goals, ie your 'rocks'. When can you plan these rocks into your diary?

- Download the free time management plans and template from **http://www.howtomakepartner.com**. Test out, and adapt if necessary, the different templates and find one which works for you.

Further resources

Books

Allen, D (2002) *Getting Things Done: How to achieve stress-free productivity*, 2002, Piatkus, London

Back, K and K (2005) *Assertiveness at Work*, McGraw-Hill, New York

Covey, S (2004) *The Seven Habits of Highly Effective People*, Simon & Schuster, London

Mills, C (2010) *Making Every Six Minutes Count*, Ark Group, London

Morgenstern, J (2000) *Organising from the Inside Out: The foolproof system for taking control of your schedule – and your life,* Hodder and Stoughton, London

Tracy, B (2004) *Eat that Frog: Get more of the important things done today*, Mobius, CA

Websites and blogs

Free time management plans and templates – http://www.howtomakepartner.com

Assertiveness questionnaire – http://www.howtomakepartner.com

Emailogic – E-mail training and tips – http://www.emailogic.com/

Catrin Mills's Lawyer Coach website and blog – http://thelawyercoach.wordpress.com/

Dr Rob Rawson's blog – The Time Management Expert – http://www.timemanagement.com/blog/

How to look, sound and be the part

12

TOPICS COVERED IN THIS CHAPTER:

- How to communicate so your message is understood correctly
- How to positively influence
- How to give and receive feedback
- How to handle a difficult conversation
- How to dress and look the part
- How to design and deliver a presentation which delivers its objectives

> *A successful partner demonstrates the ability to create an aura of 'trusted adviser' and displays the presence expected of someone in that role.*

ALAN SMITH, MANAGING DIRECTOR, ALAN SMITH ASSOCIATES LTD

Core to any professional's success is their ability to communicate. In your role as a professional adviser you are communicating with people pretty much constantly throughout your working day. For example, you could be having a difficult conversation with a client while trying to preserve the relationship, or coaching a member of your team, or delivering a presentation to potential clients. In this chapter we will explore how you can create the personal impact you want and need, utilizing the many forms of communication you are required to master.

What do we mean by effective communication?

Effective communication is when you realize that the message you have been trying to convey has been received and understood in the way that you intended it to. In theory this sounds easy. However, our message can be easily altered, and quite often we may fail to check that the message has been properly understood. In fact, your message is always distorted by the time it is received and understood by the other person. This is because your brain uses filters and associations to quickly make sense of what it is seeing and hearing. For example, if the sky is very dark and cloudy, your brain will almost definitely make an association with the fact that it is likely to rain, and wonder whether you have remembered your raincoat or umbrella.

While this filtering is essential to us as humans if we are going to be able to take in information from all our five senses quickly, and understand what is going on around us, it can make the communication process even harder as our intended message is filtered three times before it is received.

See Diagram 12.1 to see how it is filtered.

DIAGRAM 12.1   The communication process

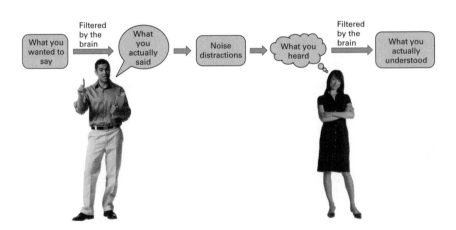

This means that before effective communication has taken place, you need to demonstrate to the person talking to you that you have completely understood them and they have understood you.

Verbal versus non-verbal communication

There are three constituents to the message we communicate: the actual words we use, how we say these words and what body language accompanies these words when we speak. You will often hear people labelling these three types of communication as the 'words', 'music' and 'dance'.

The meaning of your message is communicated by both verbal and non-verbal ways, eg the 'words', 'music' and 'dance'. This means, to increase the chances that your message is heard and understood correctly, your words, tone and body language must be congruent.

Effective listening

If you look at the communication process in Diagram 12.1, you will see that how you listen is pretty fundamental to effective communication. Very often we are not good listeners because:

- Physical problems may stop us from hearing all the words, for example trying to have a conversation on a mobile with poor reception.
- Our minds are elsewhere, such as thinking about a client project, how we will have a difficult conversation, what to make for dinner tonight...
- We perceive that the value of what someone is saying is low, eg when we believe that we are right and nothing can alter our belief or when we don't respect the other person's views, values or beliefs.
- We are tired and finding it difficult to concentrate.

To listen effectively or without prejudice is a personal choice. Very often, you will hear effective listening called active listening. This is when you choose to expend energy to really listen to someone else. This is more than just the physical act of turning off external distractions (such as taking a phone call in a quiet meeting room); it is actually a state of mind where you have to choose to suppress your own agenda or beliefs, so that you can be truly open to what the other person has to say.

To actively listen to someone:

- Minimize any distractions around you.
- Focus solely on what they are saying, and how they are saying it.
- From time to time summarize or paraphrase what you have heard to check you understand them.
- Empathize with what they are saying.

You will know when someone has been actively listening to you, as this is often the precursor to rapport being established.

What do we mean by rapport?

People like people who are like themselves or who behave like them. Sensing that someone else is like you is done at the conscious and subconscious (or unconscious) levels. Two people who sense that each is like the other at an unconscious level are said to be 'in rapport'.

Rapport is an essential component of any good-quality relationship. Therefore, if you want to build up or improve the quality of a relationship, you need to take some time to actively listen to the other person. If you observe any professional who is known for their strong relationships with clients, you will notice that they spend a large part of the conversation actively listening to the client.

Many textbooks and training workshops will teach you a technique called *mirroring*. This is where you copy the other person's body language, to try and build rapport. While this sounds fine in theory, in practice it never works. In fact, mirroring naturally happens when you have generated rapport, rather than rapport being generated because you have copied someone's gestures.

What are they not saying?

Very often you will learn more by listening out for what your clients, team or partners are not saying. For example, have a chat with any new recruit into your firm about how they are finding life in the firm. You would expect any new member of a firm to be excited about their new role and how much they are enjoying working in their new firm. Therefore, if a new recruit who doesn't say this or convey in their words enthusiasm for their new role, they are likely, even if they don't explicitly say it, to be struggling in their role.

Effective questioning

As a professional adviser, you are expected to develop excellent questioning skills, so that you can:

- find all the relevant information from a client in an unobtrusive manner;
- coach more junior members of the team around you;
- get a full brief for the work you need to do from more senior members of your team.

You will often hear people talking about open or closed questions. Open questions are ones which encourage the other person to talk more, and 'open' up. Open questions normally start with 'How…', 'Why…', 'Where…', 'Tell me…' or 'What…'. Closed questions have a tendency to 'close' the conversation down, commonly causing the listener to answer with single words such as yes/no. Closed questions often start with 'Is', 'Did…', 'Was…' and 'Who…'.

See Table 12.1.

TABLE 12.1   When to use open and closed questions

Open	Closed
When you've met someone for the first time and keen to get to know them better	When you want to keep the conversation short and to the point
In a business development meeting	Closing down a conversation
Coaching	When you want to limit the options available

Tip

Use the word 'why' sparingly. It can often cause the other person to be defensive.

Positively influencing others

Professional services firms are a complex mesh of intertwined relationships. Your ability to influence will help you positively influence your clients to take a course of action, but also achieve your career goals within the complicated informal and formal organization of a professional services firm.

> Influence is 'an effect of one person or thing on another'.

In this section we are focusing on positive influencing skills. It is a sad fact that there are some professionals in firms who achieve their objectives by using negative influencing techniques such as aggressive behaviour, shouting, bullying or harassment. While this may help you in the short term to achieve your objective, it is normally detrimental to your career and relationships in the long term. Overusing negative influencing behaviours can very often block your path to partner; see Jack's case study.

Case study: Jack

Jack was keen to make partner, and was prepared to do whatever it took to shine. His firm had a core value of always treating people with respect. When an important piece of client work arrived on his desk, he stopped one of his team from going away on a special weekend where he had planned to propose to his girlfriend. Inevitably word reached the partners about what Jack had done, and how he had upset his team by his bullish and aggressive conduct. As a consequence the partners, because they felt that Jack didn't uphold one of the firm's core values, blocked his promotion to partner, and he never made partner at his firm.

When we therefore talk about positive influence, we mean *working to achieve a positive difference*.

It does not mean:

- a compromise (a solution neither party really wanted);
- manipulation or deception;
- one side winning and the other side losing.

It does mean working to achieve:

- a genuine consensus;
- openness and integrity;
- both sides winning.

Push and pull types of influence

Influence techniques split into two different types, dependent on whose agenda you are working to. When you are working from your agenda, you are normally utilizing push influencing techniques. Conversely, if you are working from the other person's agenda to influence someone, you are using pull influencing techniques. No one technique is better than the other; it depends on the people involved and their personal influence preferences.

Push influencing

There are two main techniques here:

- stating your own views, requirements, opinions or feelings;
- using incentives or pressures.

Stating your own views, opinions and feelings

This is where you give your own views, opinions or feelings on a given topic, eg:

I believe, based on my years of experience with similar cases, that the best course of action for your business is ...

I feel worried if we were to choose to ...

Right now, I feel irritated about the progress on this project because the team is struggling to prioritize ...

In my view, the client's accounting system is inadequate for the job it is now required to do.

This is one of the most used influencing techniques in business. Very often you will hear people stating their own views confidently, as if they are proven facts. If it is overused, it can become counterproductive and aggressive, particularly when we don't seem to care about the other person's thoughts, views or opinions.

Using incentives or pressure

This is where you apply either a positive or negative outcome to persuade someone to a course of action. This is often used in a negotiation situation, eg:

> If you come along and present to our management board, free of charge, you are likely to be asked to present at the firm's annual conference.

> If you can meet this tight deadline, we will pay overtime rates to you and your team.

> If you refuse to move on this demand, then we will walk away from the contract.

If you are going to use this influencing technique, then you must make sure, to remain credible, that it is within your power to deliver on the negative or positive outcome and you are prepared to carry out your threat. Very often this technique is used in negotiation situations where you don't have the ability to compromise on certain areas and are not open to influence.

Pull influencing

There are four main types of pull influencing techniques that are normally used:

- active listening;
- finding common ground;
- exploring;
- disclosure.

Active listening

When you take the time to actively listen to someone else, it can be a powerful influencing technique. It allows you to understand the other person's views, opinions and motivations, which then allows you to adjust your demands or reasoning to make them more acceptable to the other side. Very often, just the act of being properly heard and understood makes someone more disposed to listen to and be persuaded to a course of action by others. You will often see this technique being used successfully to resolve a conflict between a client and their adviser.

Finding common ground

This is where you aim to find areas where you have shared views, beliefs, values, attitudes or common experiences. Too often individuals focus on the differences and disagreements that divide them. Sometimes it is finding the similarities and agreements, which you do share, that can help unlock a deadlock. Very simply when you believe that someone is like you, you are more likely to be open to influence by them, eg:

> As we are both short of time, I'm guessing we would both like to resolve this issue quickly.

Exploring

This is a simple technique where you encourage the other side to open up, so you can both enlarge your understanding of the situation. For example:

> Tell me more about why you want to do this ...

> What's the back story here?

The greater understanding of the situation, from both sides, makes it easier to find a mutually acceptable course of action.

Disclosure

This is where you choose to disclose facts or your own feelings which can influence a decision or course of action, eg:

> I know that everyone thinks Raj is ready for promotion to manager, but I have a nagging doubt that he is not mature enough yet to act as a good role model to the juniors.

> Before we choose to target this client, I have to let you know that I was speaking to a contact last week who informed me that they were suffering with cash flow problems.

This is a very versatile influencing technique because:

- It can disarm hostility.
- It builds closeness.
- It can be used as a response to attack.
- It can be used to successfully start a potentially difficult conversation.
- It can be creative when you don't know what to do next.

How to handle a difficult conversation

Very often, as a professional adviser, you will be required to use your influencing skills when you have to have a difficult conversation. For example, it may be:

- a fee dispute with a client;
- a piece of difficult feedback you have to give;
- some unwelcome news for a client on their case;
- having to tell a member of the team that their case for promotion wasn't accepted this time around;
- a team member is not achieving chargeable time targets.

Regardless of the subject matter of the conversation, many professionals shy away from having a difficult conversation. In our experience, these types of conversations never get any easier if you delay having them. Nor does the need for the conversation disappear the longer you leave the conversation.

To be able to successfully handle a difficult conversation, you need to be able to keep a dialogue going, so that you both reach the point where the right kind of action can be taken by each of you. However, this is not always easy since our brain uses filters and associations to make sense of the message it is hearing. Mankind's very ability to survive over thousands of years has been partly due to our sensitivity to perceived threats. This, of course, is great for the human race's survival, but not so great when you know you are having a difficult conversation. Our brains are often identifying risks that are not actually real. As we see and hear the conversation, our brains are filtering the message and associating what we hear with previous experiences. Based on the associations we make, our brain, if we feel unsafe, produces emotions and actions based on those emotions.

To be able to keep a dialogue going, when all this is going on in our brains, means you have to, as described in the book *Crucial Conversations: Tools for talking when the stakes are high*, establish and maintain a safe conversation. To do this, you need to:

- ask for permission to have the conversation;
- speak in private;
- avoid inappropriate humour;

- apologize if necessary, regardless of whether you believe you are right;
- state what you do want to happen as a result of the conversation;
- state what you don't want to happen as a result of the conversation.

As you are participating in the conversation, listen out for signs that the other person has started to make the conversation unsafe. For example, this could be:

- aggressive and emotive language;
- sarcasm;
- silence;
- agitated body language;
- avoiding the conversation by changing the subject.

To get a conversation back to safe ground, you need to help the other person master their emotions, to allow you to carry the conversation to a satisfactory outcome. Ways you can do this include:

- acknowledging that emotions are now present;
- stressing the mutual gain for having the conversation;
- focusing on the outcomes of what you do want and don't want to come out of the conversation.

How to give and receive feedback

One of the most common difficult conversations you will have is when you have to give effective feedback or ask for feedback about your performance. In Chapter 7, we talked about the requirement to be open to and seek out feedback on your performance. So what do we mean by *effective* feedback?

Effective feedback is feedback that:

- creates and delivers a specific message based on observed performance;
- describes specific behaviour so that a person can learn by repeating good behaviour or ceasing bad behaviour;
- enables the receiver to walk away understanding exactly what they did and what impact it had on you or others.

There are many models or processes around of how to give feedback to someone. We recommend you use the situation–behaviour–outcome (SBO) feedback model.

What is SBO?

The SBO model is a feedback model which can be used to structure both positive and constructive feedback. Its structure increases the likelihood the feedback will be received in a clear, non-defensive manner by the recipient. Feedback models often require you to deliver both positive and negative comments. In our experience these models never tend to work very well because the person receiving the feedback always wonders whether the positive feedback is genuine, and only really hears the negative feedback.

The SBO model:

- Situation: Describe where and when the observed behaviour occurred, and what happened. Remember to be specific.

- Behaviour: Describe what you saw or heard. Avoid interpretations and judgements such as 'You weren't listening to me.' Simply describe the person's behaviour: 'When I was talking, you pushed your chair away from the table and gazed out of the window.'

- Outcome: Share with the individual the outcome or impact of the behaviour on you and/or on others. Outcome is what you or others experienced. It can include work outcomes, client satisfaction, work team and/or the larger firm. Most often, it starts with 'I felt...' or 'I was...' or 'it appeared to me others were...'

Some examples of using SBO feedback:

Weak feedback: *Janet, you were good in the client meeting today – thanks.*

Effective feedback: *Janet, at the client meeting this afternoon (**situation**) you demonstrated your knowledge of our aerospace client particularly well when you talked about trends in their sector this year (**behaviour**). The client commented on your thorough preparation and that it portrayed true professionalism (**outcome**) to the client.*

Weak feedback: *James, the office manager is unhappy – you just didn't deliver or meet his expectations.*

Effective feedback: *James, the office manager, George, on the job appraisal forms has suggested that you weren't proactive in meeting his expectations (**situation**). Specifically, when I talked to him he said that despite your work being thorough, you provided reports late on two occasions without letting him know (**behaviour**). This led to a lot of frustration on his part (**outcome on manager**) and detracted from what has been a successful job (**outcome on individual**). Can we work through this together so that we can prevent this happening again?*

Some tips for giving feedback, which will be accepted first time around:

- Praise in public, criticize in private.
- Always ask permission to give the feedback; unsolicited feedback is rarely welcomed.
- Ask the other person first what they thought went well and not so well.
- Wait until your emotions have calmed down, before giving feedback.
- Use the SBO model to help you be specific.

How to receive feedback

Feedback, particularly when it is of the tough variety, can often be hard to swallow. The best way to view feedback is that it is a gift, but one which you can choose to accept or decline.

If you are fortunate enough to receive feedback, regardless of whether it is negative or positive:

- Always thank the person afterwards (whether or not you agree with it); people offering feedback are almost always well intentioned.
- Listen carefully to what they are saying, if necessary asking for clarification.
- Resist the temptation to get defensive or clarify your version of events.
- If you feel yourself getting emotional, request some time to reflect on the feedback before discussing it.

How to dress the part

Earlier on in the chapter we talked about the 'words', 'music' and 'dance' forming the whole message which you communicate. The way you dress also communicates a message about you. Whether you agree with it or not, your personal appearance will be judged as an expression of who you are and your approach to the job. Your hair, shoes, tattoos, piercings and clothes will be taken as indicators of your status, suitability for partnership, self-confidence, self-care and self-worth. If you get your image right, it is likely to be noticed but not commented on. If you get your image wrong, then this will materially slow your career progression within a firm. Very often you wouldn't be directly told that you are dressing inappropriately, because many managers or partners shy away from this kind of conversation as it feels far too personal and too risky.

If you are getting feedback similar to the following, then it is likely that you need to spend some time considering how to change your look at work:

- Lacks presence, charisma or gravitas.

- Doesn't look the part.

- Isn't polished enough.

Tips to help you strengthen your presence, not detract from it:

- Dress for the job you want, not the job you have. Look at how the partners in your firm dress, and as much as you feel comfortable with, copy their style.

- Do not wear clothes which are considered to be too revealing, tight or short.

- Keep your wardrobe updated and regularly ditch anything which has become worn, stained, ripped or tired.

- Do add new items to your professional wardrobe at least once a year.

- Don't become a fashion victim, but keep an eye out for what styles are current and what's not.

- Invest in classic pieces for your wardrobe which will never go out of fashion.

- Make sure your clothes fit properly.

- As you progress upwards in your career, consider investing more in clothes which are made to measure for you.

- Don't dress for comfort, dress for presence. For example, walk to work in comfortable trainers, but immediately change into work shoes when you enter your office.

- Always aim to dress slightly more formally than your clients. For example, if your clients dress casually in jeans, then dress in business casual when you go and see them.

- Always have a comb and mirror handy before you go and meet clients or go to an important meeting.

- Always have a jacket in the office in case you need to dress up an outfit or a client unexpectedly visits.

- Wear clothes which cover up any visible tattoos.

- Keep your nails and hands neat and tidy.

- Remove any excessive facial or ear piercings.

- The newer or more junior you are in a firm, the more conservatively you should dress. As you establish yourself in a firm, then you can add a little more flair to your wardrobe.

- Men: keep your facial hair tidy and neatly groomed.

- Always check your back view in the mirror before leaving home or going into a meeting – you should be aware what others are seeing when you exit a meeting while they remain. For this reason, it's worth polishing the back of your shoes as well as the front.

Delivering a presentation with impact

Being able to present confidently and effectively is a core skill for any professional to master. Great presenters will spend time thinking about what they want to achieve when they are presenting, and the best way to achieve this.

To maximize your audience's recall, break your presentation into three sections:

- the opening, where you tell your audience what you are going to tell them;

- the body content, where you use a maximum of three main points;

- the close, which summarizes your main points and tells the audience what you want them to do as a result of the presentation.

To be truly effective as a presenter, you need to be able to conquer your nerves. The easiest way to reduce your nerves is to allocate plenty of time to design and practise delivering your presentation before you have to deliver it for real.

There will be times where you are a member of a team delivering a presentation. Make sure you have a team leader who opens and closes the presentation. Each team member's part of the presentation, to maximize the audience's recall of the presentation, needs to be treated as a sub-presentation, ie have an opening, body content and close. See Table 12.2.

TABLE 12.2 Presentation dos and don'ts

Do	Don't
Think about what you need to say to influence your audience	Read off your slides
Practise before you deliver your presentation	Cram in as much information as possible
Use signposts in your presentation to help your audience orientate themselves	Use lots of jargon
Make eye contact with your audience	Stare at one person in the audience
Give hand-outs at the end	Forget to allow time for questions at the end
Use an easy to see structure for your presentation	Fiddle with pens or keys in your pockets
Use pauses to give you and the audience time to think	

There is a free guide to designing and delivering presentations with impact at **http://www.howtomakepartner.com**.

Summary

Effective communication only takes place when the person who is communicating has verified that the message has been understood correctly. Active listening is when we choose to expend energy to listen to someone else. Open questions are questions used to open up a conversation and closed questions invite a closed number of responses and can be used to close a conversation down.

Influencing techniques split into push and pull types, dependent on whose agenda you are working to.

It is not easy to give or receive feedback. When giving feedback use the situation–behaviour–outcome (SBO) model to help ensure that it is effective and acted upon.

When you are having a difficult conversation, focus on generating mutual respect and finding a common purpose for the conversation. If you notice emotions creeping into the conversation, take a step back and make the conversation safe again.

It is important to 'look the part', by being guided by the dress of the others in the business.

Action points

- Every time you find yourself having to give feedback, use the SBO model. For the first few times you use the model you will need to script what you are going to say.

- Experiment with using only open or closed questions in a conversation at home. Notice the impact your questions have on the conversation.

- When you are having a conversation with a person who primarily uses push influencing techniques, try using pull influencing techniques with them. How effective were you in influencing the other person?

- Ask your mentor, partner or counselling manager at work whether your appearance at work is helping or hindering your progression in the firm. If you are serious about advancement in your firm, then be prepared to change your appearance and book an appointment with an image consultant to make over your professional wardrobe.

- Volunteer to give a presentation to your team or department on something that they will find useful.

- Ask to go along and observe a pitch team in action. How did they work together as a team?

- If you are not a confident presenter, book yourself onto a presentation skills course.

- Identify a good presenter in your firm. Take notes on some things they do well, then apply those ideas to your own presentations. Never be afraid to ask someone afterwards how you could have improved your presentation.

Further resources

Books

Back, K and K (2005) *Assertiveness at Work*, McGraw-Hill, New York
Carnegie, D (2006) *How to Win Friends and Influence People*, Vermillion, US
Etherington, B (2006) *Presentation Skills for Quivering Wrecks*, Cyan Books and Marshall Cavendish, UK
Patterson, K, Mcmillan, R, Switzler, A and Grenny, J (2011) *Crucial Conversations: Tools for talking when the stakes are high*, McGraw-Hill Professional, New York

Websites and blogs

How to make partner blog – http://www.howtomakepartner.com
Toastmasters – http://www.toastmasters.org
Professional Speaking Association – http://www.professionalspeaking.biz
Six Minutes Speaking and Presentation Skills: http://sixminutes.dlugan.com
Alan Steven's Media Coach Blog – http://www.mediacoach.co.uk/blog.htm

How to build your network for life

13

TOPICS COVERED IN THIS CHAPTER:

- What we mean by networking, and the four reasons why people network
- How your network is core to your future success
- How to design, build and maintain a network which will help you achieve your future career goals
- How to network effectively
- How to successfully work a room

The number-one reason why professionals' careers stagnate is they neglect to build and maintain their network.

JULIAN, PARTNER

In this chapter, we will look at what we mean by networking as well as how to design, build and maintain a professional network that will help you achieve your professional career goals. Later in this book, we will look at how to use the network you have grown, to help you build your client portfolio.

What is networking?

> If you want to be prosperous for a year, grow grain. If you want to be prosperous for ten years, grow trees. If you want to be prosperous for a lifetime, grow people.
>
> Anon

Effective business networking is the process by which you find, build and maintain mutually beneficial business relationships. However, networking at its simplest is about meeting people and interacting with them.

There are four reasons why professionals network:

- to improve their profile, ie being 'found';
- to generate opportunities such as a new job or new clients;
- to extend and strengthen the community around them;
- to find answers and 'tools'.

When they talk about networking, many people connect networking merely with formal networking events without realizing that most of us are consistently networking throughout our waking hours. You may not badge all these activities as networking, but they are all ways in which we network:

- phoning your mother or a friend for your regular catch-up;
- writing and posting a new blog;
- introducing yourself to a new member of your club or society;
- exchanging some pleasantries on a phone call before getting down to business;
- logging into your Facebook account and reading your friends' status updates;
- inviting your work colleagues over for a meal;
- answering a question posted on an online forum;
- regularly attending a business networking club;
- talking to the person next to you in the queue for coffee at a conference.

Why invest time in building your network right now?

An effective business network contains strong relationships built upon a foundation of trust and mutual respect. These relationships don't magically appear at the point you need them. They take time to develop and mature. Very often you need to be thinking ahead and place bets on which professional and personal relationship are going to bear fruit in the long term. None of us has a crystal ball and is able to predict who out of our network from school, university and the early years of our professional life is going to be the one who makes it into a position of influence and power. What we do know is that this early network which you have been blessed with, if you keep in touch with it, will, five to ten years down the line, produce potential clients and well-placed introducers for you. This means that the best time to build your network that is going to sustain and facilitate your career progression upwards is *now*.

You may be thinking, 'Why can't I just develop work-winning relationships with potential clients and partners right now? After all, these are the people who are likely to be able to help me achieve my goals.' Unfortunately most potential clients and introducers are unlikely to want to build a relationship with someone who is a fairly junior member of the firm. This relationship is normally driven by a desire to have a direct contact with the decision maker and acknowledged expert within your part of the practice, rather than a personal slight on your character. It is for this reason that we recommend, in the early years of your career, focusing on relationships with your peers and people one level above you inside your firm, from other firms and professional networks and from your earlier life network. Ideally as their careers progress, your career will benefit, too.

Common concerns and myths around networking

Between us, we have heard a wide range of common concerns and myths around networking:

- Fear of rejection – 'I can't stand rejection!'

- It will create an obligation – 'If they support me in some way, what will they expect in return?'

- It takes too much time – 'I don't have time to network, *and* I already have more contacts than I know how to handle.'

- It is cold and impersonal – 'Networking seems cold, forced and impersonal. Frankly, I don't want to be one of those people who is always out for themselves.'

Stop worrying – in this chapter we debunk these myths and, if you share any of the above concerns, we will help you to overcome them by providing the framework and tips to improve your confidence when networking.

If you have any doubt at all about the importance of networking, just remember the following facts:

- A referral generates 80 per cent more positive results than a cold call.
- Approximately 70 per cent of all jobs are found through networking.
- Most people you meet have around 250 contacts.
- Anyone you might want to meet or contact is four or five people away from you.

How to design and build your network

Sadly most professionals in their early years pay very little attention to their network. The reality for most junior professionals is learning by osmosis, rather than any focused planning and activity, in establishing their networks. Very often these networks are heavily focused on their peers with whom they trained and qualified. Some of the enlightened firms, such as Bircham Dyson Bell LLP, invest in building their professionals' networking capability very early in their career. However, most firms tend to formally train their people how to network effectively only at the point when they are expected to start bringing in their own work.

If you only take one thing away from this book, then let it be the need to focus and plan your networking strategy and activity from the beginning of your career, not at the point in your career when you are under pressure to deliver results.

Focusing your networking goals

> The number one reason why some people get work done faster is because they are absolutely clear about their goals and objectives and don't deviate from them.
>
> Brian Tracy, author of *Eat that Frog*

The number one reason for professionals not achieving the results they require via their network is a lack of focus. This lack of focus is addressed by having networking goals, which are focused on helping you achieve your big life goals. Many people confuse networking goals with the big life, career and business development goals that they have or that their boss gives them, such as: 'Make partner by the time I am 35', 'Find £50k of new business every month.'

These are not networking goals. These are the big career and life goals that we want our network to help us achieve. Your networking goals need to be the activities that you will do to help you achieve your big career, life or business development objectives. For example: 'Spend one hour on LinkedIn each week to find and meet new potential introducers.' 'Attend all the department's social events and make the time to speak to all the partners who turn up.'

Identifying your big goals

Close your eyes for a few moments and visualize what success you want to achieve. What do you see in your mind's eye? What are you feeling? What does your inner voice say to you? Then complete this sentence:

My networking strategy will help me achieve _____ (fill in with what it will help you achieve) by _____ (fill in with a date by when you want to achieve this).

Designing your network for the future

In your early years as a professional you don't know who out of your current network is going to be in a position of influence and power to help you start to build your own client portfolio. So it's a matter of trusting personal chemistry and your instinct for whose career will grow quickly, and in doing so help yours along too. However, don't forget that your network is not just there to help you when you are a senior manager building your own client portfolio; it can still help you now. For example:

- It can help you find your next job.
- It can provide you with good quality business intelligence about your chosen target market, current or potential clients, and people within your industry.
- It can give you support and friendly guidance when you are having a tough time.

Network maps

In order to focus on whom you need in your network, you need to spend some time thinking about who can help you achieve your goals. To do this, you need to draw a network map; see Diagram 13.1.

DIAGRAM 13.1 Your network map

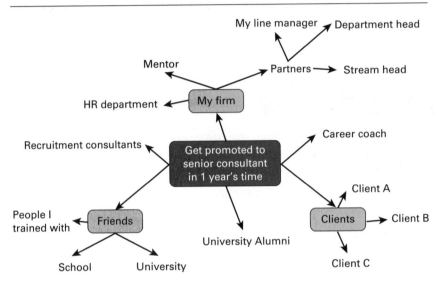

Start with a clean sheet of paper, or use a mind-mapping piece of software. In the middle of the page, write down your big goal and put it in a box.

Now brainstorm everyone who could help you achieve this goal. Do think laterally and map everyone. Wherever possible, add names to the map.

You've now designed your network. However, as the saying goes, 'Not everyone is created equal.' There will always be some people within your network who are better placed to help you achieve your goals.

Look over your map. Who are the top five to ten people who, if you maintained a positive and healthy relationship with them, would help you achieve your big goal in the shortest time possible? These we call your A-listers. Now have a look at your map and identify five people who are the least likely to be able to help you achieve your goals in the short, medium or long term. These are your C-listers. Your B-listers are everyone else. You don't want to forget entirely about your B- or C-listers; however, you really want to spend more time on building and nurturing relationships with A-listers.

Relationship plans

Now that you have identified the people in your network most likely to be able to help you achieve your big goals in the shortest time possible, it's time to write relationship plans for each and every A-lister. You may want to think about ways in which you can easily keep in touch with the B- and C-listers without having to expend too much time or resource. For example, will you be able to see some of your B-listers at the regular work social events?

What needs to go in your relationship plan?

Within each relationship plan for your A-listers and potential A-listers you need to identify the following:

- How you think the relationship may help you achieve your big goal.
- Their contact details.
- Their social media profiles, eg Twitter account and LinkedIn profile.
- Some personal details about them, eg likes, dislikes, family situation.
- How you met and know each other, plus any relationships in common.
- How you may be able to help them.
- What you are actually going to do to help them and strengthen the relationship; for example, your desired frequency of conversation by what medium (phone, e-mail, social media, etc).

For an example of a relationship plan, have a look at Diagram 13.2.

Your relationship plans need to be 'live' documents which you frequently update and maintain. They don't need to be paper based – in fact, with the great technology available today, you may find it easier to keep these plans electronically. After you have written your relationship plans, transfer the activity from the plan to your diary. This way, your relationship plans are more likely to be implemented.

For a free relationship plan template, go to: **http://joinedupnetworking.com/ free-stuff/free-networking-plans-worksheets-and-templates/**.

DIAGRAM 13.2 An example relationship plan

Name:	Eka Patel			E-mail:	Eka. Patel@address.com		
Phone:	01234 123 456			Address:	35, High Street, London		
Twitter:	@ekapatel			Role:	MD of UK PLC		
Frequency of contact	Phone:	monthly	Face-to-face	quarterly	e-mail:	fortnightly	

Their Goals and Objectives:
- Grow UK PLC to a £35 million company
- Identify companies to grow strategic alliances with
- Find international distributors for their products

Their interests outside work:
- Family – especially cooking
- Hindu, regularly attends the local temple
- Coeliac

Family situation:
- Married with 2 grown-up kids

What stuff can I send to him regularly, or invite him to?
- Articles on getting the most out of your leadership team
- Gluten-free recipes

How can I help him?
- Provide introductions to my clients – particularly marketing directors

Relationship next steps:
1. Diarize monthly and quarterly meetings and telephone conversations
2. Ask PA to look out for good gluten-free recipes
3.

Expanding your network

In your relationship plans you have probably identified groups of people you don't yet know. Part of your networking strategy has to include how you will find these people, so that you can build mutually beneficial relationships. It becomes easier to find people to add into your network when you know whom you are looking to add.

Time-saving tip

If you have a role where you have large chargeable hours targets or are away from home for significant periods of time, prioritize methods of meeting people through your work-based activities.

Here are some places in which you can expand your network of useful contacts:

- social events;
- formal and informal networking events;
- seminars and conferences;
- project teams from client assignments;
- professional association events;
- training courses;
- networking sites such as LinkedIn;
- hobbies and interests, such as sporting clubs, gym classes, music groups.

How to network effectively

> Networking takes a lot of your time and energy – and yet so many people simply go along and see what happens.
>
> Bryony Thomas, Chief Clear Thinker
> at Clear Thought Consulting

Heather devised the FITTER™ model to help professionals network in a time-efficient manner. This model gives you a simple mnemonic which will enable you to network efficiently and effectively anywhere and anytime.

What is the FITTER™ model?

The FITTER™ mnemonic is not a step-by-step process – you need to be mindful of doing *all* of these things *all* of the time when networking, regardless of where you meet people or how you meet them.

FITTER™ stands for:

Follow up.

Introduce yourself with impact.

Target specific people.

Turn social conversations into business chat.

Engage.

Research.

Follow up

> Similar to a golfer, the follow-through for networkers is as important as how you hit the ball.
>
> Jon Baker, business coach

Neglecting to follow up after a networking event is probably the biggest mistake professionals make when networking. Failing to follow up turns all your hard effort during the networking event into a waste of your time.

Very often professionals don't follow up effectively with their network because they are worried that they 'don't have anything to offer them'. While on the surface this may be true, we can all offer everyone something. For example, you could help them by:

- sending them an article which they will find interesting or useful;
- offering to connect them to someone in your network;
- sending them a link to a website or blog which will be useful to them.

What to do after an event

After the event, within 24 hours of meeting someone, sort through the contacts you made, and split them into three piles containing A, B and C-listers.

Productivity tip

Block out an hour in your diary the day after a networking event to do follow-up.

Regardless of whether they are an A, B or C-lister, everyone needs to go into your contacts database; and ask to connect with them on LinkedIn. Even if you don't have specialist relationship management software, most e-mail software such as Outlook and Google Contacts will have the functionality to manage your contacts. Make a note of where you met them. Even if you don't think you'll get in touch, keep a note of the contact – you never know who people know! When you add a contact, here are the details that you should aim to record:

- Name, address, telephone number(s).
- Company name.
- Website address.
- Twitter accounts – company and personal.
- LinkedIn profile.
- Their company on LinkedIn.
- Note when and where you met. Additionally, jot some details about them and what you discussed.
- Add in some comment to help you remember them if you met them again – eg 'Looks a little bit like Sean Connery.'

> **Tip**
>
> To keep your A-listers visible, create a list for them in Twitter, tag them in your e-mail client as 'important' as well as tagging them in LinkedIn and your relationship management software.

Effective follow-up is not purely about what you do immediately after meeting someone. It's what you do to build and maintain the relationship over the lifetime of the relationship. So, next time you meet an A or B-lister, decide on what you will do to grow and maintain the relationship, and grab a blank relationship plan and fill it in. Then diarize the next steps!

What to do with your C-listers

You may be thinking that it isn't worth bothering spending any time or effort with people who fall into your C-lister category. However, never write off a relationship; life isn't static and people and their roles, needs and wants do change over time. The lowly finance clerk in your client's organization may develop into a financial controller or finance director of a company you would love to have as a client one day. Social networking sites like LinkedIn offer a great way to still stay connected to your C-listers without having to spend any time keeping the relationship current.

Introduce yourself with impact

> The image you project, in many circumstances, is far more valuable than your skills or your record of past accomplishments.
>
> Michael Korda, author of *Power! How to get it, how to use it*

Whether you are conscious of it or not, whenever you are with other people you will have an impact on them. Research has shown that within the first seven seconds of meeting someone new, people form three judgements about the individual – male or female, their size and whether or not they like them. From this they go on to makes a series of assumptions about race, age, occupation, competence, education, mood, personality, trustworthiness and even sexuality.

First impressions are everything. Get it right, and everything becomes easier. Get it wrong and you've a hard task ahead of you to correct those all-important first impressions. As humans we can't help forming instant opinions when we meet a stranger; it's how we are programmed for survival. Studies show that we can be very reluctant to change our minds once we have formed a strong impression.

So, what do we mean by a great first impression? In both the real and virtual worlds people respond well to warm, positive and confident people. If you are meeting someone in person, this means offer your handshake (firm) first, give them a warm smile and be positive and enthusiastic. This simple act will convey credibility and a likeable personal brand.

If someone is meeting you for the first time in the virtual world, there isn't the equivalent of a handshake. But don't be fooled: they will still be forming a perception of you from that first meeting. If your answer, tweet or blog post conveys warmth, positivity, authenticity and likeability, then you are halfway there to creating a great first impression. If your first online meeting is positive, the next thing that someone will do is look at your profile, blog or website. This is why it is so important to spend time on your social networking profiles and general web presence.

Your opening sound bite

> Too often we lose an opportunity to meet someone because we spend precious time trying to think of the perfect opening line.
>
> Susan RoAne, author of *How to Work a Room*

The last piece of the jigsaw is how you introduce yourself. For many professionals, a big trap is waiting for them when asked (the almost standard question at a networking event), 'So what do you do?' Do you confess and say,

'I'm an accountant…lawyer…architect…'? Or do you describe what you do by the value you bring to your clients? For example, an accountant may describe what they do like this: 'I help my clients legally pay only the right amount of tax, not a penny more, not a penny less.'

The right answer is to have the one-sentence sound bite prepared, which succinctly talks about the value you bring to your clients. By talking about the value you bring to your clients early in the conversation, you are emphasizing the benefits of your service rather than the features. After all, every sales-person will tell you that people buy benefits, not features.

When Heather trains professionals to use an opening sound bite describing the value they bring to their clients, many people worry that the other person wouldn't know what they do. Of course this is a genuine and real concern. However, in our experience, whenever this type of opening is used, the next question is, 'Oh, that sounds interesting. How you do that?' And then you are off, the conversation is started, and you have moved straight into a business conversation.

Remember that your internal firm network is just as important as your external network. How will you tailor your opening sound bite when meeting people in your firm for the first time? Don't always assume that they will know what your department and team actually do.

Your online footprint

When someone connects with you online and likes what they see, the first thing they normally read is your profile or online biography. Why? It's to find out more about you and evaluate whether you are the type of person who they want to get to know. This may sound callous, but every time you meet someone new in person, you are subconsciously deciding whether you want to get to know them better. This may only be the quick decision whether to follow someone on Twitter, or it may be a decision to contact them with a view to hiring them in the future. Very often a potential client will check you out online, particularly by Googling your name and looking for you on LinkedIn, before they pick up the phone to talk to you.

Tip

When writing your profile in Twitter, include the people you would like to follow you. Many people use search tools to find people with certain words in their profile.

Your online presence needs to demonstrate your credibility and position your brand, eg state who you work with, and the problems which you solve for your clients. Do remember to include your photo within your online profile, as it helps people viewing your profile start to connect with the person behind the profile. Very often a social networking site, eg LinkedIn, and the profiles within it are rated very highly by Google. Therefore, to help you appear near the top of the search engine rankings for content you control, it is important to include keywords in your profile which your clients and potential clients are likely to be searching for online.

LinkedIn tip

Adding a profile photo makes your profile seven times more likely to be found in searches. Having your two most recent positions makes your profile twelve times more likely to be found (Source: The LinkedIn Blog. 'simple steps to a complete LinkedIn profile', published 14 February 2012, **http://blog.linkedin.com**).

When we meet someone in person, very often our gut instinct tells us whether we can trust them or not. When we meet someone online, we can only rely on the written word and what their photo looks like. Trust is often generated in online relationships by consistency, ie answering the same types of questions, tweeting on similar themes and having the same profile and professional-looking photo, regardless of which online networking site you meet them on.

What needs to go in your online biography or profile?

Your online biography or 'bio' is part of your networking toolkit. You need to have a couple of versions of your online biography prepared; for example:

- to use as an author credit for your articles;
- to use within marketing materials, for example if you are a guest speaker at a seminar or conference;
- in your social networking site's profiles, eg Twitter and LinkedIn.

You may find that your firm already has guidance on how to write your online profiles. Your basic biography needs to consist of your professional head-and-shoulders photo, one sentence stating what you do, then a paragraph qualifying your credibility.

Some tips when writing your basic biography:

- Keep it short and sweet; less is more.
- Don't claim to be more than three things, as it damages your credibility.
- Include links back to your firm's website presence.
- For social networking profiles, especially LinkedIn, include keywords within your profile.

To access free downloadable templates for your LinkedIn profile, go to: **http://joinedupnetworking.com/free-stuff/free-networking-plans-worksheets-and-templates/**.

Target specific people

If you've ever been to a networking event, you will know how easy it is to end up having great conversations but not actually talk to the people you have gone to the event to meet. If you have done your homework before an event (see the later section in this chapter on research), you will have a shortlist of five to ten people you want to meet at the event. How many of these people could you contact via LinkedIn before the event and arrange to meet at the event? Perhaps you could get your host to introduce you to them?

Heather was once asked to give a networking tip to a senior audit manager who was going to a networking event the very next day. She suggested that he contact people he wanted to talk to at the event via LinkedIn. He followed her advice and of the six messages he sent via LinkedIn, five people responded and he gained four sales meetings as a result of talking to these five people at the event.

Before you attend an event, tweet that you are attending and use your LinkedIn status to let people know you are going, asking if anyone else is also going. This may encourage someone who wants to meet you or get to know you better to attend the same event. Connecting up with people in advance of an event gives you an additional purpose to attend the event, as well as the opportunity to strengthen an existing relationship.

Turn social conversations into business chat

> Don't count conversations, make your conversations count.
> Rob Brown, motivational speaker and networking expert

Blurting out your objective for meeting someone, within the first minute of meeting them, is very unlikely to be constructive. Before you start talking business, take your time to get to know the person first and generate some rapport.

> Many potential partners make the mistake of thinking that business development is about telling people what you can do for them instead of listening and asking questions to find out what they really need.
>
> Amber Moore, Amber Moore Consulting

Some good questions to use to move your conversation into a business-orientated conversation include:

- How's business at the moment?
- What's your ideal client?
- What problems do you solve for your clients?
- How do you market your business?
- What challenges are you facing at the moment?
- Who is your ideal referral source?

Engage

> People don't always care how much you know, but they do know how much you care by the way you listen.
>
> Anon

When meeting someone at a networking event, focus 80 per cent of your energy on listening and finding out about them: their objectives for being at the event, who they are, shared hobbies, interests and mutual acquaintances, and what makes them tick. Remember, you are not there to sell; you are there to start a mutually beneficial relationship, which can be accelerated by being able to help them there and then. For example, how about asking them:

- what has brought them to this event?
- who they are hoping to meet at the event?
- what do they want to achieve by the end of the event?

Most people, unless they are very self-obsessed, will always reciprocate and find out about you and your agenda. If they don't, do you really want to spend time on someone who is not interested in you?

Research

Before you attend a networking event or meet someone, you need to do your homework. Your research will enable you to focus only on the events worth attending, the people who will be beneficial to you to meet or reconnect with, what you want to achieve by meeting someone and good topics to talk about. Your personal assistant can do this research for you.

Let's say you are an accountant and are looking for a new job within a private practice locally. Therefore, you want to be meeting partners within local accountancy firms and people well connected to these firms, eg partners within law firms. Your research will identify which local events they are likely to turn up to, plus who are the people from the firm you would benefit from an introduction to.

Tip

Use an RSS reader, like Google Reader, to take a feed from websites of organizations who host events you may want to attend. This way you will be automatically informed of good events for you to attend.

Once you know what event you are going to attend, the next stage is to prioritize whom you want to meet. Most event organizers will give you a delegate list in advance. See if the event is listed on LinkedIn or Facebook, and see who has listed themselves as going. If you are on Twitter, tweet that you are going and ask if anyone else is.

Tip

Don't forget to reconnect with existing members of your network at events. Strengthening your network is just as important as extending your network.

After you have a list of people attending the event, it is time to find out as much as you can about the attendees, and crucially what they look like. Your aim is to have a shortlist of about five to ten people whom you would really like to meet. Here's how you can find out more about someone:

- Search for them on LinkedIn.
- Look at their company website.
- Do a Google search on their name.
- Search for them on Facebook.
- See if any of your trusted connections on LinkedIn are connected to them, and could tell you more about them.
- See if they are on Twitter and what they tweet about.

Remember that your aim is to find five to ten target people, and something that you can ask them which gets them talking to you. It's a great way to make a first impression and quickly build rapport and credibility if you can demonstrate some shared knowledge or connection.

Spend some time thinking what you would like to achieve as a result of meeting these people. Is it a further meeting or an introduction to someone in their organization?

Before the event, have a quick scan through the news, business and sports sections of the BBC and industry-related press. This will give you conversation starters at the event and an opportunity to voice your opinion and demonstrate your professional credibility.

Summary

Effective business networking is the process by which you find, build and maintain mutually beneficial business relationships.

To make sure that your networking is effective, you need to identify how you want your network to help you achieve your big career and life goals, and then who you need in your network to make that happen. A network map will help you do this.

A-listers are the people who are most likely to help you achieve your professional and personal goals in the shortest amount of time possible. To make sure you keep the relationship strong and positive you need to write and implement a relationship plan for each A-lister.

FITTER™ stands for:

Follow up: Sort people into A, B and C-listers, add them into your database, and make contact with them.

Introduce yourself with impact: A good impression will start a mutually good relationship.

Target specific people: Your time is precious, so make sure you know who you want to meet and why you want to meet them.

Turn social conversations into business chat: Take your time to get to know the person first and then move the conversation on to business topics.

Engage: Focus 80 per cent of your energy on listening and finding out about them.

Research: Focus only on events worth attending and the people worth meeting.

Action points

- Identify a maximum of six big life, career or business goals which you would like to achieve. Now complete a network map for each of these goals.

- Using your networking maps or other ways of identifying who is important to you, identify 10 to 20 people, your A-listers, who are best placed to be able to help you achieve your big goals quickly.

- Write and implement relationship plans for your A-listers.

- Who is a rising star within the partnership within your current firm? How about approaching them and asking them to be your mentor?

- Organize a time to get back in contact with some of the people you went to university with, or trained with, whom you may be starting to lose contact with.

- Use LinkedIn to connect with people you trained with, worked with or had a good relationship with while at university.

- Consider connecting with your friends and colleagues at work on Facebook.

- Next time you go to a networking event, aim to connect with five people via e-mail or LinkedIn before the event.

- Google your name – what does your online footprint say about you?

- Review your own LinkedIn profile; how can you showcase your credibility better?

- Before your next networking event, read the news (paper or online) so that you know what's in the news, arts and sports to provide 'openers' for small talk.

Further resources

Books

Ferazzi, K and Raz, T (2005) *Never Eat Alone, Again: and other secrets for success one relationship at a time*, Doubleday Business, US

Fisher, D and Villas, S (2000) *Power Networking: 59 secrets for personal and professional success*, Bard press, US

Goleman, D (1999) *Working with Emotional Intelligence*, Bloomsbury, UK

RoAne, S (2007) *How to Work a Room: Your essential guide to savvy socialising*, Collins, US

Spillane, M (2000) *Branding Yourself: How to look, sound and behave your way to success*, Pan Books, UK

Townsend, H (2011) *The Financial Times Guide To Business Networking*, Financial Times Prentice Hall, UK

Tracy, B (2004) *Eat that Frog: Get more of the important things done today*, Mobius, UK

Websites and blogs

Joined Up Business Networking – http://www.joinedupnetworking.com

Free networking plans and templates – http://joinedupnetworking.com/free-stuff/free-networking-plans-worksheets-and-templates/

How to make partner – http://www.howtomakepartner.co.uk

Business Networking – http://www.business-networking.co.uk

Rob Brown – http://www.rob-brown.com/

The LinkedIn Blog – 'simple steps to a complete LinkedIn profile', published 14 February 2012, http://blog.linkedin.com

How your role will change as you move upwards

14

TOPICS COVERED IN THIS CHAPTER:

- The five stages of the career ladder
- How your role changes as you progress from trainee through to partner
- What skills are important at each stage

"In the big four accountancy firms you are actively managed up... or out."

HEENA PATTNI, STRESS MANAGEMENT COACH

In this chapter we explore how your role will change as you progress upwards from trainee through to partner. We describe in detail the 'grinding', 'minding' and 'finding' parts of your role as a client-facing professional adviser, and how much time you will spend on each part of the role as you gain experience and climb the rungs of your firm.

There are typically five key stages within your career:

- pre-qualification;
- qualified;
- manager or associate;
- director or senior associate;
- partner.

Depending on the size of your firm, you may have more career transition stages than this, or even less. However, while you may not have a title reflecting this structure, you will complete each of these stages to go from trainee through to partner. Typically, in a small practice, your formal transition from one career stage to another is not always clearly delineated.

What do we mean by the terms grinding, minding and finding?

Grinding: completing work on behalf of a client, while normally being supervised by others.

Minding: maintaining the client relationships, while supervising and managing others doing the client work.

Finding: finding and winning new business for the firm.

Table 14.1 shows how the focus of your role changes as you progress up through the career ladder.

TABLE 14.1   Changes in the focus of your role

Career stage	Grinding	Minding	Finding
Pre-qualification	High	Zero	Zero
Qualified	High	Low	Zero
Manager or associate	Medium	High	Low
Director or senior associate	Low	High	Medium
Partner	Low	Medium	High

Pre-qualification

Typical job title: trainee, junior, analyst, semi-senior.
Key focus of work: learning and applying your technical knowledge.

In this stage you are learning the ropes of 'how things are done around here' as well as beginning to acquire the technical foundation which will underpin everything that you do within your chosen professional field. You will likely spend significant time away from your day job attending in-house and external technical training to help you gain a professional qualification. During this period, you may also be seconded to work within a client's company to help you improve both your understanding of the client's business and the practical application of the professional advice provided to the client by your firm.

> Compliance work can be seen as tedious, but it's so much more rewarding when you get to the business end of it. For trainees, it's sometimes just about getting through the process but at the more senior level you get direct interaction with clients, which makes it more interesting.
>
> Myfanwy Neville, Audit Partner, Berg Kraprow Lewis LLP

Very often at this stage you will be doing jobs which may seem menial and boring. For example, many legal trainees will be able to recount stories of how they have spent all day photocopying files for a court hearing. While you may be given interesting work and assignments to complete, you are unlikely to be trusted with any significant level of direct contact with the firm's major clients due to your lack of experience. In a well-managed firm, risk management is also an important consideration; therefore, your firm will avoid giving you work which you are not qualified to do, yet. A wide range of people including your supervisor, assignment manager or partner will delegate work to you.

Qualified

Typical job title: assistant, solicitor, senior, consultant, management consultant, executive.

Key focus of work: gaining experience and consolidating your technical knowledge and skills.

Typically after two to three years most trainees will qualify. Already by this time several junior people will have been rooted out and left – either because they haven't passed their exams or they realized that their chosen profession was not for them. In this stage, you will start receiving more technically complex and challenging client assignments, projects and pieces of work. Although not always a certainty (dependent on the firm you are in), you will probably be trusted to have some direct dialogue with clients, although you may find that all your correspondence with clients will continue to be reviewed and signed by a partner before it is sent out. You may even be given a few assignments where you are expected to manage more junior members of the project team – for example, if you are part of an audit or surveyor team on site.

It is unusual to be expected to be actively involved in business development work. However, most firms will encourage and expect you to start building a network with your peers, inside and outside your profession (see Chapter 13) which will enable you to eventually win your own client work. Although you may not be given the opportunity to attend a pitch as part of the pitch team, you can expect to help by carrying out research, preparing presentation notes and information packs.

Manager or associate

Typical job title: associate, supervisor, manager, managing consultant.
Key focus of work: running and managing client assignments for partners.

Depending on your profession and the size of firm you have joined, at this career stage you would normally be given responsibility to actually run and manage client assignments on behalf of the partners. It is likely that you will be the day-to-day first point of contact for some of these clients. Your work and correspondence will continue to be checked or reviewed before going out to a client. While you are expected to maintain and deepen your level of technical expertise, your supervisor's and partners' expectations may begin to focus on more than just your ability to deliver to the client's expectations, eg how you get the work done, whether you are covering your costs and are making a profit for the firm. If you haven't already started to develop a personal technical or sector specialism, you would be expected to do so now.

Unless you have developed a very niche specialism for your firm's practice, you would normally be expected to manage or supervise more junior staff, either by having your own fixed team, or more usually on an assignment-by-assignment basis.

In most firms, as you are now the client's first point of contact for day-to-day matters, you will be expected to get involved in business development initiatives. While you are probably not expected to find and convert new clients, you will be encouraged to develop more work from your existing client portfolio. It is also likely that you will be routinely involved in preparing for pitches and tenders, and may also be a member of the pitch team.

Director or senior associate

Typical job title: senior associate, director, assistant director, associate partner, principal, senior executive, senior manager.

Key focus of work: winning your own work and taking on day-to-day management responsibilities for your part of the practice.

You are now considered to be a senior member of the firm and expected to stand in occasionally for the partners. To be promoted to this stage of your career, you need to be regularly winning work from existing clients and you will be finding that you are often being helped (or expected!) to start to win your own clients and build up your own portfolio.

Also included in this level are highly experienced technical specialists who may or may not have staff. Such people have strategic importance to the firm without necessarily heading for partner. People at this level of seniority are often authorized to sign off files and client work, on behalf of the partnership.

Depending on the size of your firm or practice area within your firm, you may be expected to participate in the day-to-day management of your department or practice area and so free up partners' time to concentrate on clients, business development and wider partnership responsibilities.

Partner

Typical job title: partner, full equity partner (FEP), fixed share or junior partner, principal.

Key focus of work: overall performance of your part of the practice and winning new client work.

You are now responsible for the performance of your part of the firm. The full equity partners within a department are responsible for the overall performance and financial performance of their practice department. As a partner, you are responsible for delivering your agreed personal financial targets. You will ultimately be measured and rewarded according to your practice department's financial performance and against the other key performance indicators which your firm deems are important to the profitability and long-term sustainability of the practice. Your key responsibilities as partner are:

- winning work from existing and new clients;
- leading and managing employees within the practice to achieve the firm's strategic objectives;
- agreeing and delivering the strategic goals for your practice department.

Partners are expected to be able to 'feed' themselves – ie generate all their own work and work for the people in their part of the practice. This may be from an inherited client portfolio or a portfolio personally built up over time. In short, it is the partner's responsibility to bring in the work, make sure it is done at the agreed price, billed and paid at a profit.

Summary

As your career progresses, the key focus of your work will change as you gain experience:

Pre-qualification: learning and applying your technical knowledge;

Qualified: gaining experience and consolidating your technical knowledge and skills;

Manager or associate: running and managing client assignments for partners;

Director or senior associate: winning your own work and taking on day-to-day management responsibilities for your part of the practice;

Partner: Overall performance of your part of the practice and winning new client work.

With the career stages from trainee through to partner comes a progression of increasing experience, maturity, responsibility and contribution to the business.

Action points

- Refer to your firm's competency framework, which should align with the roles described in this chapter. Identify what stage you are in now. With your immediate manager, find out which competencies you

already demonstrate. Record these on your career action plan.
(If your firm does not have a competency framework, you may find it helpful to look at role descriptions for your area of the business.)

- For competencies you have not achieved yet, add actions to your plan and discuss timing with your immediate manager and mentor.

- The action points at the end of Chapter 10 required you to find a reason to interact with other people in your firm. Find some who are further advanced in their career and set up a casual meeting to ask about their transition from the level you are on now to the next level. In particular, ask about what support they needed.

Further resources

Books

Charan, R, Drotter, S and Noel, J (2011) *The Leadership Pipeline: How to build the leadership powered company*, Jossey-Bass, US
Maister, D (2001) *True Professionalism*, Simon & Schuster, US

Websites

How to make partner – http://www.howtomakepartner.com

15 Keeping your eyes on the prize

TOPICS COVERED IN THIS CHAPTER:

- Being focused when you are too busy to think
- Keeping yourself constructively busy and motivated when work is light

> *Optimism is the faith that leads to achievement.*
> *Nothing can be done without hope or confidence.*
>
> **HELEN KELLER**

In the last chapter we looked at how your role will change as you move from trainee through to partner. However, many potential partners don't become partners because either they find the grunt of the early years demotivating and boring, or the long hours and stress involved in these roles become too much for them.

How to stay focused when you are too busy to think

Staying focused on your ultimate career goal of making partner gets pretty tough, when you are so busy that all you can think about is getting through the day (If this hasn't happened to you yet in your career as a professional adviser, then we can assure you that it will happen at some point!). However, if you are going to stay on partnership track, then you need to keep plugging away at advancing your career, regardless of how much client work is on your desk at the present time. Very understandably, when you are 'too' busy it can become all too easy to lose sight of your career goals. However, unless you have recently experienced a life-changing event, most people don't suddenly wake up in the morning and completely change how they work and what they do to remain focused on their end game.

To keep yourself mentally focused on your career progression, you need to build personal routines designed to help you achieve your long-term career objectives, which you then religiously follow daily, weekly and monthly. These are routines which you build up over time to help keep you personally effective as well as always working towards your personal objectives. It is essential that you learn to do this early in your career. We have seen numerous professionals fail to make partner because they have not maintained a good enough level of contact with their clients and work-referring contacts. These professionals make the mistake of not thinking about where the next piece of work will come from, or how to progress their career to the next stage, because they only concentrate on the work on their desks. We are not saying that this is easy but you must learn to do it and then keep doing it. We will now look at some of those routines, which the very successful professionals use to keep themselves focused.

Write down your daily and short-term objectives and make them visible

In Chapters 2 and 7 we talked about the importance of having long-term career goals. Cialdini, in his bestselling book *Influence: The psychology of persuasion*, identified that people were more likely to achieve their goals if they committed themselves to their goals by writing them down and telling others about them.

Looking back at your career action plan:

- What are your major milestones to reach your career goals?
- What small achievable objectives can help you achieve these career goals?
- Who will you tell about these objectives?
- Where will you write down these objectives so they are easily visible to you at home and at work?

> **Tip**
>
> Write out your objective in big letters, and in as few as words as possible, eg 15 minutes, client relationship strengthening calls, daily. Then put this objective in a place where you will see it, such as your computer or fridge.

Work with a mentor or coach

As one of our clients, Jonathan, found out, working regularly with a coach helps you to keep focused on your career goals. After working with Heather, Jonathan achieved his long-held ambition of making partner in a law firm nine months earlier than planned. He found the services of a coach were invaluable to helping him keep his career ambitions alive and visible, even when the workload was high.

Spending time with a mentor is a great way of keeping your career intentions known and visible. When you are getting bogged down by client work and can't see further than the next week, your mentor will be there to keep you connected to your long-term career goals. Working with a mentor was discussed more fully in Chapter 8.

Any time spent with a mentor or a coach is time in which you can reflect and review. These are two activities which very often don't happen when we are very busy with client work. Normally we are under pressure to start and finish the next piece of client work; we don't get time in our working day to spend time reviewing what's going well and reflecting on how we are doing and feeling. Slightly controversially, we would suggest that very often professional services firms don't encourage personal review and reflection time on the firm's time. Look down your firm's list of timesheet codes; how many of them are related to review and personal reflection time?

Keep it simple

Trying to do too much is one of the easiest ways to sap your energy and motivation. If just keeping up with client work is becoming too much, it will feel even harder if you are putting pressure on yourself to achieve multiple big career goals. So take the pressure off yourself and recognize that when the going gets tough you need to focus on achieving just one small career goal at a time. You may find that talking to your manager about your workload may help you understand your major work priorities, and what you *have* to get done by when.

How to keep yourself constructively busy and motivated when work is light

If you ask any professional what they want from their work, they will probably talk about these three things:

- interesting and mentally stretching work;
- interesting clients;
- regular career progression.

This means that when there is less work, or even no work around, it can become very demotivating. There are always times when work is light on the ground – that's the nature of any business which sells its time for money. In particular, the deal-led departments, such as corporate finance, will often oscillate between times of intense work and 'downtimes' between deals. In fact, many professionals, when there is less work available, stop delegating work downwards because they hate the thought of having nothing to do. Also, your partner may be poor at delegating work down because they are more concerned about meeting their own targets. This actually compounds the problem because the busier they are doing client work, the less time they have to spend on finding and bringing new client work into the department.

These slow times at first are a joy as it gives your body time to recover from what's gone before, and also allows you to get stuck into those lists of things that you have promised you would do when the workload dips, ie your 'will do' lists. However, if this downtime stretches on and on, it can start to be demotivating and concerning for everyone in the department – particularly if in your role you have little influence on the flow of work into the department.

Heather used to be involved in organizing a fast-track management programme for newly qualifieds. As part of this programme, Heather worked with the participants as they moved between assignments. She remembers that the participants always found it hard to start in the deal-led environments. They always had a period of 'bedding in' while they waited for a new piece of work to come into the department and to be assigned to that project team. Some participants found it easy to deal with this bedding-in time, while others really struggled.

What can you do to keep yourself positively busy when work is thin on the ground? One of the best ways to keep motivated is to do meaningful activities. For example, you can build up a 'will do' list of activities for you to do when work gets light. This means that when you are faced with a 'light' day, then you can refer to this list and meaningfully fill your time until the client work picks up again.

Ideally the items on this list should align with things in your career action plan.

Your 'will do' list will typically have four different kinds of meaningful activity:

- holiday;
- invest in relationships and your profile;
- invest in your (and others') professional development;
- marketing and business development activities, eg research.

Holiday

The most obvious thing you can do is to take holiday when times are quiet. While this doesn't necessarily keep you 'constructively' busy, what it does do is allow you to take some rest and relaxation at a time which can benefit both you and your department. Taking a holiday will also enable you to recharge your batteries and return to work more energized. However, for those people who have children, and have to plan their holiday time months in advance around school holidays and other people's timetables, it may not always be possible or practical to take holiday when the workload is light.

Invest in relationships and your profile

In Chapters 17 and 18 we will examine what you need to do to increase your personal profile, and what the key relationships are which you will need to nurture. You have already identified, in Chapter 13, the key relationships for your career and life goals. Utilizing your downtime or 'slow time' to invest in relationships and build your profile across the firm is a very valuable and useful use of your time.

Eight ways to invest in relationships and build your profile at the same time:

- Have you had a recent catch-up with your mentor and people whom you regularly work for?

- Which A or B-listers from your network have you not spoken to recently? How about picking up the phone and arranging to meet? These could be people from your firm, clients, other professional advisers or introducers/referral sources.

- Spend some time raising your visibility by walking around the office. A common complaint when you are busy is that people see less of you. This way, you also get to hear what has been happening around the firm while you were busy.

- Ask the partners and senior managers in your department if there is anything you can help them with.

- Volunteer to help out another department or team if their workload is high.

- Who is relatively new in your department? How about arranging to spend some time getting to know them better?

- Organize a lunch/after-work drinks for you and your peers.

- What networking events are taking place that you could usefully attend? (See Chapter 13.)

Invest in your (and others') professional development

Continuing professional development, or CPD, is something which every professional body requires its members to complete. Depending on the body to which you belong, how formally you are required to complete and declare it will vary. Very often, professionals tend to forget about this and at the end of the year there is a sudden desire from people in the firm to complete it for the year. In an ideal world your CPD would be a planned activity that takes place uniformly during the year, strongly linked to the department's business goals, your career action plan and long-term career aims. (See Chapter 7 for more details on this.)

Ideas to help you use your slow time to invest in your personal development

- What personal or professional development could you complete to help you advance your career action plan? For example, what book, blog or articles have you been wanting to read but so far have not had time to do?

- Who in your team can you invest some time helping them with their development?

- Refer back to your career action plan, and find a course or seminar which would advance your development.

- Can you get ahead on an assignment that you will need to submit some time in the future for a professional qualification you are studying for?

- Could you deliver a presentation or learning session for people in your department on subjects such as:
  - changing regulations;
  - lessons learnt from a recent pitch or client assignment;
  - business development skills;
  - a technical area in which you are particularly skilled.

Marketing and business development activities

When work is light on the ground and the pipeline is also looking a bit patchy, you may find that there is a directive from management that everyone is required to focus on marketing and business development activities. Whether or not you have a choice about where you focus your time when the workload is light, this is a great place to spend time which will help you develop skills for the future, as well as be noticed by the people who matter in your department, and maybe even generate some new client instructions.

In Chapters 17 and 18, we go into more detail about how to build up a client base and be seen as the 'go to' expert for your particular field. Regardless of your own particular comfort zone around marketing, there is always something you can be doing to help the practice's marketing and business development efforts. If you are unsure of what you can be doing, then ask the partner for your practice area what you can do to help. Most practices welcome anyone who volunteers to do the following:

- Research any company or person on the department's target list of prospects.
- Write an article, blog post or white paper.
- Help with the organizing of any department seminars.
- Attend a networking event.
- Maintain and deepen their relationships with current or potential referrers and introducers.
- Shadow a partner at a business development meeting or pitch.
- Follow up on conversations with people who have hinted that they may have some work for you in the future.

Most professionals' workload has a cyclical or seasonal nature. It becomes easier to accept the slow times when you realize that it is balanced out by busy periods, and that this is all part and parcel of a professional adviser's life. One of the ways which you can keep your own motivation high during slow times is ask the more experienced people in the department about this particular slow time. Are they worried? Or are they enjoying this period of relative calm before the phone rings again with new client instructions? What do they do in these times? If they are concerned, how can you contribute to any business development initiatives to win more work?

Summary

When work is light on the ground, consider these things to keep yourself positively busy:

- holiday;
- invest in relationships and your profile;
- invest in your professional development;
- marketing and business development activities, eg research.

Use a list of things you want to do when the workload is low, which is linked to your career action plan.

Building a core of daily, weekly and monthly personal routines into your work pattern will help you keep focused on your career progression even when you are too busy to think. A coach and mentor will provide you the space to review and reflect, while keeping you committed and accountable to your career and life goals.

Action points

- Refer back to your career action plan and pull out objectives which could be worked on during times when your workload is light.
- Start a 'will do' list for when your workload starts to get light.
- If not already involved in your practice's business development effort, then ask how you can help.
- Look at your diary and plan in some holiday or personal development time when you know that your department is traditionally quiet.

Further resources

Books

Cialdini, R B (2007) *Influence: The psychology of persuasion*, Collins Business Essentials, UK

Websites and blogs

Leo Babauta – Zen Habits Blog – www.zenhabits.net

How to keep your body working at peak performance

16

TOPICS COVERED IN THIS CHAPTER:

- The relationship between pressure and performance
- The importance of regularly feeding your soul
- The role adrenaline plays in keeping us at peak performance
- Signs of stress
- Dealing with stress

"You don't have a soul. You are a soul. You have a body."

C S LEWIS

In this chapter, we explore how you can keep your body working at peak performance so you stay healthy, both mentally and physically, to give yourself the optimum chance of making partner. The authors are indebted to Chris Williams of Momentum 4 for his help with this part of the book.

In the previous chapter we explored how you can remain motivated on your journey to partnership, even when the going gets tough. Sadly many talented professionals never make it to partnership, because their body and consequent health are unable to handle the lifestyle that the commitment to making partner so often demands. If you are going to maintain your peak performance so that you can make partner, and enjoy your life when you get there and beyond, then you need to be serious about your long-term health and wellbeing, now.

This short health questionnaire, which will only take a few minutes to complete, will help you to relate the contents of this chapter to your particular circumstances. Do write down your responses, and record the date so you can compare your answers over time.

The Health Audit

- How healthy are you now? (Rate yourself on a scale of 10–100.)
- If you continue with your present lifestyle, how healthy do you expect to be in 20 years time? (Rate yourself on a scale of 10–100.)
- What could make you healthier?
- What can you identify in your life currently that contributes to your health and sense of wellbeing?
- What could you do to get more of this?
- What is there in your life currently that detracts from your health and sense of wellbeing?
- What could you do to ensure that there was less of this negative influence in your life?
- Do you need an alarm clock to wake you up each morning?
- How good is the quality of your sleep?
- Do you suffer from constant time pressure, as if you are always behind?

Taken from *Manage Yourself, Manage Your Life*
(McDermott and ShirCore)

> Stress is still not something lawyers are comfortable talking about.
> Catrin Mills, author, *Effective Stress Management Techniques for Lawyers*

Don't worry, this is not going to be the section in the book where we tell you to eat your five fruit and vegetables a day or tell you to go to the gym at least three times a week. Let's be realistic. Many of us have gym memberships, which only a few of us use regularly. In addition, if you ask a clearly stressed professional whether they need to go on a stress management programme, most of them wouldn't volunteer – often because they either don't realize they are stressed, or owning up to stress is perceived to be a sign of weakness. This isn't a question of access to facilities; this is about you thinking differently about your health and wellbeing, and taking steps to put in place good practices now – or as Chris William calls it – 'alternative asset management'.

Signs of stress:

- constantly feeling angry or getting angry easily;
- feeling down or depressed, often without knowing why;
- always feeling anxious, nervous, or constantly worried;
- either feeling hungry all the time, or having no appetite at all;
- feeling constantly overwhelmed;
- crying, or feeling like crying, a lot of the time;
- feeling constantly tired, and having trouble sleeping;
- not being able to concentrate;
- having to use alcohol or recreational drugs to be able to relax or wind down at the end of the day;
- poor skin, eg eczema, acne;
- hormonal swings or imbalances, particularly for females;
- digestive discomfort, for example irritable bowel syndrome and heartburn.

If you find that you can personally relate to three or more of the signs on this list, then you need to seek professional advice and take action to reduce your stress levels.

Pressure vs performance

If you were to plot a person's stress levels versus their performance, you would see a graph similar to Diagram 16.1.

Everyone is different, and so the right amount of pressure for one person may be drastically different from another's. Over time, people create coping strategies and mechanisms to be able to increase the level of pressure that they can deal with, while still maintaining peak performance. It's when either you don't create these coping strategies and mechanisms or they become insufficient that your health really starts to suffer from effects of this unmanaged stress.

DIAGRAM 16.1   Pressure versus performance

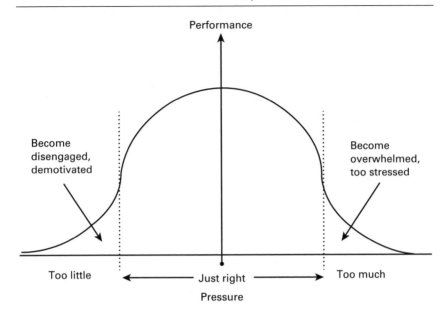

Most partners are normally working at the boundary of healthy and unhealthy stress.

Chris Williams

In the rest of this chapter we are going to look at what those coping strategies and mechanisms may be, as well as what happens to your body when you spend too long in the 'too much' part of the curve.

Feed your soul

Many partners and potential partners completely marginalize all other areas of their life so their entire success is now their business success.

Chris Williams

When people start their career in professional services, they can often become so immersed in their work (or the amount of chargeable hours they are required to complete) that they stop doing many of the things that they enjoyed, looking after their own health and wellbeing, and isolating themselves from their friends and family.

When times are tough at work, you need to be able to fall back on your life outside work, to sustain you and keep you going until you get back on your feet. Your support team (see Chapter 8) outside work are there to help, as long as you have spent time nurturing those relationships.

In our research for this book, the phrase 'sell your soul' popped up numerous times. There is a definite perception – and some might even say, belief – that within the professional services industry you have to sell your soul if you are ever going to make partner. We beg to disagree. Actually, in our view you need to 'feed your soul' if you are successfully going to make the transition and be happy and healthy as a partner. The choice is in your hands.

> I started singing in a barber shop choir, as I realized that I had no life outside work.
>
> Myfanwy Neville, partner, Berg Krapow Lewis LLP

So what is meant by feeding your soul? Chris Williams explained that we all have three boxes: career; relationships; and self.

For our long-term health and happiness, and ability to successfully absorb the slings and arrows of professional life, we all need to be regularly feeding these three boxes. Too often we only focus on the career box and neglect the others; we sell our soul. The relationships and self boxes are very important for coping strategies and mechanisms to deal with the stress and the daily bumps in the road. Releasing the pressure of a tough day could be by going to the gym, sinking into a long hot bath or phoning a friend. If the relationships and self boxes are continually neglected, this is when mental ill health may begin to take root.

Before you read the rest of this book, take a moment to stop and think and answer these questions:

- How full are your career, relationships and self boxes?
- Are you overinvesting in one box at the expense of the others?
- What could you do now to balance out your investment in your three boxes?

Use the Wheel of Life exercise in Chapter 2 to help you work on improving your balance in these three boxes. If you are going to achieve your career ambition and make it to partner *and still have a life*, you will need to plan and set goals for all three boxes. Obviously, your investment will change over time but unless you consciously balance your investment in all three boxes, it is likely that you will concentrate on your career box.

Alternative asset management

Let's think of your body as an asset which needs to be managed. If you treated your body in the same way in which you handle a client's affairs, you would spend time nurturing it to make sure it was running at peak performance.

Tip

A 30-minute brisk walk five times a week will reduce your chance of a heart attack by 55 per cent.

To see how easily you could be improving your overall health and general quality of life, take a few minutes to consider and write down your answer to the following question: What could I do to build up my health?

Your answers may be quite predictable, such as:

- Eat a more balanced diet and cut out snacks.
- Walk around the block for 20 minutes at least once a day.
- Start running.
- Take up yoga.

However, you don't need to make big changes to your lifestyle to make a positive difference. For example you could:

- Walk part of your journey to and from work rather than using the car, bus, train, tube, etc.
- Take an active part in fun things to do with your family, eg ride bikes around the park, play football, go swimming together.
- Have a 15-minute walk at lunchtime – which could be to buy your sandwich (rather than asking someone to get it for you!).
- Get the taxi to stop slightly before your destination so you walk the last 15 minutes of the journey.

The importance of physical activity

The human body was designed for physical activity – often walking 10 km in a day to forage for food and get water. How many professionals would now be able to walk 10 km every day?

Physical activity, as well as being a great stress-reduction tool, is vital for our mental wellbeing and stamina. Think of physical activity as time when you are investing in your self box. Earlier in the chapter, we saw how just 30 minutes of brisk activity five days a week could significantly reduce your chances of having a heart attack. Let's now look in more detail how just a small shift in our level of activity helps our all-round general wellbeing and consequently enables us to maintain more periods of peak performance, regardless of the amount of pressure we are under at the time.

> **Tip**
>
> Next time you are struggling with a complex problem, take a break and have a walk around the block. On your return you will probably find it easier to solve your problem.

When you exercise, your body starts to produce serotonin. Serotonin enhances your mind and helps you clarify your thinking. This is why it often gets easier to take a decision, work out what's going on or cope with an event if you go for a walk or run. However, serotonin has even more benefits to our health. It is the precursor to melatonin, which is the chemical our body produces to help reach deep sleep. When you sleep deeply you wake up in the morning fully refreshed and ready to tackle the day. In turn, you've more energy left to do more exercise and therefore produce more serotonin, which makes you a happier and more effective person because you can think more clearly … and so on, in a virtuous circle.

Dealing with stress

Our bodies come hard-wired with the *fight or flight* response which is only meant to be triggered once or twice a week, for example when hunting for food or being under attack from a predator.

> A great way to help you reduce your daily stress is to take 30 minutes out of the working day to recharge your batteries.
>
> Heena Pattni, stress management coach

In the *fight or flight* response, a series of complex hormonal changes occurs, which prepares our body to take emergency action. Adrenaline is produced – the equivalent of giving our body a shot of rocket fuel. The only way we can dissipate this rocket fuel is to either do some activity or proactively relax. Unreleased, adrenaline will accumulate in the body.

Over-adrenalizing

However, in the workplace many professionals may find that they have already triggered their *fight or flight* response three times *before lunch* – without having an opportunity to reduce the amount of adrenaline in their systems. The body becomes over-adrenalized and we become grumpy and sometimes even withdrawn. We get hard-wired for longer and become less able to experience deep sleep. At night, we cycle between two different types of sleep: *deep* sleep and *light* sleep. As the night goes on, we experience shorter cycles of deep sleep and longer cycles of light sleep. If we've become over-adrenalized, we still may sleep for the same amount of time, but with significantly less deep sleep. This is the reason why when we are stressed we wake more often during the night, and often feel as if we have had a bad night's sleep even if we've not been woken during the night. When we are in deep sleep this is the time when our body's cells repair themselves. Consequently if we become routinely over-adrenalized, we feel tired, run down and our immune system significantly reduces, making us susceptible to illness.

Sick holiday syndrome

> Many professionals almost accept they're going to be sick on holiday because so many of the people at their level of business do become sick on holiday.
>
> Chris Williams

The demands of our job mean we often have to run our bodies at peak performance for concerted periods of time, working 12+-hour days. The only way we can keep this up over time is to keep hitting the adrenaline button to obtain the energy that we need to get through the day. We can only keep doing this for so long before our bodies start to wave a white flag. Normally what happens is when we consciously downshift our mental gears, such as at the end of a long and complex transaction or when going away on holiday, we then fall ill. You see this happening all the time, where people have finally taken a 'much needed' holiday and then spend part of the holiday being ill with minor (and sometimes not so minor) bugs and ailments.

How to stop over-adrenalizing

There are only two ways of stopping you becoming over-adrenalized: adding in periods of exercise, such as a walk at lunchtime, or consciously taking steps to relax. If you have got into a vicious cycle of over-adrenalizing just to get the work done, the only way to break this cycle is to take a break from work, ie take some annual leave. You don't actually have to go away on holiday, just ensure that you are not working, and focus on spending time investing in the relationships and self boxes.

Summary

We all have three boxes – career, relationships and self. To maintain our peak performance, general wellbeing and mood, we need to balance our investment across all three boxes.

Your future career success depends on your ability to find coping strategies and mechanisms to deal with the pressures you may face at work. This means that you need to take steps to invest in your relationships and self boxes. If your life is unbalanced, it is also highly probable that it will be unhealthy. Ignoring your own needs can lead to resentment, cynicism and loss of job satisfaction.

The earlier you invest in activities that bring a balance to your life, the better the returns you are likely to achieve.

Action points

- Review your answers to the Health Audit. Now that you have read the above, what steps are you going to take to improve your health and sense of wellbeing?

- Look at your typical working week over the last six months: how often were you investing in your career, relationships and self boxes? What can you remove from your career box to allow extra investment in the self or relationship boxes to redress any imbalance? Discuss your findings with members of your support team.

- Consider your current workload and stress levels, and decide whether taking some annual leave might be sensible.

- Get into the habit of switching your e-mail off when you finish work for the day.

- Start spending some of your weekly non-work time on something you enjoy which helps you relax and unwind.

- Plan to take a minimum of a 15-minute brisk walk or activity every day. What opportunities do you have to do this activity with family and friends inside and outside work?

- Ask your children, if you have them, what they would like to do with you regularly at weekends.

- Get into the habit of having a regular 'date' night with your partner or friends.

- Find a form of exercise which you enjoy, such as swimming, yoga, Pilates or running, and participate in this activity at least once a week. Add this exercise into your career action plan and weekly planners.

- See if other colleagues will accompany you to an exercise class.

Further resources

Books

McDermott, I and Shircore, I (1999) *Manage Yourself, Manage your Life*, Piatkus (Publishers) Limited, UK

Mills, C (2010) *Effective Stress Management Techniques for Lawyers*, Ark Group, UK

Websites and blogs

Momentum 4 – http://www.momentum4.co.uk

Cognitus's distress at your desk blog – http://cognitusuk.com/blog/

Beyond Excellence's blog on stress management – http://www.beyond-excellence.co.uk

How to become the 'go to' expert for your firm and profession

17

TOPICS COVERED IN THIS CHAPTER:

- Why your personal profile is important
- How to choose your specialism and niche
- How to build your personal profile and become the 'go to' expert
- How to manage your relationships to keep your profile high

> *The only people who get on in this world are the people who get up and look around for the circumstances they want, and if they can't find them, they make them.*
>
> **GEORGE BERNARD SHAW**

In this chapter we look at the importance of your personal profile within your firm and the wider profession. Your profile is how visible and well known you are to the people inside and outside your firm. Although people see a partnership environment as very collegiate, and partners are 'in it together', each partner's success depends on their ability to build and develop their external, internal and online profiles. This chapter shows you how to build your profile so you become known as the firm's 'hot property' and also become the 'go to' expert in your field for your firm and profession as a whole.

What do we mean by profile?

One of the most common pieces of feedback that we hear given to professionals is: 'You need to build your profile.'

At this point, there is normally a lot of scratching of heads, and often this is when we are called in – first to help the professional understand what this piece of feedback means, and then what they can do to change this perception. When you have built a profile for being the 'go to' expert for your specialism, then you will find that you will more easily attract new clients to you.

It is possible to build a very visible personal profile within a firm, but for all the wrong reasons. Once you've gained a bad reputation as a poor performer or for a 'bad attitude', then it is often very difficult to shake this off, regardless of how well you develop from this point. Sadly, often the only way to ditch the bad reputation is to change firms.

What do we mean by your personal brand?

If you are going to gain a reputation for being the 'go to' expert, then you will need both a marketable personal brand and awareness of you, and your profile, within your firm. A personal brand is how others perceive your identity, whereas your profile is how visible you are to others. Go to Chapter 2 for more information on your core values, identity, vision and purpose.

Frequently, when we talk about someone not 'fitting' in a firm, it is because their personal brand does not fit with the firm's brand, culture and values. However, if you haven't invested in your personal profile it doesn't matter how marketable your personal brand is within the firm, because you must be seen as member of 'the club' (see Chapter 10). As the saying goes, 'You've got to be in it to win it.'

> Personal branding is about figuring out what makes you special and then communicating it to a specific audience.
>
> Dan Schawbel, Author, *Me 2.0*

There are four main ways that we position and package our identity, ie outwardly communicate our personal brand to people around us:

- What you do:
  - what service or product you provide;
  - the niche, sector or community within which you operate.

- How you do it:
  - what processes, systems, communication media you use;
  - where you choose to spend time physically and virtually.

- How you show yourself to the world:
  - how you conduct yourself in a social setting, eg your social airs and graces;
  - the possessions you surround yourself with, eg your car, phone, your laptop case;
  - how well you handle your emotions in professional situations, particularly when under stress, ie your emotional intelligence or maturity.

- How you let the world know about what you do:
  - what you say, how you say it and how you sound saying it;
  - how well you navigate the new standards in media, eg social networking, Twitter;
  - how much of your personal life and circumstances you choose to share.

Why invest in both your personal profile and your personal brand?

Before we go any further, it's worth stating that how marketable your personal brand is and how visible your profile is within a practice are inextricably linked. Typically when Heather coaches potential partners on how to build their client portfolio, she tends to focus them on building a marketable brand and their profile within the firm and marketplace. You need both for your career to progress within a firm. For example, your profile and being known by the right people can help you get access to the assignments which will help you build your specialism and your personal brand. However, your developing specialism can then help you increase your profile as you get known as the specialist in 'X'.

Quite simply, if people don't know you exist – ie you have a low personal profile – then you won't be first in the queue for any of the opportunities available to develop yourself, such as invitation-only leadership development programmes, secondments into industry, high-profile assignments, etc.

> ### Case study: Suzanne Dibble
>
> Suzanne's personal profile in her firm meant she was given the chance after qualification to do a secondment with Virgin. The prestigious industry award for her work at Virgin resulted in her being put on the fast track to partnership.

It's not just development opportunities that you miss out on by having a low profile; it's the chance to be seen by and work with the best partners for what you do and your preferred specialism – once again strengthening your personal brand. Partners, rather understandably, only want the best people in the firm working for them. Not only the partners, but also managers in a practice will compete with each other to get the best trainees, juniors and newly qualified staff working for them. Think how positive it will be for your career if the rising stars or senior members of the firm want you on their team. It's your personal profile and personal brand, resulting from working for influential partners, which will ultimately determine whether a particular partner decides to mentor and champion your career and progress within a firm.

What we mean by a specialism and a niche?

Normally, when people ask you what your specialism is, they want to know what your technical speciality is. For example, are you an environmental surveyor or a mineral and wastes surveyor? Your niche is a specific industry sector, social demographic or type of person that you decide to focus on working with. You might be the company commercial lawyer specializing in working with training and coaching companies, for instance.

In the early days of developing a reputation as the 'go to' expert, it is better to aim to be the expert for a clearly defined niche. The smaller your niche, the quicker and easier it is to develop a reputation as an expert for that niche. With the exponential growth in people's networks today, you need to have both a technical specialism and a niche within which your practice can really stand out in the marketplace and distinguish you from your peers.

Let's look at some examples of real-life niches, which we have heard professionals specialize in:

- General practitioner accountant for local owner/managed manufacturing businesses;
- Architect specializing in Yorkshire residential properties who want to do a loft conversion;
- Divorce lawyer specializing in London-based couples who want to use mediation rather than the courts to amicably settle their divorce.

Choosing the right specialism and niche to turbocharge your career

During the early stages of many professionals' career they resist specializing and try to become jacks-of-all-trades. The normal thinking behind this resistance is: first, they like the variety of work; and second, if they have a broad level of technical knowledge then they will be able to work on a larger range of assignments, and so be more valuable to the firm. While this is very true in the first four to five years of your professional career, there comes a point, as Ian Brodie, ex-management consultant found, when, if you are going to take your career to the next level, you have to specialize.

Sometimes you have the luxury of choosing your specialism and niche and sometimes it finds you. For example, if you work for a boutique firm of consultants, naturally your specialism will become the firm's specialism. However, consciously choosing your specialism is the second biggest strategic decision you will take for your career – after, of course, deciding who you will work for!

So, why does choosing a specialism and niche have such a major impact on your future career progression? Very simply, this will dictate how marketable you become to a firm. For example, the banking, property and financial sector market crashes in 2008 in the UK meant that vast swathes of professionals, who specialized in these sectors, were made redundant.

Your chosen specialism and niche will directly influence how easy it is for you to get accepted into the partnership. The partners are looking for people who will be able to increase the size of the pie, ie increase future firm profit. Anyone who is able to attract new business due to their specialism and niche will be someone whom the partners will be keen to invest in and promote when the time comes.

Price Bailey

Price Bailey is a 23-partner accountancy practice. It is likely that any new partners for the firm will come from areas seen as strategically important to the future health of the firm. These are areas in which they either have strong growth, and need more partner-level capability, or are sectors, service lines or locations that would benefit from more business development effort at a partner level. These are likely to include newly created or expanded service lines such as corporate finance or insolvency and recovery.

Another very important reason for picking your specialism carefully is that in most cases it defines you for the rest of your career. This is especially true in the legal profession where it is almost unheard of to change your specialism after qualification. The last thing you want to do is get stuck in a field or with a certain type of client which you struggle to be passionate and enthusiastic about. Your ability to work at peak performance, win work from clients and be picked for jobs is heavily influenced by your passion and enthusiasm for what you do. There is no point in selecting a specialism which bores you rigid just because in ten years' time it may help you make partner within your firm. You are better off choosing a specialism which you love, and if necessary changing firms at a later date to facilitate your progression to partner.

> True work–life balance only comes when you are totally passionate about your work.
>
> Rakesh Shaunak, Managing Partner,
> MacIntyre Hudson LLP

Exercise: Finding your niche

In order to determine your niche, think about the answers to these questions:

- What type of work do you love doing?
- How are you known to others?
- Where are you considered to be an expert?
- Which types of clients do you love working with?

- If you were to look at your current client base, what trends or common themes are there?
- What sort of clients does your firm tend to attract?
- Which sectors anticipate a growth in demand for your technical services?
- For what types of work do you find clients who arrive at your doorstep 'pre-sold'?
- What types of clients or assignments do you find that the partners readily put you forward to do?

The answers to these questions will provide you with signifcant clues to finding and selecting the right niche and specialism for you to adopt and develop.

When you develop your chosen specialization and niche, you normally start to attract more rather than less work. While this probably seems counter-intuitive, it works for the following reasons. Clients want to work with experts – ie people who are considered to be a very capable and competent safe pairs of hands who *will* be able to solve their problems. Specialists are, therefore, easier to 'market' and 'sell' to clients, even with the higher charge-out rates they command. As you become more senior your charge-out rate will increase, which if you have a specialism makes it easier to justify your rates to clients.

How to build your personal profile and become the 'go to' expert in your field

Broadly speaking your strategy here has two main parts:

- How to build your niche.
- How to get noticed by the right people.

How to build your niche within your specialism

Generating a reputation as a specialist for your niche is down to a mixture of passion, enthusiasm, focus and a little bit of luck. Let's look at the four steps in the process, once you have found your niche, to develop it and examine all the tools that are available using social media to help us at each stage.

Steps to help you develop your niche:

- Decide on what niche area you want and tell people that you are going to do this. Tools to help you do this:
  - information readily available via the internet, eg blogs, articles, white papers, industry trends;
  - firm knowledge and management information;
  - trade press and newspapers;
  - advice and expertise from mentor, partner and counselling manager/partner.

- Undertake a course of study in your specialist area – this could be self-study or a formal qualification. Tools to help you do this:
  - formal qualifications, online study courses, distance learning courses;
  - information readily available via the internet, eg blogs, articles, white papers, industry trends;
  - firm knowledge and management information;
  - trade press and newspapers;
  - client knowledge;
  - advice and expertise from mentor, partner and counselling manager/partner.

- Write about things that are valuable to your niche, and which showcase your expertise and credibility. Tools to help you do this:
  - writing for a blog, contributing or writing the firm's newsletter for your specialist area;
  - writing articles and white papers which are published in the trade press (online and print) but also on your firm's website;
  - recording podcasts and video clips of you talking about your specialism which are put on YouTube, iTunes, SlideShare and other websites where you can share audio and visual clips;
  - tweeting and sharing your and others' content about your specialist subject;
  - sharing your specialist knowledge via your LinkedIn profile page, internet forums, social networking sites generally;
  - publish a book or e-book.

- Participate at events where you speak about your specialism to your niche. Tools available to help you do this:
  - delivering presentations at internal and external events, such as seminars and conferences;
  - delivering webinars and teleseminars to existing and potential clients;
  - running online virtual text-based chats via facilities such as Skype, social networking sites, Twitter;
  - run internal and external training courses for your specialist area.

If you do these four steps well, and this is where that little bit of luck comes in, then in time you will find clients coming forward asking to use your specialist skills on their behalf. After you have passed this major milestone, it gets much easier. Your first clients then become your case studies and marketing 'war stories', and provide you with testimonials. These emblems of credibility, ie testimonials, case studies, references, will enable you to appear more credible to future clients, who in turn, because you now have an established track record in being able to solve their particular problem, will want to engage you.

How to get noticed by the right people, for the right reasons!

In Chapter 5 we discussed how to get tagged as partnership potential. If you succeed in becoming known as partnership potential, this means you have solved the problem of how to get noticed by the right people for the right reasons. The same attributes and skills to becoming known as partnership potential are therefore applicable if you want to raise your profile; ie

- being commercially minded;
- exhibiting maturity;
- being likeable and having enthusiasm;
- staying fit;
- being open to opportunities and taking responsibility;
- having a reputation for being trustworthy and reliable;
- demonstrating initiative and going the extra mile;
- being career-driven;
- displaying commitment to the firm's vision.

These factors, combined with a strategically important specialism and niche, all help you create a highly marketable personal brand. However, to keep your profile high with these people will still require you to actively manage your relationships both with people inside and outside your firm.

Relationship management

As 80+ per cent of the new work you win will come from people you have existing relationships with – clients, people in your firm, or introducers – so how you build and maintain these relationships is key.

The five-level relationship level model

When Heather was researching for *The Financial Times Guide To Business Networking*, she discovered that the strength of a relationship can be categorized into one of five levels. How useful or helpful your relationship is to you will depend on the level which the relationship is currently at.

DIAGRAM 17.1   Five-level relationship level model

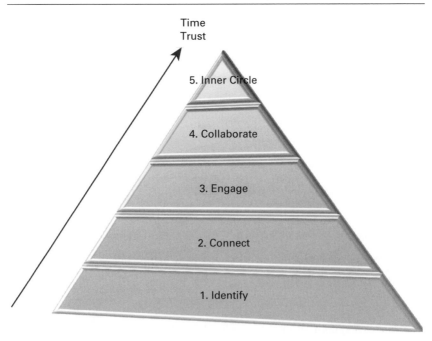

Level 1: Identify – on your radar:

- You become aware of someone.
- No communication, either online or in real life, has yet taken place.
- Low trust.

Level 2: Connect – polite conversation:

- One-way or two-way communication is taking place, either online or in real life.
- Both sides are thinking, *Do I like this person?* and *Can I see a benefit to continuing the conversation with this person?*
- Low trust.

Level 3: Engage – one-to-one conversation:

- Both of you commit to having a one-to-one conversation in real life to deepen the trust in your relationship.
- Increasing trust.
- Minimum level you need your relationship to get to, before you will both actively help each other.

Level 4: Collaborate – professional friends:

- Regular communication is taking place, via phone, e-mail, social media, face-to-face meetings.
- High trust.
- Often helping each other out.
- Your mentor needs to be at this level (or higher) for your relationship to be effective.

Level 5: Inner circle – personal friends:

- Your relationship is both a personal and professional relationship.
- High trust.
- You will regularly communicate on matters relating to work, home, mutual hobbies/interests and family life.
- The friends, both inside and outside work, who are on your support team need to be at this relationship level.

Often many junior professionals subscribe to the view that they want to keep work and their life outside work completely separate. As your career progresses, this will become less and less possible – regardless of whether you decide to remain in the profession or not. Over time your personal and professional worlds will start to merge – and considering we all spend two-thirds of our waking hours at work, we should expect this.

If you think about how long it has taken to grow and maintain your relationship with your close friends, you will quickly realize it is not always possible to take everyone to a Level 5 relationship. For a start there may be no chemistry between you, or not enough hours in a day to maintain a Level 5 relationship with everyone you know. The skill in relationship management is knowing which relationships to invest in, and how to do this in a time-effective manner.

How to identify your key relationships

Your key relationships are those we previously identified in Chapter 13 as your A-listers. These are the people who, if you positively nurture the relationship, are most likely to help you achieve your career and life goals.

Your key relationships will be split into people within your firm and people outside your firm.

Internal firm relationships

Every firm is different, so there is no one right answer which fits all. However, the people who are most likely to be able to achieve your goal of making partner are these:

- Managing partner and anyone involved in the partnership selection process.
- Your departmental lead, who is most likely the partner who 'puts you up' or sponsors you for selection to the partnership.
- Your firm's HR and learning and development team.
- Influential people within your department or practice area.
- Your mentor and manager.
- The person in your department who allocates people to client assignments.
- Partners and senior managers in other departments within your firm who are able to refer work to you and your team.

Exercise: Running your own internal PR campaign

Take a sheet of paper and brainstorm all your key internal relationships. Now rate each relationship on a scale of 1–10 for your profile or visibility with each person, where 10 = they are my greatest fan and 1 = they don't even know about me. Now rate each relationship for how much they know about your career ambitions, on a scale of 1–10, where 10 = they know my career ambitions and are actively helping me to achieve these, and 1 = they don't know my career ambitions at all.

Now plot the relationships on a grid like the one in Diagram 17.2.

DIAGRAM 17.2   Profile versus career ambition grid

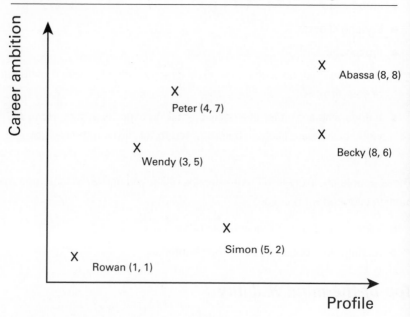

Looking at your grid:

- Which relationships need the most work?

- What are their personal agendas?

- What do you think they think about you – how can you verify this?

- What messages do they need to start hearing about you?

- Who can help to broadcast the right messages about you?

- What three things can you do *now* to start this internal PR campaign?

- What do you want to add to your career action plan?

External firm relationships

Your external network is also important. It will help you to:

- win work;
- find a new job if required;
- get information about your marketplace;
- find friendship and support, eg your 'support team'.

These people are most likely to be able to help you build up your own client portfolio:

- introducers;
- existing clients;
- prospects;
- people you trained with and worked directly with who have moved out of your firm;
- friends who are either in a decision-making capacity at their place of work, or who are likely to be promoted to this level in the next couple of years.

These people are likely to be extremely helpful if you decide to look for a role outside your current practice:

- partners and senior managers in other firms;
- recruitment consultants and headhunters.

Top-of-the-mind visibility

To keep your personal profile high with the people that matter to you, part of your effort needs to be focused on keeping your name at the top of their mind.

In *The Financial Times Guide To Business Networking*, Heather defined top-of-the-mind visibility as:

> When someone within your network sees or hears of an opportunity, you are the first person they think of.

To help you achieve top-of-the-mind visibility with the people who matter for you, you could:

- regularly be present at firm formal and informal social events;
- accompany partners to networking events, such as conferences;
- attend your industry-related events;
- post on the firm's intranet regularly;
- ask questions during partners' presentations, workshops and road shows;
- tweet on behalf of your practice area or firm;
- blog on behalf of your practice area or firm;
- connect to your partners, clients and prospects on LinkedIn and Twitter;
- update your status daily on social networking sites, particularly LinkedIn;
- contribute to or organize the firm's regular newsletter for your part of the firm;
- send regular articles of interest to people within your network;
- volunteer to be on cross-firm project teams or committees, or industry focus groups.

Exercise: Relationship plans

In Chapter 13, we talked about the importance of relationship plans that you are actively implementing. For each of the key relationships you have identified to help you achieve your career and life goals, build a relationship plan which will help you achieve your goals.

Now look at your career action plan; as a result of writing these relationship plans, do you need to add or change any of your milestones or objectives?

Summary

Developing a strategically important specialism to your firm is a great way of becoming the 'go to' expert in your firm, and be seen as partnership potential. Even when you have developed your profile and strong personal brand, you still need to make sure you have top-of-the-mind visibility with the people who matter to you. Key to achieving the right level of profile with your network is to actively manage the relationships within your network.

Social media has provided today's professional with many more tools to help them be noticed by the right people, eg blogging, Twitter, webinars (ie virtual seminars).

Action points

- Talk to the partner responsible for business development in your part of the practice, and ask how you can become more involved in business development initiatives.
- Volunteer to take an active part in cross-firm project teams.
- Ask the partners in your firm what industries, sectors or specialist skills are likely to be in demand by clients and the marketplace generally over the next five years.
- Reflect on what work you really enjoy and for what type of clients – this is likely to become your specialism.
- Read the trade newspapers and magazines to increase your industry knowledge of one or two sectors which you would like to specialize in.
- Ask your counselling/line manager/partner for their thoughts on what you are really good at. Also find out what you are becoming known for around the firm. Document in your career action plan any actions you want to take to correct any unhelpful preconceptions about you.
- Look at the firm's current partnership. Ask yourself the following questions:
  - Which practice areas are partner heavy (especially junior partner heavy)?
  - Which practice areas are doing well, but are partner light?
- Add into your career action plan any of the milestones or objectives you have identified from your relationship plans.

Further resources

Books

Brogan, C and Smith, J (2010) *Trust Agents: Using the web to build influence, improve reputation, and earn trust*, John Wiley and Sons, US

Brown, R (2007) *How to Build Your Reputation: The secrets of becoming the go to professional in a crowded marketplace*, Ecademy press, Penryn, Cornwall

Overhaus, J (2009) *Juggling the Big 3 for Lawyers: A career-building plan to develop your personal brand, client business, and leadership mindset*, ProvechZiel Ltd, UK

Schawbel, D (2012) *Me 2.0: 4 steps to building your future*, Kaplan Trade, US

Townsend, H (2011) *The Financial Times Guide To Business Networking: How to use the power of your online and offline network to generate career and business success*, Financial Times Prentice Hall, UK

Websites and blogs

Dan Schawbel's personal branding blog – http://www.personalbrandingblog.com/
Rob Brown's blog – http://www.rob-brown.com/blog.html
Twitter – http://www.twitter.com
LinkedIn – http://www.LinkedIn.com
Wordpress – http://www.wordpress.org
Ian Brodie – http://www.ianbrodie.com

Building your own client portfolio

"You must sell yourself to sell your firm."

FORD HARDING, AUTHOR, *RAINMAKING*

The number-one reason why people don't make it to partnership, regardless of the size of the firm or their specialism, is their lack of a significant client portfolio or, as it's known in the trade, 'a following'. As an associate or senior manager you are expected to be able to develop more business from existing clients. However, these pieces of work are generally credited to the partner who 'owns' the client rather than you personally. Therefore, in order for you to develop your own client portfolio, you must be prepared to go out into the marketplace and win your own clients. Some people are lucky and inherit their client portfolio from a retiring partner – however, this is now the exception rather than the rule.

This chapter will help you build your own client following, thereby making you eminently more employable and promotable – regardless of what size of firm you are working for or where you want to take your career.

> When times are tough, a firm will hang on to those who bring in business longer than those who provide technical support.
>
> Ford Harding

The business development process

Business development, or 'BD' as it is often known within the professions, encompasses the three disciplines of marketing, sales and account management. It covers everything that you do to help you win either more work from existing clients or work from new clients.

> Eighty per cent or more of all new business for a professional services firm will come from one of three sources: new instructions from existing clients; recommendations from existing clients to their network; business being passed to them, or 'referred' to them by introducers.

Marketing: Everything that you do to get yourself known within your target market and demonstrate your credibility in your chosen specialism, so that they ask you if you can help them. This could include:

- writing articles, blogs, white papers, case studies, books, reports;
- presenting at conferences, seminars and webinars;
- generating testimonials from clients;
- face-to-face networking events;
- being active on social networking sites, especially LinkedIn;
- undertaking research.

Later on in this chapter, we will take you through the eight areas you need to consider to help you identify your own personal marketing plan to help you build a client portfolio.

> ### Tip
>
> It is very common to meet a prospect, ie someone who may be interested in instructing you, before they are ready to buy. Have 'keeping in touch' processes and systems in place that allow you to stay close to them until they are ready to buy.

Sales: Everything you do to turn a lead, ie someone who has come forward and expressed an interest in using your services, into a client. Before a sale can take place, the buyer needs to progress through a sales process. See later in this chapter for more details on the sales process.

> ### The buying criteria
>
> Regardless of what any book on sales will tell you, there are only three fundamental reasons why someone will not want to buy from you. These are:
> - They don't believe you are capable of doing the job.
> - They don't like or trust you.
> - They don't believe that they are getting value for their money, possibly because they have no need for your services.

Account management: Everything that you do to delight your existing clients and stay in touch with them so they want to buy more services from you or your firm. Very often a new client will test out your capability by initially instructing you on a small matter. If you do a good job, then as time goes on you will be asked to act for them again on bigger and more complex assignments.

The role of introducers

Most services offered by professionals are complex, expensive and very often one-off 'distressed purchases'. A distressed purchase is something that a person needs to buy because of their circumstances, which if they had a choice they would not buy. Distressed purchases include services such as litigation, divorce, insolvency, tax investigations, etc. Typically these services are difficult to market directly to a potential buyer. For example, you can't just pick up the phone and ask a company if they are in financial difficulty and need some financial or legal help! Consequently most professionals find that a significant portion of their work comes to them from introducers. These may be formal 'panels' within banks and public sector organizations, strategic partners or informal relationships.

Panels

Many banks and public sector organizations will set up 'panels' of suppliers for typical pieces of work that they require. These 'panels' are the equivalent of a preferred supplier list, eg an NHS trust will have a 'panel' of heavily vetted law firms to whom they pass all their medical neglience work.

How to build your own personal marketing plan to build your client portfolio

There are eight areas you need to consider for your own personal marketing plan. Remember to make sure that your plan is aligned with your department and firm's business development strategy. How much detail and thinking you will need to do personally for your marketing plan, will depend on the level of sophistication and maturity of your firm's business development processes and support.

1 *Decide on your niche*
   In the previous chapter we talked about the need to adopt a specialism and niche. When you are clear about your niche you are able to pinpoint your marketing messages more effectively – thus increasing your client attraction and conversion rate.

2 *Understand your prospect's 'pain'*
   Unless a potential client is suffering some form of emotional pain, they will not buy from you. Emotional pain could be as simple as *Unless I sort this problem out I will have the board members asking me difficult questions* or serious as *If I don't sort this problem out, then the business will fail.*

3 *Decide on your services and how you will deliver them*
   When you understand your potential client's pain, you can then devise services to help them solve their problems.

Case study: Joseph Fraiser

Joseph Fraiser specialize in working with deaf and hard-of-hearing clients. Such people find it very difficult to work with solicitors as most solicitors require a face-to-face conversation or phone-based communication. So Joseph Fraiser have tailored their services to this market by:

- training all their staff in sign language;

- providing the option for their clients to talk to their solicitors by Skype message rather than having to use the phone;

- specializing in industrial deafness personal injury claims.

4   *Differentiate yourself – 'Why you?'*

If we asked you today why we should buy your services rather than one of your peers or someone from another firm, could you answer this question succinctly? At this stage we are not talking about you having a 'USP' (unique selling proposition), just some clear statements why your potential clients will benefit from working with *you*.

Very often it is not the services you offer, but *how* you deliver those services that will help you to differentiate yourself. After all, for most professionals it is very hard to differentiate themselves based on the services they offer. For example, one accountant doing your tax return offers a very similar service to another accountant doing a tax return. Like Joseph Fraiser who actively promote in their marketing messages how they are equipped to work with hard-of-hearing clients, you need to be able to articulate 'why you' in your marketing messages.

5   *Decide how you will get your messages in front of your target client*

There are many different ways you can get your message in front of your potential clients. These include telemarketing, social media marketing, direct mail marketing, search marketing, content marketing, seminar speaking, print advertising, PR, etc. Frequently, choices you have on which marketing methods you will use will be dictated by your firm and its overall marketing strategy. However, you need to decide which methods you will use and how much you will utilize these methods. For example, if you decide to build your portfolio by referral, which relationships and networking events/groups will you invest time in to generate new client leads?

Marketing is the process of 'buying' leads. Every hour that you spend on your own marketing is an hour that you could be doing chargeable work. Therefore, you need to spend your time on marketing methods that will yield the greatest return for your time investment. The only way to find this out is to measure and monitor where each lead comes from, the quality of the lead and how much time you need to invest to gain the lead. Your firm's CRM (client relationship management) system may record this for you automatically. If you don't have this at your disposal, then a simple spreadsheet will do the job for you.

6 *Do a great job for your existing clients*
Your existing clients are normally the best source of referrals for you. After all, if they like you and how you work, and the results you achieve, then they are more likely to buy again from you and recommend your services to others. What account management systems or processes have you got in place to make sure you deliver a great job every time for every client? These could include formal or informal:

- project management or case management systems and procedures;
- ways of gaining client feedback both during and after the job has finished;
- end-of-project reviews.

Once again, the size and sophistication of your own practice will determine how many of these things are provided as 'standard', and how many you will have to build into your own ways of working.

7 *Cross sell*
Many of your firm's clients originally hired the firm for one particular service. However, this automatically qualified them as potential clients for other services that the firm might offer. For example, clients needing the services of a divorce lawyer will almost definitely need some advice on their will. Where could potential clients for you already exist within your firm? How could you cross sell other services to your current client base?

8 *Keep in touch with your prospects and existing clients*
Most potential clients, at the point you meet them, don't yet have a burning need for your services. What systems and processes do you have in place to keep both existing and potential clients in touch with your fee earners until they *are* ready to use or recommend your services?

Your marketing activity plan, or what you will actually do to market yourself

Now that you have thought about how you will generate leads, the time has come to decide on *what* you will actually do. Your level of marketing activity needs to be sustainable regardless of the amount of client work on your desk. For most professionals there is a delay between marketing activity happening and client leads being generated. This can lead to professionals oscillating between manic busy periods and very quiet periods. For this reason you need to commit time every week to making sure your personal marketing plan is delivering results.

Exercise: Write your own personal marketing plan

To help you write your own personal marketing plan, there are free downloadable marketing plan templates on the How to make partner website, **http://www.howtomakepartner.com**.

Allocate three hours, and write your own personal marketing plan to help you build a client portfolio. Then make sure you have updated your career action plan so that you have incorporated goals, milestones and objectives from your marketing plan.

The sales process

We are often conditioned to think that we will make a sale the first time we meet a potential client. For most professionals this is an unrealistic expectation and very unhelpful. Any potential buyer of professional services needs to go through a series of defined steps before they are ready to sign on the dotted line. This is what we mean by the 'sales process'. Sometimes the buyer can go through all the steps in one meeting; however, normally each step takes a certain level of activity and amount of time, depending on the service you are selling. Unsurprisingly, the bigger the price tag for your services, the longer the sales process tends to be. A typical sales process for professional services will look something like this Diagram 18.1.

DIAGRAM 18.1 The sales process

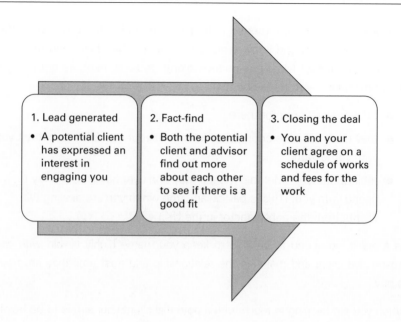

1. Lead generated
- A potential client has expressed an interest in engaging you

2. Fact-find
- Both the potential client and advisor find out more about each other to see if there is a good fit

3. Closing the deal
- You and your client agree on a schedule of works and fees for the work

Your aim within the sales process is to progress the potential client to the next stage of the sales process. For example, a potential client has asked for a meeting to talk about some help they need. This means they are at step 1 in the sales process. Your aim is to complete the fact-find, step 2, and see whether there is scope for the two of you to work together. Before you enter into a detailed and time-consuming fact-find you want to qualify early in step 2 whether this is the sort of client you want to work with. This is often called pre-qualifying your lead. As business development is a non-chargeable activity, your aim is to only focus your time and attention on potential clients who you want to work with, and who will be profitable.

Relationships and the trust which goes with good relationships are among the most significant factors in the time it takes a potential client to buy and whether they choose to go with your or another firm. In fact, one of our clients, a top-ten accountancy practice, found that they had a three times better conversion rate for competitive tenders when they had an existing relationship with the potential client. Strong relationships within your network, as well as your networking activities, can help every stage of the sales process. See Chapter 17 for more information on relationship management.

The importance of keeping in touch

In an ideal world you will meet a potential client and at the point when they will be ready to buy and know exactly the service that they need from you. Now back to reality! Most prospective clients you will meet are not ready to buy from you just yet. It may be that:

- the time isn't right for them;
- they don't yet have enough confidence in your capability to entrust you with some work;
- their budgetary timetable means they don't yet have the money to spend with you. (This is particularly true when you are dealing with clients from the public sector in the UK.)

As a result, you need to be able to keep your name highly visible with your prospective client and maintain the relationship and trust until they are ready to buy.

When you are keeping in touch with a potential client your aim is to be helpful but non-intrusive. For example you could:

- regularly send them articles which they will find interesting;
- interact with them on social networking sites such as LinkedIn and Twitter;
- invite them to join you at events such as conferences or seminars;
- arrange regular catch-up conversations or meetings;
- send them (with their permission) the firm's regular newsletter.

Many professionals leave the keeping in touch to chance, partly because this isn't a chargeable activity! However, if you are going to successfully build your own portfolio, then you will improve your ability to win work considerably by having processes and systems to enable you to maintain a good level of contact with potential clients.

> **Tip**
>
> Always ask your potential clients for permission to stay in touch with them.

Summary

The business development process normally involves three key stages: lead generation, fact-find and closing the deal. Depending on the service that you offer, you may find that it is impossible to market to your client directly and you need to use introducers to win new clients.

In order to progress towards partner, you need to build your own client portfolio.

Action points

- Build your own personal marketing plan and incorporate this into your career action plan.

- Draw your own network map of people (see Chapter 13 for an example of a network map) who can help build your own client portfolio. Where are the gaps in your map? How can you fill these gaps?

- Find a mentor who can help you and guide you to build your own client portfolio.

- If your firm runs any internal courses on marketing and selling yourself, book yourself on those courses.

- Talk to a partner in your part of the practice and find out how they grew their client portfolio, and where they get their main sources of referrals.

- Observe a partner in action during some sales meetings. What did they do well to progress the sale and increase the prospect's motivation to buy?

- Spend time with people from other departments in your firm to identify the likelihood of cross sales from your department to their department and vice versa.

Further resources

Books

Cooper, I (2012) *The Financial Times Guide To Business Development*, Financial Times Prentice Hall, UK

Harding, F (2008) *Rainmaking: Attract new clients no matter what your field*, Adams Media Corporation, US

Tovey, D (2012) *Principled Selling: How to win more business without selling your soul*, Kogan Page, London

Townsend, H (2011) *The Financial Times Guide To Business Networking*, Financial Times Prentice Hall, UK

Websites and blogs

Principled Selling – http://www.principledselling.org/
Free templates to help you build a marketing plan –
    http://www.howtomakepartner.com
Ian Brodie's blog – http://www.ianbrodie.com
Joined Up Networking – http://www.joinedupnetworking.com

Managing and leading your way to success

19

TOPICS COVERED IN THIS CHAPTER:

- What we mean by 'managing' and 'leading'
- How to build and develop a team
- What motivates people
- How to run a performance review and set objectives
- How to coach
- How to set quality controls to mitigate any risks

> *Management is doing things right; leadership is doing the right things.*

PETER DRUCKER

In the last chapter we looked at how you can build your own client portfolio. Many of the mid-tier practices will expect their partners to develop a client portfolio worth in excess of over £1 million of fees annually. Understandably you can't find and service all that work by yourself. So you need to place as much focus on managing and leading your team as you do on building your client portfolio. Without a team of committed and skilled people who want to work with and for you, your ability to build a client portfolio as well as have success as a partner will be limited. This means your ability to lead and manage a team will be vital to you both making partner and succeeding as a partner. This chapter shows you the essential management and leadership skills you will need if you are going to successfully make partner.

What are 'management' and 'leadership'?

> Leading is not about dictating specific behaviour. It is not about issuing orders and commanding compliance. Leading is about getting others to see a situation as it really is and to understand what responses need to be taken so that they will act in ways that will move the organization toward where it needs to be.
>
> Noel M Tichey

The nature of professional services is that the people have their specialisms and mostly belong in a 'group' of similar specialists, working within a partner's department. In addition, when a client engages the firm, the firm pulls together a 'team' of different specialists to that project, and the team has a senior person appointed as the assignment leader. The partner role attracts with it the additional responsibilities of leading their part of the practice.

Until you have made partner, you will have a career manager and you will also have an assignment leader, for the client matters which you are currently working on. And they have two different roles for you. The career manager is concerned with helping you with your career action plan and general development. Your assignment leader is focused on getting the whole team delivering the work to the client. This chapter describes the roles and responsibilities you will have when acting as a career manager and assignment leader for others in your firm. Both roles are about 'getting people to do stuff', and you have to be effective as a manager and as a leader. When we talk about your team in this chapter we are referring to both the client team you will lead on an assignment and the direct reports who you act for as a career manager.

Typically, a manager's job is to plan, organize and coordinate, while the leader's role is to decide on direction, motivate and inspire. You will need to be able to do both if you are going to make partner.

When you are acting in a senior capacity within a professional services firm, there are normally four different elements to balance:

- the needs of the *client*;
- the needs of the *team*;

- the needs of the *task*;
- the needs of the *individual*.

Very often these needs are in conflict. For example, the nature of a busy deal-led department, such as corporate finance, means that there is often too much client work to let individuals take time out of the workplace to focus on their own development. The temptation sometimes is to let the short-term needs of one element overshadow the others. Over time if one or more of the four elements are neglected, a backlash may result. For example, if the needs of individuals are ignored over the long term (such as regularly cancelling their annual leave or planned training), this can result in high sickness and absence levels and high staff turnover.

How to build and develop a team

> All of us perform better and more willingly when we know *why* we're doing what we have been told or asked to do.
>
> Zig Ziglar

Part of your progression towards partnership will be to take on more responsibility as an assignment leader, in addition to being a career manager for more junior people in your department. This means that you will need to build and develop teams and individuals who will be able to service the work, you and others bring into the firm. The teams you lead will vary in size, longevity, location, composition, performance and effectiveness. The quality of the team you build is just as important as the quality of your client portfolio. A motivated and capable team around you will free up your time to focus your energies on making partner, ie taking on strategic-level responsibilities in your firm, as well as building and maintaining a profitable and loyal client portfolio. Typically a team, as opposed to a group of people, will share a mutual purpose, eg service all the firm's residential surveying clients, similar performance goals and hold themselves mutually accountable.

You will often hear the phrase 'high-performing team' bandied about. A high-performing team is one where:

- The whole team is focused on achieving the team goals.
- The team achieves superior results.
- There is a high level of respect and mutual trust within the team for the skills, knowledge and expertise that each team member brings along.

- The team is excellent at overcoming any obstacles to achieve their team goals.
- The team has shared values, standards and beliefs.
- There are clearly defined roles and responsibilities for each of the team members.
- Open and clear communication is present between the team members, regardless of their location in the world.
- Effective decisions are taken at the right time by the right people.
- There is a collaborative and positive atmosphere between the team members.
- Conflicts are surfaced and resolved quickly and effectively.

Your role as a team leader is to build your own high-performing team. Typically, as a team leader you will be performing, at any one time, three roles within the team:

- Direction finder: You will be working with your team to identify, clarify and build commitment to achieving the team's ultimate destination; eg bill £1 million in the next 12 months. Part of your role is to help the team identify the right journey for them as a team to achieve the ultimate destination.
- Facilitator: You will be helping your team to work together effectively and knit together as a high-performing team.
- Coach: Similar to any sports team coach, you will be working with the team as a whole and on an individual level to make sure that people have the right skills and behaviours for the job they are required to do.

Your team does not become high-performing overnight; it takes time, focus and energy to get it to this level. The Tuckman model of team development explains that as the team develops maturity and ability, and relationships establish, the leader must change and adopt different styles of leadership. In the model, there are five distinct stages of team development:

- Forming
- Storming
- Norming
- Performing
- Adjourning

Forming

At this stage, the team is very new and freshly formed. Every time someone joins or leaves a team, the team reverts to this stage again. The team members look to the team leader for guidance and direction, plus clarification on each team member's roles and responsibilities. As a team leader, be prepared to be very 'present' with the team to communicate its purpose, objectives and facilitate any external relationships.

Storming

The team is becoming clear on its purpose and how to get there. However, there is still plenty of uncertainty, and decision making may be slow within the group. Inevitably there will be some conflict as people within the team jockey for positions. Sometimes you may find that there may be power struggles and challenges to the team leader's authority. A team may never get through the storming phase where unresolved conflict is left to fester. It is the team leader's role to focus the team on its goals and resolve relationship and emotional issues.

Norming

Only if conflict is resolved from the storming stage does the team move on into norming. The team now is fully committed to its mutual purpose and goals. The dust has settled, meaning that roles and responsibilities within the team are now clear and accepted. Collaboration across the team is established. Unlike the storming stage, big decisions are taken as a whole team, whereas the smaller decisions are delegated to the appropriate people within the team. You may find that the team is starting to socialize outside the working environment. At this stage the team is working together to develop its working processes and team dynamic.

Performing

When the team starts to display the characteristics of a high-performing team it moves into performing. The team leader role is still generally required as the team will still need ongoing coaching, delegation and guidance from the team leader. However, generally, the team is self-supporting, ie the team no longer needs much instruction or assistance as it is pretty much self-sufficient.

Adjourning

This is where the team breaks up as it has fulfilled its purpose. If the team has been particularly strongly bonded, the ex-team members may experience a sense of loss during this stage. As a team leader it is your role to celebrate the success of the team and facilitate team members' journeys on to new projects and roles.

What motivates people

To get your direct reports, ie the people whom you act for as a career manager, and client teams to perform to the best of their abilities you will need to know how to motivate them, ie find out what makes them 'tick'. Different things motivate different people and these may change as we grow older and our lives change.

Typically you will find that three simple things motivate most professionals in a firm:

- career progression;
- interesting and challenging work;
- feeling valued for who they are and what they bring to the firm.

To help your direct reports progress their career:

- Provide on- and off-the-job training.
- Coach them on the job, helping them gain new skills.
- Set meaningful targets for their career progression.
- Provide timely and regular feedback on their performance.

Being able to provide interesting and challenging work is not always easy within a professional services firm. Many lawyers can tell stories of the number days that they had to spend photocopying as a trainee. However, when you regularly act as an assignment leader you have greater control over who gets what work.

For example:

- Do you know what kind of work each of your team members, for all the teams you are part of, likes and wants to do more of?

- Are you aware of the skills gaps in your team and have a career action plan in place for your whole team to be able to fill these gaps?
- What on your desk can you delegate to your team?
- Have you identified and agreed stretching objectives in place for all your team members?

Making people feel valued is an interesting one because not everyone feels valued in the same way. Further, you may not yet be in a position in your firm to influence some of the tangible rewards, such as a pay rise, in recognition of the value your people bring to the firm. Here are some simple ways in which you can help people in your teams feel valued:

- taking an interest in what they do both inside and outside work;
- giving regular praise (when it is due);
- showing individuals why their work and efforts matter;
- spending time with them during the working day to help them achieve their goals and objectives;
- creating an atmosphere of mutual cooperation;
- truly listening to your team members' ideas and concerns – not just brushing them under the table.

How to develop your people

As an assignment leader and career manager, you have a responsibility to develop your people. See Chapter 6 for more on all the different ways that people can learn, develop new skills and behaviours. In order to get the maximum effectiveness from a training intervention for a member of your team your responsibilities include those shown in Table 19.1.

Development needs analysis

Before you can decide what the appropriate training intervention is for your direct report or team member, you need to fully understand the extent of the training requirement, by completing a development needs analysis (DNA). A development needs analysis is a process that helps you identify the gap between an individual's performance and the desired performance for that role and individual, and how you will close that gap. For example, is this

TABLE 19.1   Responsibilities for developing your team members

Before	During	After
Agree how this time spent on training will help them in their role	Give them the time away from the workplace to complete the training	Spend time with them to help understand what they learnt while doing the training
Agree what specific behaviours, knowledge, skills or attitudes you want them to acquire while doing the training	Support them to try out new behaviours	Find out what long-term support they need to embed their new knowledge, behaviour or skills
Agree when and how to measure progress		Give them work which will help them to hone and perfect their new skills
		Give them feedback on how well they are doing on applying their new skills and behaviours
		Coach them to overcome any hurdles to applying their new skills or behaviours
		Measure progress

a piece of mandatory technical training which their institute requires them to do at a certain point in their career? Or is this a deep-seated behaviour issue which is affecting their performance?

A DNA needs to be completed when you have someone who is:

- new to a role;
- wanting to develop into a new role;
- underperforming in part of their role;
- keen to be promoted to the next level;
- returning to a role after a long time away, eg after a sabbatical or maternity leave;

- experiencing a significant change in their department's strategy, processes or systems;
- part of a team or department which as a whole is underperforming.

Steps to complete a DNA:

1 Collect data to identify the desired future state and compare with the current performance levels, using:
   - informal or formal feedback on the individual;
   - your own personal observations;
   - any grievance or disciplinary issues;
   - any tasks or behaviours that the individual is highlighting as a problem for them;
   - if your firm has it, a competency framework;
   - role description;
   - team or department business and action plans;
   - KPI reports for the individual, team or department.

2 Investigate the gap between the current state and the desired future state.

3 Agree with the individual a career action plan with defined actions from the two of you to enable the performance gap to be closed.

4 Agree with the individual how and when to measure progress.

Tip

To speed up the time it takes your direct report or team member to acquire a new skill or behaviour, choose development options that appeal to their preferred learning style.

How much time should you spend on developing and managing your people?

The simple answer is as much time as they need to enable them to achieve their goals and what you require of them. However, their level of competence and commitment to the task at hand will define how much time you need to spend with them. Your role as their career manager or assignment leader is to assess each direct report or team member's level of competence and commitment to the tasks you are allocating them. Broadly speaking, if either of these is low you will need to spend significantly more time with them to:

- clearly define what they need to achieve;
- discuss with them how they will go about the task;
- agree milestones and points where they will come back to you to check on progress;
- monitor their progress;
- be available for any questions or queries they may have.

How to run a performance review and set goals

What is a performance review?

It is good practice to sit down with all the people you act for as career manager, ie your direct reports, at least twice a year to talk about their performance. Very often your firm will have a set way of doing performance reviews, with requirements to do them at certain points during the year. Sometimes the performance review is called an 'appraisal'. See Table 19.2.

Between performance review times, plan to spend time each month with your direct reports to see how they are doing, and talk about their progress on their goals, milestones, objectives, plans and specific client assignments.

TABLE 19.2 A performance review

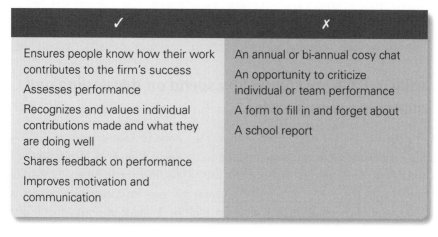

✓	✗
Ensures people know how their work contributes to the firm's success	An annual or bi-annual cosy chat
Assesses performance	An opportunity to criticize individual or team performance
Recognizes and values individual contributions made and what they are doing well	A form to fill in and forget about
	A school report
Shares feedback on performance	
Improves motivation and communication	

TABLE 19.3   Responsibilities throughout a performance review

Before	During	After
Agree date, time and private place to hold the review Allocate sufficient time for the review Compile feedback on the individual	Give praise and share feedback on performance Discuss and agree goals and objectives Discuss how they are finding things in general Take notes Provide advice and support, coach if necessary Communicate how well the firm and department are performing Boost individual's motivation if required	Write up the notes from the performance review Follow up on actions agreed Book in monthly 1:2:1s to monitor progress against objectives

How to run a performance review

To make sure that the performance review is a positive and meaningful experience for both you and your direct report, Table 19.3 shows your responsibilities before, during and after the performance review.

Your firm may already have a predefined structure for how to run a performance review. If they don't, you may find this simple four-part structure useful to structure the review:

1 *Look back*
   In this part of the review you look back at the last six months (or 12 months, if you only do performance reviews annually), and discuss:
   - performance against their goals and objectives, plus reasons for achieving or not achieving these goals or completing their objectives;
   - highlights for the individual;
   - lowlights for the individual.

2 *Look forward*
   In this part of the review you need to look forward to the next six to 12 months and agree on:

- what the individual needs to deliver, ie goals and objectives, to help the department and firm achieve their goals;

- help and support the individual will require to achieve these goals and objectives.

3 *Development planning*

This is the part of the review where you switch your focus onto the individual's short-term and long-term career goals.

- What's the next step for their career? How can you and your firm support this?

- What's the long-term vision for their career? How can you and your firm support this?

- What skills, knowledge, behaviours or attitudes do they need to acquire or change to achieve their short- and long-term career goals?

- What can you do to help them achieve these career goals? For example, what type of client work can you pass to them to help them acquire these new skills and behaviours?

In this part of the review you will help your direct report to further refine their career action plan to enable to them to achieve their career goals. Use the development needs analysis process, as detailed earlier in this chapter, to allow you to create the plan.

4 *Next steps*

As we stated earlier in the chapter, a performance review is not a cosy chat. It needs to lead to action. Therefore, you need to agree action plans and next steps for both you and the individual to complete to make good on all your intentions.

Setting goals and objectives

Your role as leader of a team is to work jointly with each of your team members to set goals and objectives. These objectives when combined across the team will enable the team to hit its goals and each team member to progress their career at their desired rate. Your team's goals will need to cascade from your department's goals, which will flow from the firm's business goals for the year. See Diagram 19.1; and see Chapter 7 for more detail on setting meaningful and motivational goals, milestones and objectives.

DIAGRAM 19.1 How your team members' goals and objectives relate to the firm's strategy and headline performance goals

Firm's strategy and headline performance goals

Your practice area's strategy and goals to achieve its share of the firm's goals

Your personal goals to achieve the practice area's goals

Your team members' goals to help you achieve your goals

How to give feedback as part of the performance review

You may have noticed that as part of the review, you are required to give feedback to the individual. We strongly recommend that you give the feedback using the SBO model as outlined in Chapter 12. If you have been regularly sitting down with your direct report during the year and discussing their performance, any feedback shared as part of the performance review should not be a surprise.

The feedback that you provide during a performance review needs to be a rounded and balanced assessment of their performance. In many firms you find that you are required to run performance reviews with direct reports whom you don't regularly work with. In any case, it is always good practice to seek feedback on them from others. For example, you could ask for feedback from:

- partners or managers whose clients they have worked with;
- team members who have worked with them on jobs;
- clients whose work they have been involved with.

Depending on what your firm provides, you may find these invaluable sources of information to find feedback on the individual:

- job appraisal forms;
- notes from end-of-job completion meetings;
- feedback and notes from any assessment or development centres the individual has attended;
- recent letters or reports written by the individual.

How to coach

In your role as assignment leader and career manager you will need to be able to coach your team, its members, and also your clients and potentially your peers.

Typically a coaching conversation is one where the coach helps their coachee to find their own way to develop a skill set, achieve a goal or overcome a problem. To do this means that the coach normally focuses on their coachee's agenda and helps them come to a conclusion or course of action by asking them a series of questions. There are many excellent coaching models available to help you with a coaching conversation; however, we have selected the GROW model because it can be used by anyone without special training and successfully applied to most situations.

The GROW model

The coach asks their coachee a series of questions to progress through the GROW model:

- Goal: This is the end point, where the person wants to get to.
  - What do you want to achieve? And by when?
  - Where do you want your career to be in 12 months?
  - What do you want to achieve by taking on this project?

- Reality: This is where the person is currently.
  - What's happening right now?
  - Where do you feel your career is now?
  - What skills do you have now to help you get to your goal?
  - What skills are you missing to help you progress to partner?
  - What's stopping you from starting this difficult conversation with a client?

- Options: These are things that the person could do to achieve their goal.
  - What could you do to take the first step to progress your career to the next level?
  - How could you start the conversation with your client about fees?
  - What would you feel comfortable in doing?
  - If your mentor were advising you, what would they tell you to do?
  - What do you think I would suggest you do?

- Way forward: What will you commit to do to achieve your goal?
  - What are you going to do as a result of this conversation?
  - What first step will you do to achieve your goal?
  - Write down the steps you will take to achieve your goal
  - What feels like the easy next step for you to take?

Coaching tips

- Find a place to have the coaching conversation free from interruptions and distractions.
- Focus on what the other person is saying.
- Listen out for what they are saying and what they are *not* saying.
- Don't be tempted to give them your solutions.
- Spend your energy listening to them, not thinking about what's the right next question to ask.
- Be comfortable with silences in the conversation; they give the coachee time to think and process.
- Don't feel as if you both have to resolve the problem or find a way to achieve a goal in the one conversation. Very often the power of coaching comes in having the conversation rather than achieving anything in the conversation.

Quality controls

The demise of Arthur Andersen

Arthur Andersen was once one of the global Big Five accounting firms. In 2002 it had approximately 85,000 employees globally and generated annual revenue of over US$9.3 billion. On 15 June 2002 Andersen was convicted of obstruction of justice for shredding documents related to its audit of Enron, resulting in the Enron scandal. As a result of the conviction, the firm surrendered its right to practise in the USA – effectively putting the US arm of the firm out of business. The damage to the Andersen brand and reputation destroyed trust in the firm's international practices. Across the globe the firm disappeared overnight and most of its practices were taken over by the other major international accounting firms.

As an assignment leader it is your role to make sure that the firm's quality controls are applied. A professional services firm's reputation is vital to its future health and viability. See the Arthur Andersen case study for a real-life worst-case scenario of what can happen to a firm without appropriate quality controls.

Quality controls could be:

- defining who is responsible for what in a firm;
- deciding on what circumstances a partner will need to be involved before a report, e-mail or proposal is published or sent to a client;
- agreeing on limits of expenditure, eg expenses, for each member of the firm;
- designing policies and processes which need to be followed to minimize risk to the firm, eg recruitment processes which involve checking potential employees' references.

Summary

Your route to partner is intrinsically linked to your ability to successfully lead and manage your assignment team and develop the people whom you act for as a career manager. Building a successful team around you will free you from client work and enable you to focus on growing both your client portfolio and your part of the business.

In your role as a manager of people and leader of a team, you are responsible for making sure the client's work is completed to the right quality standard and within budget, while building a team and individuals within the team who are able and willing to achieve your goals for the team. To do this means you will need to allocate regular time with each team member to:

- review their work;
- review their progress against their objectives;
- help develop them to acquire new skills and progress their career.

Action points

- Have a private conversation with each of your direct reports to find out what they like about their role and where they would like to progress their career.

- Ask three people you trust and work with regularly for some feedback on your abilities as a assignment leader and career manager. What can you do, and add to your career action plan, to act on their feedback to improve your abilities as a leader and manager?

- Diarize regular conversations with your direct reports to find out how they are doing and progress they are making on their personal objectives and current client assignments.

- Book some time in with your mentor and ask them how they learnt to manage people and lead teams.

- Ask a member of your firm, such as a member of the HR team, to sit in on a performance review that you run, to give you feedback and suggestions of what you could have done differently to be more effective.

- Identify a current performance or skill gap that you or one of your direct reports has. Write a development plan to close that gap, ideally without going on a classroom-based training course.

- Think about the teams you are either a member of or lead. What stage of team development are they at? What three small actions could you do to increase the performance of each team?

- Work with a coach to help improve your people management and leadership skills.
- Volunteer to mentor or coach a more junior member of your firm.

Further resources

Books

Blanchard, K, Zigarmi, P and Zigarmi, D (2000) *Leadership and the One Minute Manager*, Harper, US

Selden, B (2010) *What to Do When You Become the Boss: How new managers become successful managers*, Business Plus, US

Whitmore, Sir J (2009) *Coaching for Performance: GROWing human potential and purpose – the principles and practices of coaching and leadership*, Nicholas Brealey Publishing, UK

Websites and blogs

How to make partner website for details of Executive Coaches – http://www.howtomakepartner.com

Overcoming the final hurdles to making partner

20

TOPICS COVERED IN THIS CHAPTER:

- Undertaking your own due diligence
- The partner admission process
- What happens on a partner assessment centre
- The partner admission interview
- Creating your personal business development plan
- Checking that promotion to partner at your firm is right for you

In this chapter, we look at what you should be asking your firm and what might happen to you as you overcome the final hurdles in the long process of making partner. These hurdles are like your driving test – if you have done your study and practise along the way, you will find the test far easier to pass. This chapter describes the final steps in the admission process to make partner.

Undertaking your own due diligence

It is important to find out as early as possible what the expectations are. What does your firm really want or expect? Only when you know this fully can you make an informed decision about whether partnership is right for you.

Amber Moore, Amber Moore Consulting

Most people are flattered to be asked to put themselves forward for partnership, and often forget that the partner admission process needs to be a two-way process. Remember *you* are auditioning *the firm* for its suitability *for you*, just as much as it is assessing you for your partnership capability.

Once you begin the partner admission process, you must ensure that you are in a position to ask appropriate questions about the business, its financial performance and strategic goals. Becoming a partner is not just a promotion but also an invitation to run and own a share of the business. Most firms require their new partners to invest capital within the firm, at the point they are admitted into the partnership. This capital could be anything from tens of thousands of pounds to hundreds of thousands of pounds, depending on the size of the firm. You owe it to yourself to take this financial investment seriously.

> I am constantly surprised at how little interest potential partners show
> in the financial indicators of their firm other than their profit shares.
>
> Robert Chambers, consultant
> and Interim Finance Director

Based on our years of experience developing, coaching and preparing potential partners for admission to partnership, here are the essential things that we believe you should know or ask:

- Your firm's current and future financial health. *Look for:*
  - How the business is funded and how your capital will be used.
  - Any trends in the financial performance of the firm over the last three years.
  - Profit forecasts for the firm and by partner over the next three to five years – do these seem realistic? Find some benchmark data to compare your firm with others.
  - Are the current levels of partners' drawings sustainable?
- Your firm's business development strategy. *Ask:*
  - Does the firm have a clear strategy and business plan for client and business development?
  - How will you be involved in delivering this business development strategy?
  - What support does your firm's marketing and business development team offer to new partners?

- The quality of your firm's leadership and management. *Find out:*
  - What is the strategic plan for the firm and why is the firm's leadership following its particular strategy? Can you support this strategy?
  - What are the firm's core values and culture? Are they something that you can role model both internally and externally?
  - Does the firm have a clear idea of how current and future changes in their marketplace will impact it and a strong vision as to how to deal with this?
  - Is there a culture of robust leadership in the firm with well-defined strategy as to how the firm will develop in the future, with the management having the authority to implement the actions necessary to achieve this?
  - To what extent will you, as a partner, be able to participate in/affect decisions concerning the future of the firm?
- Risk management. *Find out:*
  - What are the key risk issues facing the firm?
  - What is the firm's professional indemnity (PI) record? Are there any major outstanding PI issues/claims?
- Partner role and responsibilities. *Ask:*
  - Do I fully understand the responsibilities of becoming a partner and proprietor of the business as opposed to being an employee?
  - To read a copy of your firm's partnership agreement.
  - What are the financial and tax implications of switching from salaried to self-employed status?
  - How will expectations of my personal performance change when I become a partner?
  - How and when am I expected to make my capital contribution – will the firm arrange a bank loan or do I have to raise the cash and when is it payable?
  - How much coaching and development support will the firm offer to help make a successful transition to partner?
  - To what extent do the current partners look happy and healthy?
  - What extra responsibilities will I be asked to take on when I become a partner?

- Does partnership at this firm fit with my career and life goals?
  Ask yourself:
  - Am I excited about the prospect of becoming a partner in this firm?
  - Do I feel like 'one of the club' and have I been actively encouraged to take the final step to partner?
  - What will I (or the people around me) potentially have to sacrifice if I make partner?
  - How passionate am I about being able to influence the strategy of the firm?
  - What will I need to make happen if I make partner at this firm if I am going to still achieve my career and life goals?

To give yourself as complete a picture as possible, you should make time to talk to the following people in your firm, and seek their views and opinions:

- the finance director (or equivalent);
- the HR director (or equivalent);
- the business development director (or equivalent);
- your head of department, mentor and other partners and peers in your firm;
- decision makers from the firm's key clients;
- the firm's marketing department;
- your personal support team, particularly your family members.

What are you being offered?

Very often when people are asked if they want to join the partnership, it isn't made clear what they are being offered. Are you being offered the chance to be 'full equity' or a 'fixed share equity' partner? Or are you being given the title of partner but remaining on a salary with the expectation that if you prove yourself you will become an equity partner in two to three years' time?

The terms 'full equity' and 'fixed share equity' refer to how partners are remunerated, and typically their seniority and voting rights within the practice. New partners will normally join the firm as a junior fixed share equity partner and progress to senior fixed share equity partner over a number of years, after which they are expected to become full equity partners.

Newly promoted partners are typically admitted at the lowest point of a profit-sharing scale. The scale is usually based on a percentage or a number of points. Over a period of time, the percentage is increased according to the next step on the scale, which is agreed and approved by the full equity partners. A fixed share equity partner will receive a monthly 'drawing' from the firm based on the percentage of points they have accumulated, and the firm's anticipated financial performance.

At the end of the financial year if the firm has performed strongly, the equity partners share the profit based on the individual percentage of points they hold. In a number of large firms, up to 25 per cent of the profit is held back and paid as a bonus to a full equity partner based on their performance during that year or, in some firms, based on their performance over the last three years.

Full equity partners have typically demonstrated their ability to build a sustainable and profitable client portfolio. Unsurprisingly, full equity partners are almost always the most senior and influential partners within a practice, and have full voting rights.

The partner admission process

Many professionals make the mistake of thinking that making partner will only take a concerted effort during their last couple of years on the partnership track. However, making partner is a political process, and people in firms have long memories! You need to garner the support of the partners not only in your department but also throughout the firm. Finally, don't overlook your relationships with clients, juniors and business support staff. Their views may also be taken into consideration, since client service, supervising and managing others, and management skills are important attributes of partners. Therefore, you need to be positioning yourself as a potential partner – and act accordingly – from your early days in a firm.

> **Tip**
>
> Participating in firm committees and attending all firm social activities are some of the ways to get to know those partners that you don't work with on a regular basis.

The process may be more informal, that is, less documented in some small and medium-size firms. However, the business rationale for admission to partnership is essentially the same. Once you understand this, it's your job to decide what experience you need in order to fill the gaps in your capability, to establish yourself in an area of expertise and acquire the skills required to become a partner.

What firms look for in their partner admission process

Most selection processes have been designed to assess a candidate's suitability for the role as partner, and future potential as a partner. Typically, the selection process is looking for the key must-have qualities for a partner. These will vary from firm to firm. However, most, if not all, managing partners will tell you that for a firm to be successful the role of partner must include the following attributes:

- Business development:
  - Can you demonstrate your ability to win work for yourself and others in the firm?
  - Is your client portfolio now of the size, or your reputation in the marketplace such that the partnership would be worried if you left the firm?

- Client service and relationship management skills:
  - Have you a track record of solving client problems and working effectively with client teams?
  - Do you have a strong understanding of your clients' businesses, sectors and markets in which they operate?
  - Have you a strong network of contacts, and clients that routinely refer work to you?

- Financial management:
  - Have you and your team consistently hit your financial targets, including billing, cash collection, WIP and lock-up for the last three to five years?
  - Are you and your team known for complying with the firm's financial systems and procedures?

- People management and development:
  - Can you detail your ability to develop and build a team both within your department and across the firm, depending on the client requirements?
  - Have you got examples where you have motivated others to generate great performance?
  - Have you a good reputation for your people management skills?
- Partnership participation and contribution:
  - How have you successfully promoted the firm to the outside world?
  - Is your day-to-day behaviour role modelling the firm's core values and culture?
  - Do people within the partnership see you as a good 'fit'?
  - Have you got verifiable examples when you have gone 'the extra mile' for the firm?
- Future potential:
  - Where have you already shown your potential to grow and develop the firm?
  - What are your proven abilities to run your part of the practice?

Exercise: How ready am I for partnership?

Look back at the attributes needed by most successful partners. Ask yourself:

- What am I already doing that meet these criteria?
- What examples could I already use to show my firm that I am operating at this standard?
- Where are my gaps in experience or verifiable examples?
- What could I add to my career action plan to plug these gaps?

The typical process

Most mid-size and large firms publish their partner admission process, usually six months before admission to partnership. These firms may also have a partner selection committee who, with support from the HR director, are responsible for managing the selection process for the firm. In small firms creating new partners sometimes takes place every two or three years depending on the requirements of the partnership and availability of suitable candidates.

Usually, the selection process is as follows:

- Determine the size of the firm's partner pool. The firm's management board will decide, based on business cases submitted by heads of departments, how many new partners are strategically and financially viable.

- Identification of suitable candidates for promotion to partner. Partners will 'sponsor' people within their department who they believe are ready to be admitted into the partnership. In the majority of mid-size and large firms, potential partners will know at least one to three years ahead when they will be eligible for partnership consideration.

- Partnership nomination packs are prepared with input from the head of department, sponsoring partner and the candidate. At this stage in some firms, potential partner candidates may be required to attend an assessment centre (see below), following which a report will be prepared for consideration by the partner selection committee.

Contents of a partnership nomination pack for a candidate will normally include:

- their personal business development plan (see below);
- a self-assessment;
- report on their financial performance;
- their performance and development reviews for the last three years;
- psychometric assessment reports;
- any reports from assessment and development centres, in particular if they have attended a partner assessment centre;
- the head of department and sponsoring partner's business and financial case reports;
- feedback from clients and internal feedback;
- the management board recommendations for the candidate.

- The partner selection committee will then interview the candidate, their head of department, and sometimes their sponsoring partner. Depending on the firm, the number of candidate interviews can be as many as six. In some firms, there is a technical competency interview that is conducted by a partner who specializes in the relevant area.

- The partner selection committee will then discuss the merits of each candidate, and submit their recommendations for approval by the management board. In most firms, the equity partners will then vote to approve each new partner.

The partner assessment centre

The partner assessment centre is normally only one part of the partner admission process. The purpose of the centre is to help your firm gain insight into your broader leadership skills that are important in making the business a success. Apart from familiarizing yourself with your firm's competency framework, you do not need to prepare anything in advance of the centre.

What happens on a partner assessment centre?

An assessment centre is an intensive and personally draining experience, which will normally take between one and three days to complete. Over the course of the centre, you will be involved in a number of exercises based around real-life situations, and some interviews. At the end of the centre the assessors will review the individual's performances and make recommendations on who is ready for the challenge of partnership.

The exercises

These exercises could be individual or group work, role plays or written work. Very often a business case is used throughout the exercises, which is not based within a firm's technical specialism. You will be asked to tackle issues to do with external clients, internal colleagues and suppliers. There may be strategic and tactical issues to deal with across the full range of functions such as finance, HR, IT and operations.

> **Tip**
>
> If you believe that you have performed badly in one exercise, keep calm and move on. You will be taking part in more than one exercise, so there will be lots of opportunities for you to show what you can do. Your performance will be evaluated as a whole, rather than just on one exercise.

Although there will be other participants on the assessment centre, there is no need for you to compete with each other during the exercises. You are being evaluated based solely on your performance. Sometimes you will find that actors will be involved in the exercises. The basic rule is to be yourself and use your current knowledge and experience to deal with the situations you are asked to deal with during the centre.

> **Tip**
>
> The assessors can only assess you on what they see on the day. If you don't involve yourself in the group exercises, the assessors can't assess your abilities. Accept the imaginary situations, and don't make assumptions about how you should respond or what the assessors are looking for; you may be wrong.

Interview

Typically there will be a one-to-one competency-based interview with an assessor. This interview will last between 45 minutes and an hour. Rather than talking about your achievements, the assessor will ask you for examples of actual projects or pieces of work that you have done. You will be asked to describe these in a great level of detail. By understanding the detail, the assessor will probe your style and approach in handling a variety of problems and other work situations.

Feedback on your performance

Depending on the firm, you may or may not receive feedback on the last day. Where feedback is not given, the assessor's report recommending whether you should be recommended for admission to the partnership will be given to the management board and the partner selection committee. You will be debriefed as soon as the management board, heads of department and sponsoring partners have reviewed the results.

Where feedback is provided on the last day, the assessor who interviews you will be the person responsible for giving you feedback based on your performance in all the exercises. Based on this, the assessor will provide feedback on your strengths and development needs against all of your firm's competencies. A copy of the assessor's report and recommendations will be given to the management board and the partner selection committee.

Creating your personal business development plan

Your personal business development plan is where you set out your market stall and show your readiness for partnership. Your ability to manage and grow existing clients, as well as winning new clients, is essential for a successful partner career. For your own sanity, if you haven't already started to do so by this stage, you must do everything that you can to build and develop your own client base and following. See Chapter 18 for how to build your own client portfolio.

> **Tip**
>
> If you are not excited by the challenges of building and developing your own practice, you should think long and hard about whether you should give up the comparative security of being a relatively well-paid employee to become a self-employed partner.

There are typically two parts to making the business case for your promotion to partnership: part A is the business case which is prepared by your head of department and sponsoring partner with some input from you; part B is your personal business development plan, which you are responsible for researching and writing in consultation with your head of department and relevant people within the firm. Your plan should be linked to your department's business plan, presented and agreed with your head of department and your partners.

Typical contents of a personal business development plan, with strategic goals set over three to five years, are:

- Market overview.

- Commercial viability.

- Barriers to success.

- Competitors.

- Resources and investment you will require to implement your plan.

- Why should they select you rather than hiring a new partner from outside the firm?

- The development you personally will need to achieve the plan.

On the How to make partner website **http://www.howtomakepartner.com** there are a free personal business plan template and worked example.

Again, if you have set career goals and created a career action plan to achieve them, writing your personal business development plan should be a lot easier because you will have already done a lot of thinking about what you want from your career and what you need to do to make it happen. You should also reread Chapter 13: How to build your network for life, and Chapter 9: How your firm makes money.

Creating a personal business development plan enables you to do the following:

- To make your 'pitch' for partnership by setting out what you believe you can and will contribute to the partnership.

- To communicate and explain the services, clients and practice that you intend to build and develop as a partner in the next three years.

- Identify the key areas for development, the resources and investment required from the firm to help you promote and grow your practice.

- Show how you propose to generate revenue and financial prospects for your practice.

Moreover, your personal business development plan provides the basis on which your partners will be able to assess the strengths, weaknesses and future potential of your practice to the partnership.

If, as recommended in this book, you have made time during the last few years to seek out key people and they have explained how things work 'around here', then tackling writing your personal business development plan and undertaking your due diligence will be easier. If you are starting now, don't panic. Most people will be only too delighted to help and guide you but, if you leave things until the last minute, you will run the risk of finding that they are too busy to fit you in.

The partner admission interviews

In mid-size and large firms, partner candidates can expect to be formally interviewed for one to two hours, by either the partner selection committee or the management board. The partnership nomination packs will have been made available to all members of the interview team.

Tip

From the day you started with the firm, you should build yourself a personal dossier of achievements. This is best done quarterly and you select one or two examples of successes. Over time, as you move closer to partner, the dossier will contain actual samples of your work, matched to the firm's competency framework and the items suggested in this chapter. Each example should have a half-page executive summary and list where the hard evidence can be found in the firm's filing system.

Exercise: Interview preparation

To help you prepare for these interviews, formulate your answers to these questions:

- Give me an overview of the work you do and the marketplace you operate in.

- How have you contributed to your department's development and growth?

- How have you helped your part of the firm become more profitable, and reduced WIP and lock-up?

- How have you specifically helped the firm?

- In relation to the promotion criteria, explain how you qualify for promotion.

- How, in your everyday working life, do you support the values of the firm?

- What additional contribution do you feel you are going to make once promoted?
- What do you think are the key issues and challenges facing the firm?
- What do you think the future direction of the firm should be?
- What will you have achieved five years from now?
- What do you want your legacy to the firm to be?

Don't forget that a successful interview is a two-way street and you should also prepare and have ready some questions for the interview team. If you have been thorough in undertaking your due diligence, you should have a few pertinent questions to ask. By being prepared with intelligent questions you can obtain the information that you need to make an informed decision about the next stage of your career, while demonstrating that you have what it takes to be promoted to partner.

Final stage

After your interview, if the management board and the partner selection committee recommend that you should be promoted to partner, the partnership will be invited to vote on the recommendation. The results will be communicated to your head of department and sponsoring partner, and they will inform you.

If you are reading through the admissions process and thinking, 'This sounds very gruelling,' yes, it can be. However, the more you do earlier in your career the easier this process becomes. Remember that your support team, particularly your coach and mentor, are there to help you through this last hurdle to making partner. Don't forget to ask for their support.

Your moment of truth – is partnership right for you at this firm?

The partner admission process is a gruelling affair that will almost definitely take its toll on you on some way. However, before you sign on the dotted line and accept the offer of partnership, it's time to stop and take stock (if you haven't done this already!). You should be talking to trusted colleagues, family and friends regarding how you currently feel about the prospect of being promoted to partner. People will always respect you for taking the right decision for you personally, even if it isn't what they want for you.

Case study: Myfanwy Neville

Becoming a partner never occurred to Myfanwy, until one day she spent some time with a personal development coach. She had just been made up to junior manager at the time and felt like she was treading water a little bit trying to keep up with the other, more experienced managers. The coach asked her about her long-term goals, and she said, 'Get better at managing.' The coach asked why she wasn't aiming to be the next female partner at BKL. From that point on, Myfanwy went for partner and was made partner in 2010.

Case study: Daniel

Daniel was offered the chance to go for partner in one of the major accountancy firms. He realized that becoming a partner in this firm would be a big undertaking not just for him but also for his wife. If he was successful at making partner he knew that there would always be three people in his marriage: his wife, himself and his firm. Even though Daniel knew he would have done some fantastic work, been at the top of his game in a brilliant organization and become a very wealthy man, he wasn't prepared to make the personal sacrifice partnership would have demanded. So he turned down the opportunity to go for partner and took his career in a different direction.

Consider these questions to check whether making partner at this firm is right for you:

- How do you feel about what you have learnt about your firm?
- Have you worked out a strategy to grow your part of the practice, hit your financial targets and still have a personally satisfying life outside work?
- Do you really respect and like your partners?
- Do you have what it takes to build a sustainable and financially strong practice?

- Are you happy that someone else will be doing the majority of the technical work for your clients?

- Are you looking forward to taking on additional roles and responsibilities?

- Can you cope with being responsible for generating sufficient work to keep a team of three people fully employed, or will this keep you awake at nights?

- How much of your time will you have available to spend with your family and friends over the next three years?

- How quickly can you develop the skills you will need to be a successful partner?

There is nothing wrong with having concerns and doubts – you should expect this; after all, making partner is a major career and life event. However, if considering the questions above fills you with dread and anxiety, you should seriously reconsider whether partnership at this firm is really for you. It could be that this is not the right time for you personally or that you don't feel sufficiently self-confident about your ability to deliver what is required by partners in your firm.

If you still want to make partner, but not at this firm, remember that, as the saying goes, there are still plenty more fish in the sea. You owe it to yourself and the people dear to you to create the life and career that you want to live. If this means you have to change firm to achieve this, then so be it. Your future happiness is worth more than a few extra quid in your bank balance.

If you can't wait to get going and feel that this is the right firm for you and the future that you have in mind, then we wish you all the best!

Summary

The partner admission process is a two-way process. Your firm is assessing you for your fit as a future partner, and you need to be assessing it against your own values, career and life goals.

To make partner, you must demonstrate to the partnership that you can think and act like a partner by:

- your ability to understand the business, clients, the marketplace, the financials and how these things affect the firm's performance;

- how you will participate in leading and managing the practice, ie contributing to business development, client service and client relationship management.

It is important to take stock before you sign up for partnership. Is partnership within this firm right for you?

Action points

- Assess yourself against the partner criteria outlined in this chapter. Where are your strengths and gaps? What do you need to add into your career action plan to improve your readiness and suitability for partnership?
- Find out about the partner admission process at your firm.
- Do your due diligence on your firm, making sure that you read a copy of your firm's partnership agreement.
- Talk to your support team, especially your family and mentor. What do they think about you making partner at this firm?
- Have a go at writing your own personal business development plan.
- Talk to new partners in your firm. How did they find the partner admission process? What tips can they pass on to you?

Further resources

Books

Ennico, C (2009) *The Partner Track: How to go from associate to partner in any law firm*, Kaplan Trade, US

Websites and blogs

At the *How to make partner website* – http://www.howtomakepartner.com:

- guidance on doing your own due diligence;
- sample personal business development plan;
- practice interview questions;
- templates for personal business development plan.

21 First steps as a partner

Becoming a partner in effect is resetting the clock to zero and starting again. You've got to make the transition to thinking and behaving like a partner.

DAVID, PARTNER

The purpose of this chapter is to help you take your first steps as a successful partner. Although this book has been written as *what you will need to know and do to make partner*, now that you are there, this chapter points you back to key chapters for your reference.

Your first few steps as a new partner

Congratulations on making it to partner – you have succeeded where many people haven't. Do take some time to celebrate your achievement and reflect on what you have achieved.

> ## Tip
>
> Your promotion into the partnership is a massive achievement, a good news story and marketing opportunity – spread the word using LinkedIn, Twitter, Facebook, e-mail and the phone. Make sure you personally ring all your A-listers, especially clients and professional intermediaries, and your support team to tell them about your good fortune.

Making partner is not a destination, but the first step in a far more rewarding role. The number of equity partners in professional services firms is decreasing. Remaining a partner has become tougher as firms of all sizes in every type of practice have de-equitized partners and lengthened partnership progression structures to defend profitability and maintain the size of the profit pie.

> Being in the club is a wonderful feeling; however, there is always a constant pressure to deliver more and more. I have known about partners who have been asked to leave the partnership, so I know that being a partner does not necessarily mean a job for life.
>
> Muna, partner

The one thing that you cannot afford to do on making partner is to continue working and behaving as though nothing has changed. You must stop acting and behaving as a senior associate or a director from the outset! What very few partners will tell you is that over the next six to 12 months the work that you were given by partners as a director or senior associate will dry up – the tap will be turned off, as you are now expected to be able to feed yourself and your team. Remember all the things that you promised the partnership that you would do in your personal business development plan? Well, you will be expected to deliver these things starting from day one. But, remember, you wouldn't have been asked to join the partnership if the partners didn't believe in your ability to implement it successfully.

'Inheriting' a partner's portfolio can be both a blessing and a curse: it initially saves you time to grow your own business. However, you shouldn't rely on it, assume it will be profitable and in good health, or expect it to sustain you for the rest of your partner career. You must build on what you have been given and prove that you can get your own clients.

As a new partner it's highly likely that you will be given management responsibility either in your department or firm wide. In fact, your personal business development plan probably stated where your management and leadership skills would be best applied in the firm! Even though your new management responsibilities will limit the amount of time you have for developing your people and practice, do accept your new responsibility. Your new responsibilities will help to increase your profile in the partnership generally, and almost definitely help you acquire new skills.

What has changed now you are a partner?

Your immediate goal is now to demonstrate and reassure your partners, who are now your peers, that they made the right decision in making you a partner. This means it's your job to grow a sustainable business, which increases the size of the profit pie for the benefit of all the partners. In today's world of increasingly competitive and performance-driven firms, partners who fail to increase the partnership's profits year on year are unlikely to survive for long.

> People that would have talked to you in one way will not talk to you the same way now because you're a partner.
>
> Darryn Hedges, divisional business director,
> Addleshaw Goddard LLP

Expect your relationships with colleagues and staff to change. Some people will make it clear that you have 'changed sides' and view you differently from now on. You should maintain close links with them while you adjust to being a partner.

As a new partner, you will need time before you become comfortable with your partner colleagues and they with you. It may help to remember that you are the new member of their club. Don't rush the relationship – making the wrong first impression may set you back. Make time to listen and learn from more experienced and successful partners – ask questions, listen and think carefully before you proceed to tell them your views on what is wrong with the partnership and how you would change things around here!

Tip

Find a partner mentor who can guide you through your first year in the partnership.

You are now self-employed and that will change how you are paid and how you will need to report your financial affairs to the taxman. For example, will you receive a monthly payment (drawings) from which taxes and cost of any benefits have been deducted on your behalf by your firm? Or will you be responsible for paying for these things? If you are responsible, then you must be disciplined and set aside money for making these payments. Your finance team should know what you need to do and may help you to set up an account for this purpose.

Your time will be typically spent *finding* and *minding*, which means that you will spend most of your time getting close to your clients and potential clients, while supervising your team who deliver these services to your clients.

You are now an owner and a shareholder of the business and will have invested a sizeable amount of capital in your firm. Therefore, ask questions and read partnership papers and information packs when they are sent to you. They are provided to help you to improve your knowledge and understanding of your business.

How you will be measured as a partner

What gets measured gets done.
John Harvey Smith

In coaching new partners, Jo stresses the importance of finding out and understanding their firm's partner performance and compensation criteria:

- How are partners measured and rewarded?
- What are partners' annual earnings targets and charge-out rates?
- What does this mean for you, at the first rung of the equity ladder?

Performance management has become more common in professional services. Consistently meeting these performance criteria will drive your progression as a partner.

The standard partner performance criteria cover:

- client service and relationship management;
- revenue and profit generation;
- management and leadership;
- supporting the firm's values and vision;
- contribution to strategic goals.

Deliver on your financial targets

See Chapter 9: How your firm makes money.

The quickest way to take the shine off your promotion is to fail financially. The first rule is that you must cover your costs plus your share of the overheads. This is the very minimum that is expected of you by your partners. Unlike when you were a senior associate or director, it is your responsibility to make sure that your team's client work adds value to the firm by making a profit for your team, even a small one. Your personal business development plan sets out how you expect to make a profit for the firm. If you acquire a reputation for continually failing to achieve your targets, you are highly unlikely to progress up the equity, and may even be asked to leave the partnership.

All your excellent work won't count if you don't record, bill and collect the cash. What is more, it will undermine your relationship with your partners particularly if it affects their profits. This will also make you unpopular with the management board for failing to comply with the firm's financial policies and processes.

Grow your practice

See Chapter 17: How to become the 'go to' expert for your firm and profession, and Chapter 18: Building your own client portfolio.

A partner who doesn't grow their practice will not progress far up the equity ladder. This means that you must make marketing and business development your top priority. You may have already demonstrated your potential for marketing and business development, but from now it is essential to frequently and consistently devote time to it. A partner without a following (except a highly valuable technical expert) is regarded as a 'glorified senior associate or director' and vulnerable when times become tough. You cannot rely on other partners to generate and bring work to your desk.

> **Tip**
>
> To kick-start your business development, engage a business development coach who will be able to help you become a confident and reliable business generator for the firm. You may find that your firm is prepared to pay for this coach's service.

Use your personal business development plan and create an action plan with specific tasks and dates for identifying business development activities. Enlist the guidance and research support of your business development team if you are uncertain about any of your potential markets and target clients.

Partners are expected to cross sell other partners' services and look for opportunities to refer clients to them. The rule is: do unto others as you would be done by – you can't expect other partners to refer you to clients if you are not prepared to do the same for them. It's now more important that you make time to get to know what your partners do and have to offer. It is important that partners share information on their capabilities with each other, formally at partnership meetings, via internal communications such as newsletters, e-mail, blogs, and informally around the drinks machine.

> **Tip**
>
> Set up a business development group within your firm, for ideas generation, knowledge sharing, mutual support and to encourage cross selling between the group member's clients.

Make sure you don't neglect your existing clients in your quest to build your client portfolio. Generating referrals and new instructions from existing clients is one of the easiest ways of winning work. However, this relies on you and your team delivering great client service regardless of what new opportunities are on the horizon.

> **Tip**
>
> Use keeping-in-touch processes and systems to maintain a regular dialogue with your existing clients, regardless of whether you are currently engaged by them. Diarize these communications to make sure that they happen.

Develop your team and others

See Chapter 8: Building your support team, and Chapter 19: Managing and leading your way to success.

Now that you are a partner, you are responsible for developing the capabilities of your team, so that they can deliver your client's work. Passing on your knowledge and experience also ensures that you have a team of capable people to whom you can confidently delegate work as your practice expands. This team doesn't magically appear, so you have to make time to develop them. If you are going to hit the profit targets you have committed to deliver, you will not have the time to do all the work yourself! Generally in our experience, associates and fee earners are always keen to work for a partner who involves and develops them – which helps when you are facing a tight deadline and competing with your partners for the services of the brightest people in the firm.

Tip

Now you are a partner, consider mentoring someone in the firm who has partnership ambitions. Part of our inspiration to write this book was the number of people within professional services firms who wanted to buy this book for their other half, child or mentee – even those who are not aspiring to make partner. How about giving your new mentee a copy of this book as you start your working relationship together?

Creating your legacy

See Chapter 2: What do you want from your career and life?, Chapter 7: Creating and writing your own career action plan, Chapter 11: How to find the time to fit it all in, and Chapter 17: How to become the 'go to' expert for your firm and profession.

We know that it is possible to make partner and still have a life, otherwise we wouldn't have written this book. We also know that maintaining the balance requires focused and disciplined planning of your non-chargeable time inside and outside work. Looking after yourself and staying healthy are essential to enjoying the rewards and benefits that come with being a partner in your firm.

Reading this book is a great start to helping yourself achieve your career goals, and have a happy and fulfilling life outside work. However, reading is not enough – you need to take action to achieve the promise of this book. What will you do?

Summary

Now that you are a partner you are, in effect, starting at the bottom of another career ladder and the newest member of an established club. Give yourself the time and space to re-establish your relationships with the people in your firm.

Use your personal business development plan to help you to start to grow and develop your part of the practice. Remember to make time to develop the people in your team so that you know you have a reliable full crew to service the work you have toiled hard to win.

Action points

- Execute your personal business development plan. Don't get stuck in the detail or strive for perfection. Start working on delivering this plan today.

- Identify what you will do to maximize the amount of business you receive from your current clients, introducers and other partners within your firm. Add this to your career action plan.

- Take your career action plan and everything that you have collected on your journey to partner, and archive it. You have 'graduated'. Then start a brand new career action plan for the successful partner journey you are embarking on. This will have new goals and will require deep thinking about your new work role and possible impacts on your life outside work.

- Keep an audit of how you are spending your non-chargeable time at work. Aim to minimize any time which is not spent on delivering your personal business development plan or developing your team around you.

- Ask for feedback from your clients, colleagues and staff and use it to help your team to develop. Use the feedback to write a team-wide development plan, which commits each person to doing at least one thing each month to develop themselves.

Further resources

Websites and blogs

Free guide to *Making a success of your first 12 months as a partner* and details of Executive Coaches who can help you successfully make the transition to partnership: http://www.howtomakepartner.com.

INDEX

NB page numbers in *italic* indicate figures or tables

360-degree feedback   81–82

Abamentis Limited   126
Accenture   62, 67
active listening   155–56, 160
activist (Kolb learning style)   76, 78
Actual People Limited   53
Addleshaw Goddard LLP   61, 282
admissions process   267–76
  admission interview   275–76
  attributes needed   268–69
  nomination   270
  partner assessment centres   271–73
  personal business development plan, your
    273–75
  voting and selection   276
Alan Smith Associates Ltd   153
Aligning the Stars: How to Succeed
   When Professionals Drive
   Results   59
Amazon EU   13–14
Amber Moore Consulting   10, 15, 116,
  121, 130, 186, *186*
approachability   69
Arthur Andersen   260
assertiveness   137–39
  client expectations, managing   138–39
Assertiveness at work: A practical guide for
   handling awkward situations   137
AW Consultants   100

Back, Ken and Back, Kate   137
Backley, John L   140
Baker, Jon   180
BDO LLP   45, 67, 171
Beck, Jonny   125
Bell, Alexander Graham   18
Berg Krapow Lewis LLP   63, 69, 193, 211
Bircham Dyson Bell LLP   174
BKL LLP   42, 277
body language   130
Brinkerhoff, Robert   77
Brodie, Ian   221
Brown, Rob   185
Buckingham, Marcus and Clifton, Donald
  81

business development process
  account management   236
  marketing   235
  sales   236

career action plan, writing a   87–99, *96*
  feedback, getting   98
  goal setting   88
  intentions vs action   88–89
  milestones   88, 91, *92, 93*
  objectives   88, 94–95
  priorities, identifying   89–91
  weekly planner, using a   95–96, *97*
career change   53–54
  negative aspects of   54
  positive aspects of   54
career decisions, making
  career progression, taking responsibility
    for   19–20
  identity, understanding your   *21,*
    21–37
    changes over time   23
    purpose   21, 36–37
    questions to ask   22
    values   21, 23–29
    vision   21, 30–36
  student debt   19
career manager, being a   49–51
  negative aspects of   50–51
  positive aspects of   50
career options, alternative   49–56, *55*
  career change   53–54
    negative aspects of   54
    positive aspects of   54
  career manager, being a   49–51
    negative aspects of   50–51
    positive aspects of   50
  in-house, moving   51–53
    negative aspects of   52–53
    positive aspects of   52
career stages
  director or senior associate   195
  manager or associate   194
  partner   195–96
  pre-qualification   192–93
  qualified   193–94

case studies
   Abi (playing to strengths)   81
   Arthur Andersen (reputation)   260
   Daniel (turning down partnership)
      277
   Dibble, Suzanne (personal profile)   220
   Fraiser, Joseph (USP)   238
   Gillman, Peter (opportunity)   42
   Jack (core values)   158
   Louise (pressure to progress)   49
   Neville, Myfanwy (long-term goals)
      277
   Neville, Myfanwy (people)   42
   Newton, Mike (moving in-house)   51
   see also Mace Group
   Robert (competition)   16
   Simon (company culture)   132
   Stylianou, John (career change)   53
Chambers, Robert   264
Cialdini, Robert   199
Clear Thought Consulting   179
client portfolio, building your   234–43
   business development process
      account management   236
      marketing   235
      sales   236
   inheriting a portfolio   234, 281
   introducers   236–37
   keeping in touch   242
   personal marketing plans   237–40
   sales process, the   240–41, *241*
closed questions   157, *157*
Clutterbuck, David   103
coaching
   benefits of   80
   coaching vs mentoring   102–03
   executive coaching   79
   GROW model   258–59
   internal coaching   79
   life coaching   79–80
commercial sense   64–65
commitment   61, 62
communication, effective   70, 153–57
   active listening   155–56
   filtering and associations   154, *154*
   mirroring   156
   non-verbal communication   155
   omissions   156
   questioning   157, *157*
   rapport   156
concerns and doubts   277–78
conscious competence   79
conscious incompetence   79
corporate culture   125
Covey, Stephen   140
cross-referring, to other partners   285

Davis Langdon   111
delegating   149–50
Dibble, Suzanne   52, 220
difficult conversations, handling   162–63
distractions, minimizing
   e-mail   146–47
   interruptions   146
   paperwork   145–46
   phone calls   147–48
DLA Piper   43
'dressing the part'   166–67
Drucker, Peter   245
due diligence, doing your own   263–66
   business development strategy   264
   career and life goals   266
   financial health   264
   leadership and management   265
   risk management   265
   role and responsibilities   265

Eat that frog: get more of the important
     things done today   144, 174
Effective Stress Management Techniques for
     Lawyers   208
emotional intelligence   67
Enron   260
enthusiasm   69
Eversheds   51

Facebook   187, 188
feedback
   360-degree feedback   81–82
   and a career action plan   98
   from a mentor   107
   giving   163–65
      effective feedback   163
      SBO model   164–65
   and performance reviews   257–58
   receiving   165
finances, understanding your firm's
     111–22
   capped fees   116
   charge-out rates   115–16
   delivering, as a partner   284
   financial glossary   114
   fixed fees   116
   payment, chasing   117
   profitability
      financial management   120
      fixed costs   120–21
      lock-up   120
      recovery of time spent   119–20
      utilization of fee earners   118–19
   questions to ask   121–22
   timesheets   117–18
   working capital   116–17

Financial Times Guide To Business Networking, The 230
'fitting in' 68, 124–33
  corporate culture 125
  office politics, handling 126–31
    black and white, being 131
    body language 130
    flexibility 128
    'gatekeepers' 127
    gossip 129
    influential partners 128
    initial impressions 130
    political correctness 129
    respect 129
    self-control 128
    senior management 127
    tools and tactics 130–31
  profile, raising your 131–32
  questions to ask 126
fixed share equity partnership 266–67
focus, keeping your 198–205
  when you're busy 198–201
    coach, your 200
    doing too much 200–01
    mentor, your 200
    objectives 199–200
  when you're not busy 201–05
    continuing professional development (CPD) 203–04
    holiday 202
    marketing and business development 204–05
    profile-building 202–03
    relationship-building 202–03
Fraiser, Joseph 238
Franklin, Benjamin 79
Fresh Professional Development Ltd 115
Freshfields Bruckhaus Deringer 28
'frog eating' 144
Frost, Julian 171
full equity partnership 266–67

George Hay Chartered Accountants 102, 112, 120
Gilbert, Andy, Frisby, Nicky and Roberts, Kathryn 24
Gillman, Peter 13, 42, 62–63, 65
Go work on your career 24
gossip 129
Gould, Stuart 45
Green, Charles H xiii–xiv, xv
'grinding, minding and finding' 192, *192*
GROW model 258–59

Hamlet 19
Harding, Ford 234, 235

Harry Potter and the Chamber of Secrets 21
Harvey Smith, John 283
health, protecting your 207–15
  exercise 212–13
  Health Audit 208–09
  outside interests 210–11
  over-adrenalizing 214–15
  pressure vs performance 209–10, *210*
  stress 209, 213–14
Hedges, Darryn 61, 282
Henrique Griffiths 125
Horner, Jeremy i, xv
How to Work a Room 182
Hunter, Toni 102, 106, 112, 120

identity, understanding your 21, 21–37
  changes over time 23
  purpose 21, 36–37
    and motivation 36
  questions to ask 22
  values 21, 23–29
    changes over time 27
    examples values 24
    and the firm's values 27–29, *28*
    values exercise *25–26*, 27
  vision 21, 30–36
    example life roles *31*
    life roles exercise *32, 33*
    Wheel of Life *34*, 34–35, *36*
    and work-life balance 30–31
importance-versus-urgency 140, *141*, 142–43
influence 158–61
  pull influence
    active listening 160
    common ground, finding 161
    disclosure 161
    exploring 161
  push influence
    incentives 160
    pressure 160
    views, opinions and feelings 159
Influence: The Psychology of persuasion 199
Ingwersen, Sarah 52
in-house, moving 51–53
  negative aspects of 52–53
  positive aspects of 52
initiative 63–64
Insights Discovery 83
introducers 236–37
iTunes 224

Keller, Helen 198
Kim Whitaker Legal Services 45, 46

knowledge, industry   84–85
Kolb's learning styles   76, 76–77, 78
   Honey and Mumford's Learning Styles
     Questionnaire   77
Korda, Michael   182
KPMG LLP   45, 58

Larbie, Jo   19, 148
Lawyer, The   52
lawyers4mumpreneurs   52
leaders (partner type)   46
leadership *see* management and leadership
Legrand, Janet   43
Lewis, C S   207
Lewis, Michael   124
Liar's Poker   124
likeability   69
limited liability partnerships (LLP)   11
Lines, Suzanne   126
LinkedIn   179, 180, 181, 183, 184, 185,
    187, 188, 224, 231, 235, 242
Lorsch, Jay and Tierney, Thomas   59
Lovells Hogan LLP   43

Mace Group   51
   see also Mike Newton under case studies
MacIntyre Hudson LLP   30, 44, 64, 222
Maister, David   66, 115, 149
management and leadership   245–61
   coaching   258–59
     GROW model   258–59
   definitions of   246
   developing people   251–54, 252
     development needs analysis (DNA)
     251–53
   motivating people   250–51
   performance reviews   254–58
     feedback, giving   257–58
     goals, setting   256–57, 257
   quality control   260
   team building   247–50
     adjourning   250
     forming   249
     high-performing teams   247–48
     norming   249
     performing   249
     storming   249
Managing the Professional Service Firm   115
maturity   67–68
McKinsey & Company   28
Me 2.0   218
meetings, effective   148–49
mentoring   101, 102–09
   choosing a mentor   104–05
   coaching vs mentoring   102–03

and diversity   103
and your first year as a partner   282
and focus   200
getting the most from   108–09
relationship with   108
role of   102, 103–04
what to expect   105–08
   challenge   106
   constructive criticism   107
   feedback   107
   pep talks   106
   problem solving   107
   role modelling   106
   support   106
Mills, Catrin   208
mirroring   156
Momentum 4   207
Moore, Amber   10, 15, 116, 121, 130, 186,
   186
Morrisey, George L   87
Murphy, Frances   51
Myers Briggs Type Indicator (MBTI)   83

networking   171–90
   expanding your network   178–79
   FITTER model   179–88
     engage   186
     follow up   180–81
     introduce yourself   182–85
     research   187–88
     target specific people   185
     turn social conversations into business
       chat   185–86
   for junior employees   173
   forms of   172
   myths about   173–74
   planning your network
     for the future   175
     goals   174–75
     network maps   176, 176
     relationship plans   177, 178
   reasons to network   172
Neville, Myfanwy   42, 63, 69, 193, 211,
   277
Newton, Mike   51
*Now, discover your strengths: How to
    develop your talents and those of
    the people you manage*   81

office politics, handling   126–31
   black and white, being   131
   body language   130
   flexibility   128
   'gatekeepers'   127
   gossip   129

influential partners 128
initial impressions 130
political correctness 129
respect 129
self-control 128
senior management 127
tools and tactics 130–31
Oglethorpe, Antoinette 62, 67
Oh, the Places You'll Go! 19
online biography, your 183–85
open questions 157, *157*
over-adrenalizing 214–15

Pannett, Alan 115
paperwork 145–46
partner assessment centres 271–73
'partnership potential' 58–73
exercise 71–72
skills and characteristics 60–71
approachability 69
commercial sense 64–65
commitment 61, 62
communication 70
drive for career 65–66
drive for results 66
embracing opportunity 62–63
emotional intelligence 67
enthusiasm 69
'fitting in' 68
initiative 63–64
leadership skills 65
likeability 69
management skills 65
maturity 67–68
reliability 64
resilience 68
responsibility 62–63
responsiveness 62
self-confidence 69–70
team building 66
teamwork 67
thinking skills 70–71
trustworthiness 64
'stars', definition of 59
value to firm, importance of 59–60
external market value 60
future value 59
internal market value 60
see also skills, developing your
Pattni, Heena 58, 191, 214
Pennington Hennessy 118
Pennington, Jamie 118
performance reviews 254–58
feedback, giving 257–58
goals, setting 256–57, *257*

personal marketing plans 237–40
PJR Consulting 126
political correctness 129
Power! How to get it, how to use it 182
pragmatist (Kolb learning style) 76, 78
presentations, giving 167–68
dos and don'ts *168*
nerves, overcoming 168
Price Bailey LLP 13, 42, 62–63, 65, 222
Principled Selling 14
procrastination 143–45
professional services firms (PSFs)
characteristics of 11
and communication technology 13
corporate world, influence of 14
and globalization 13–14
partnership structure of 11–12, *12*
and price sensitivity 13
size of firm 39–41
assessment and development 40
diversity of skill set 41
talent management 40
profile, building your 131–32, 203–03,
217–32
and finding a mentor 220
getting noticed 225–26
'personal brand' 218–19
relationships, managing
external relationships 230
five-level relationship level model 226,
226–28
internal relationships 228–29, *229*
specialism and niche, finding your
220–23
developing your niche 223–25
top-of-the-mind visibility 230–31
psychometric tools 83–84
emotional intelligence tools 84
Insights Discovery 83
Myers Briggs Type Indicator (MBTI) 83
pull influence
active listening 160
common ground, finding 161
disclosure 161
exploring 161
push influence
incentives 160
pressure 160
views, opinions and feelings 159

Raggett, Patrick 126
rainmakers (partner type) 46
Rainmaking 234
rapport 156
reflector (Kolb learning style) 76, 78

relationships, managing
    external relationships   230
    five-level relationship level model   226,
        226–28
    internal relationships   228–29, 229
reliability   64
resilience   68
responsibility   62–63
responsiveness   62
RoAne, Susan   182
Robbins, Antony   29
routes to partnership
    going it alone   45–46
    in-house route   44
    lateral route   43–44
    traditional route   42
Rowling, JK   21

sales process, the   240–41, 241
SBO model   164–65
Schawbel, Dan   218
Schwartz, David J   136
self-confidence   69–70
self-employment   283
Seuss Geisel, Theodor (Dr Seuss)   19
Seven Habits of Highly Effective People, The
    140
SG Associates   45
Shakespeare, William   19
Shaunak, Rakesh   30, 44, 64, 222
Shaw, George Bernard   217
Skaife, Dona   46
skills and characteristics, of potential partners
        60–71
    approachability   69
    commercial sense   64–65
    commitment   61, 62
    communication   70
    drive for career   65–66
    drive for results   66
    embracing opportunity   62–63
    emotional intelligence   67
    enthusiasm   69
    'fitting in'   68
    initiative   63–64
    leadership skills   65
    likeability   69
    management skills   65
    maturity   67–68
    reliability   64
    resilience   68
    responsibility   62–63
    responsiveness   62
    self-confidence   69–70

team building   66
teamwork   67
thinking skills   70–71
trustworthiness   64
skills, developing your
    coaching
        benefits of   80
        executive coaching   79
        internal coaching   79
        life coaching   79–80
    identifying missing skills   81–84
        360-degree feedback   81–82
        Assessment and Development Centres
            (ADCs)   82–83
        competency frameworks   84
        psychometric tools   83–84
    knowledge, industry   84–85
    Kolb's learning styles   76, 76–77, 78
        Honey and Mumford's Learning Styles
            Questionnaire   77
    stages of learning
        conscious competence   79
        conscious incompetence   79
        unconscious competence   79
        unconscious incompetence   77
    strengths, playing to   80–81
skills, of partners today   14–16
    client service   15
    collaborative working   16
    decision making   16
    financial acumen   15
    relationship building   15
    strategic thinking   15
    technical skills   14
Skype   225
Slaughter and May   51
SlideShare   224
Smith, Alan   153
social networking   143, 145, 179, 180–81,
        183–85, 187–88, 219, 225, 232,
        235, 242
stages of learning
    conscious competence   79
    conscious incompetence   79
    unconscious competence   79
    unconscious incompetence   77
strengths, playing to   80–81
stress
    managing   213–14
    signs of   209
Stylianou, John   53, 54
support team, building a   100–10
    executive coach   101
    family   101

importance of   101
mentor   101, 102–09
  choosing a mentor   104–05
  coaching vs mentoring   102–03
  and diversity   103
  getting the most from   108–09
  relationship with   108
  role of   102, 103–04
  what to expect   105–08
non-work friends   102
work friends   101
Sutherland, Gillian   111

Taylor Root   52
team building   66, 247–50
  adjourning   250
  forming   249
  high-performing teams   247–48
  as a new partner   286
  norming   249
  performing   249
  storming   249
teamwork   67
technical specialists (partner type)   46
theorist (Kolb learning style)   76, 78
thinking skills   70–71
Thomas, Bryony   179
Tichey, Noel M   246
time management and productivity   135–51
  assertiveness   137–39
    client expectations, managing
      138–39
  calendar, using your   139–40, 141
  delegating   149–50
  distractions, minimizing
    e-mail   146–47
    interruptions   146

paperwork   145–46
phone calls   147–48
focus   139
importance-versus-urgency   140, 141,
  142–43
meetings, effective   148–49
mindset, importance of   136–37
procrastination   143–45
Tovey, David   14
Tracy, Brian   75, 144, 174
trustworthiness   64
Tuckman model of team development
  248–50
Tutu, Desmond   1
Twitter   183, 184, 187, 219, 225, 231, 232,
  242
types of partner   46–47
Tzu, Lao   89

unconscious competence   79
unconscious incompetence   77

Virgin   220

WBS Accountants   46
Whitaker, Kim   45, 46, 137
Williams, Chris   207, 209, 210, 211, 214
Woodcock, Anita   100
work-life balance   30–36
  and assertiveness   138
  example life roles   31
  life roles exercise   32, 33
  Wheel of Life   34, 34–35, 36

YouTube   224

Ziglar, Zig   136, 247